AF594173

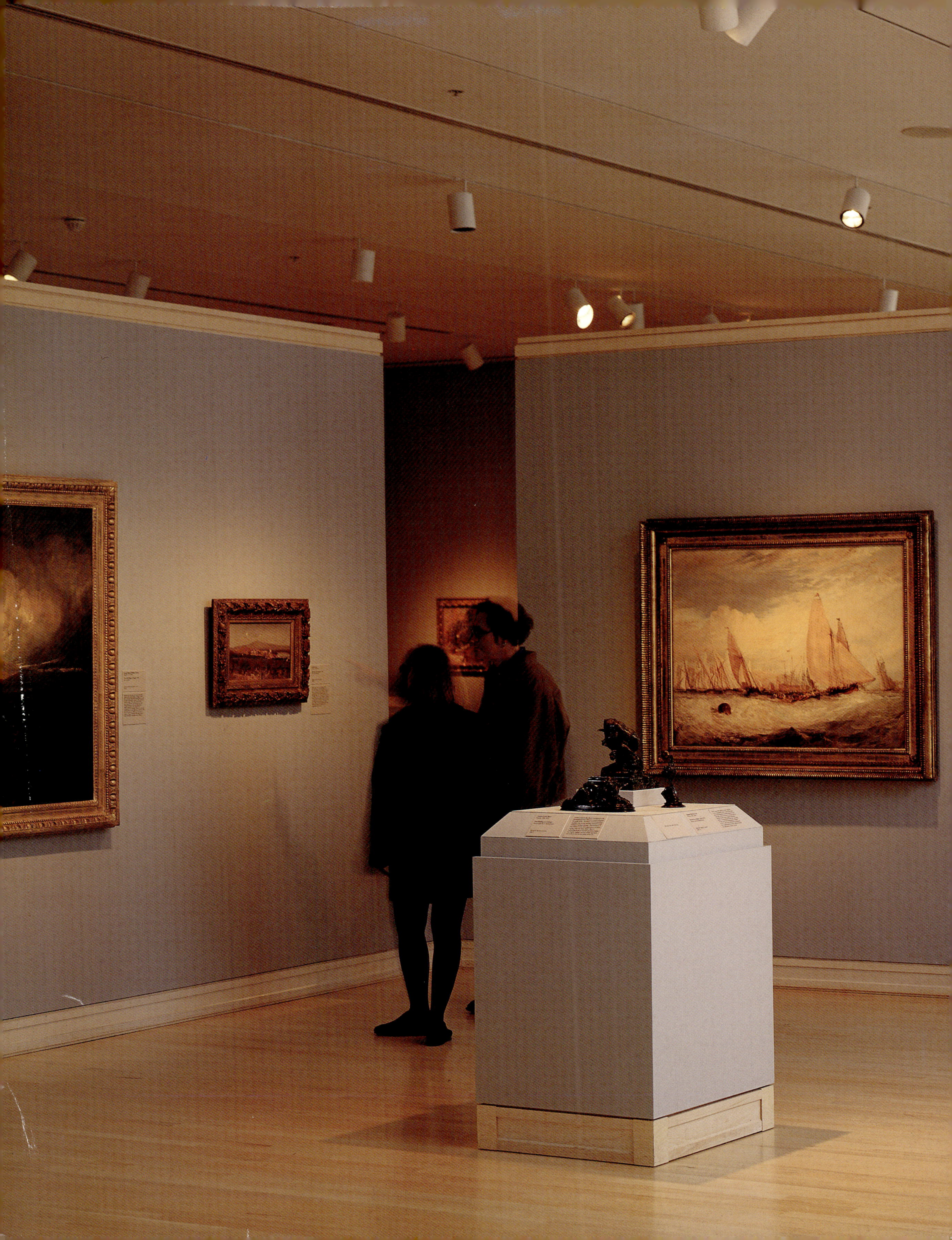

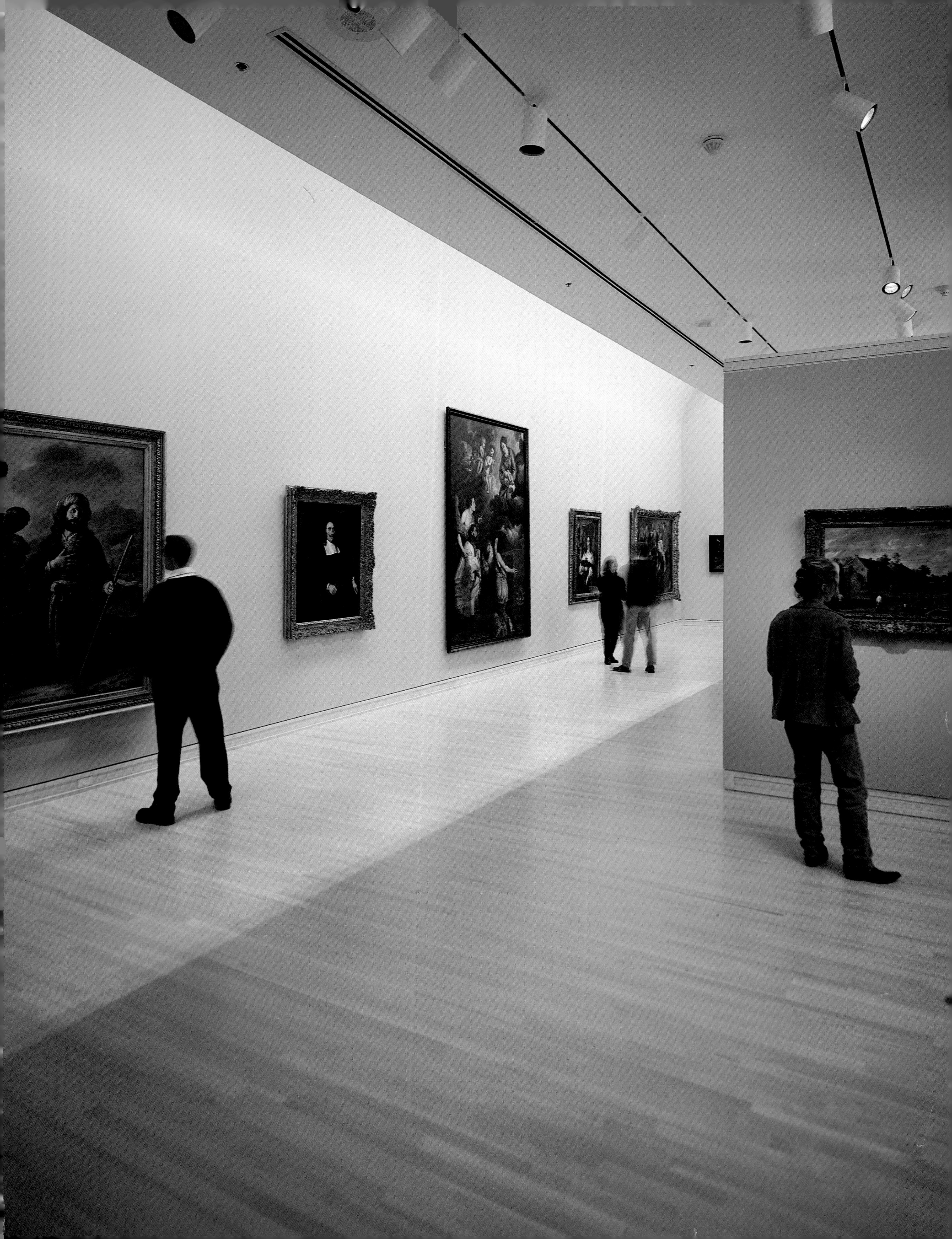

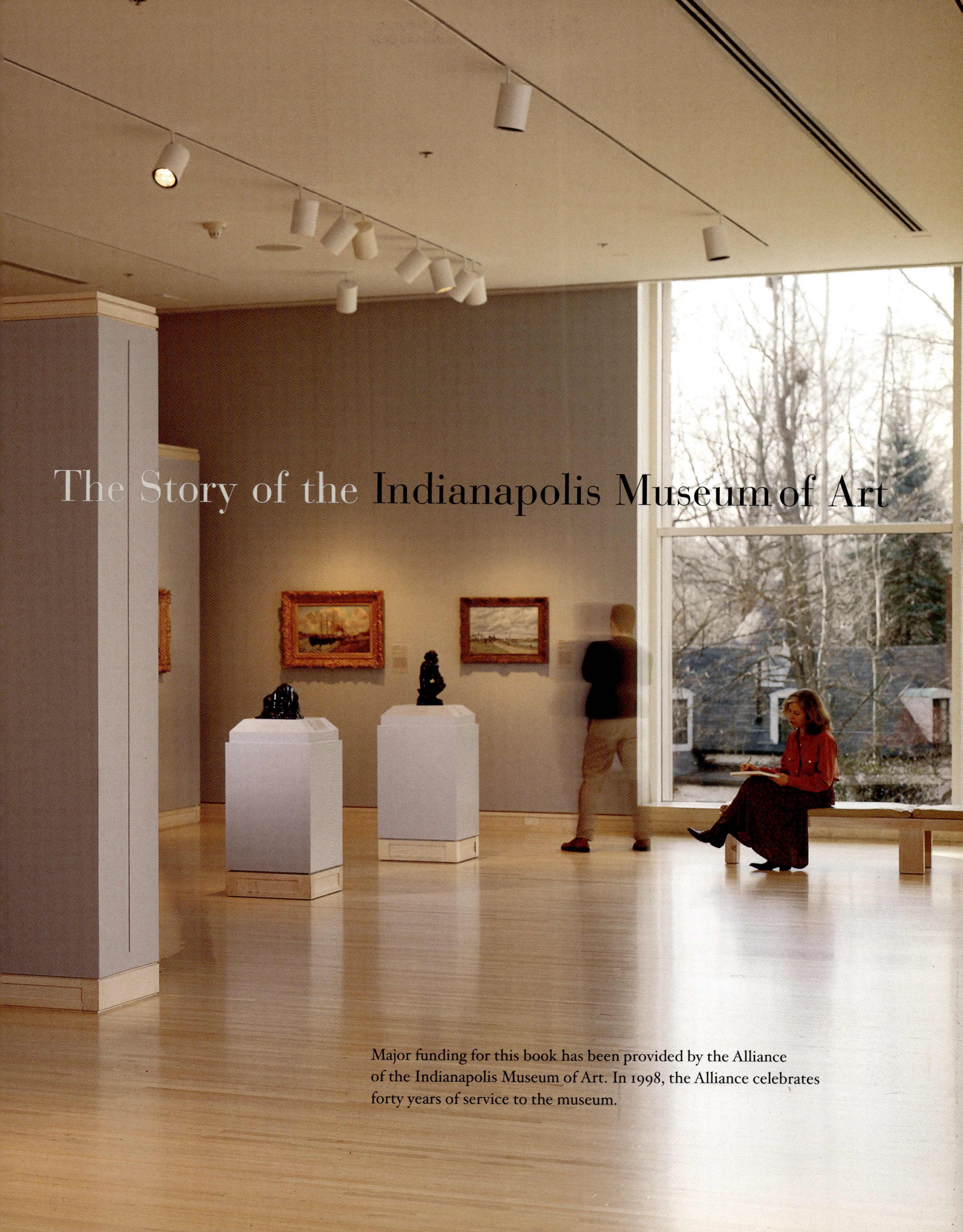

The Story of the Indianapolis Museum of Art

Major funding for this book has been provided by the Alliance of the Indianapolis Museum of Art. In 1998, the Alliance celebrates forty years of service to the museum.

5/13/98

To Sandy and Richard

Thanks for your support of the IMA!

(Go Pacers!)

Published by the Indianapolis Museum of Art
1200 West 38th Street, Indianapolis, Indiana 46208-4196

ISBN 0-936260-67-X

Edited by Jane Graham, Indianapolis Museum of Art
Designed by Antenna Commercial Artisans, Indianapolis
Printed by Design Printing Company, Indianapolis

Photography credits:

Photography of the collections by Hadley Fruits, John Geiser, Kent Jolly, Stephen Kovacik, Melville McLean, and Robert Wallace

Photography of the grounds and gardens by Hadley Fruits, John Geiser, and Ruth Roberts

© Garry Chilluffo, pp. 1-3, 78 (bottom right), 88
© Wilbur Montgomery, pp. 6 (Japanese Gallery), 9 (top)

Contents

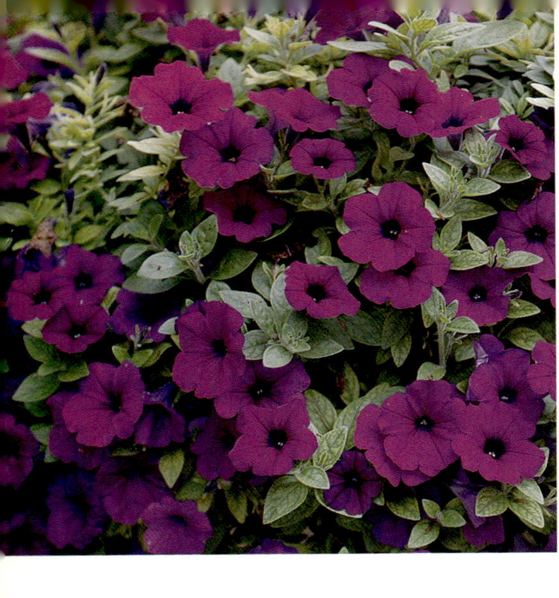
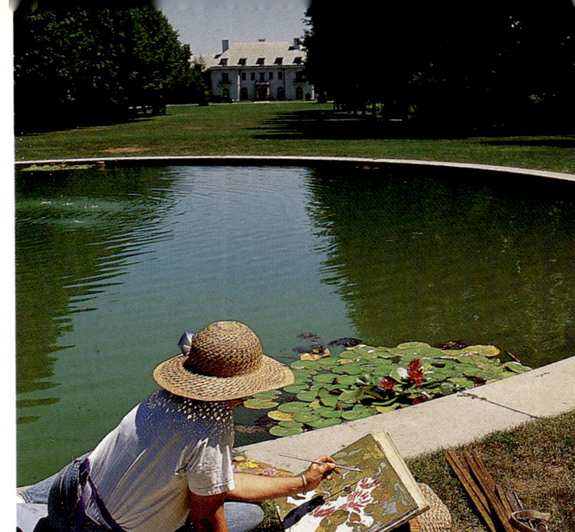
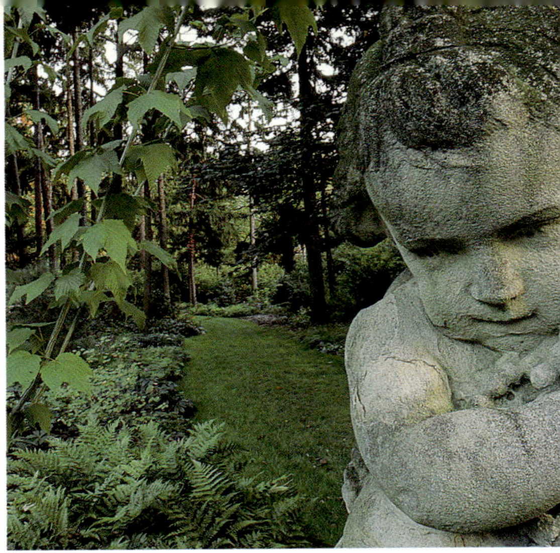
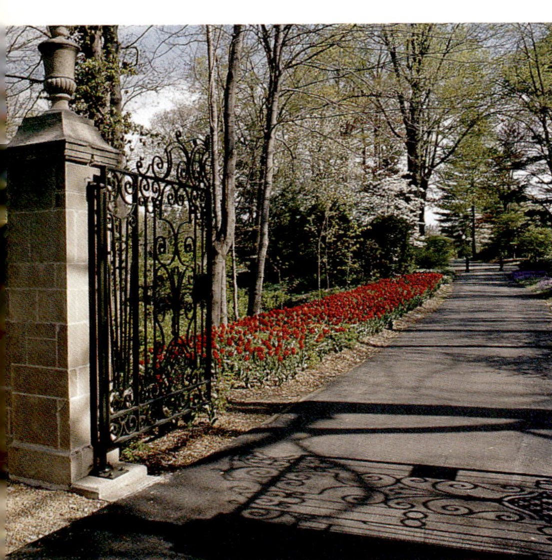
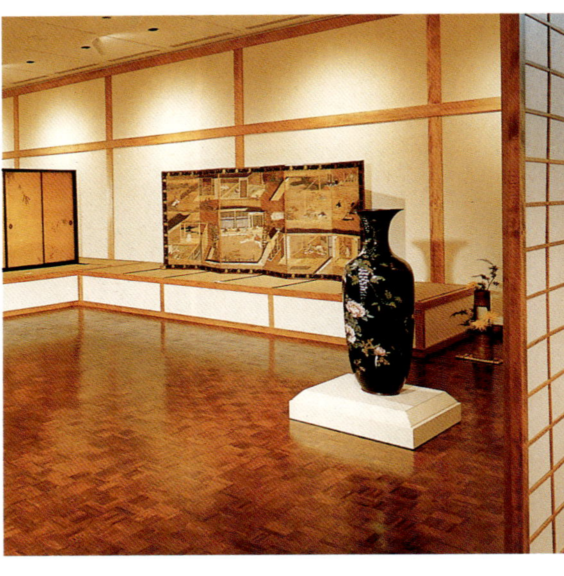
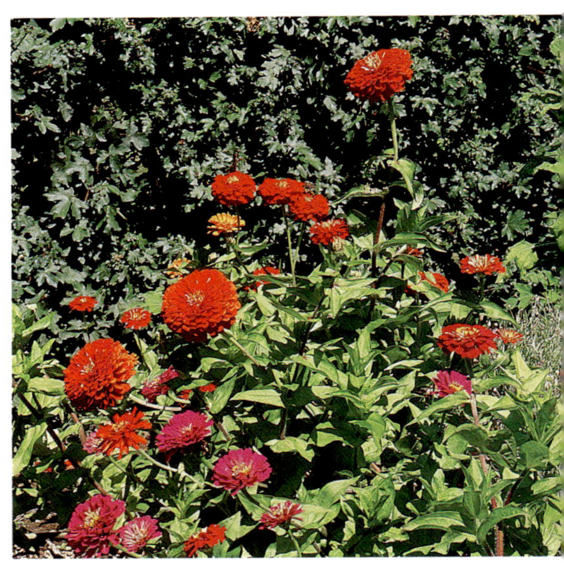
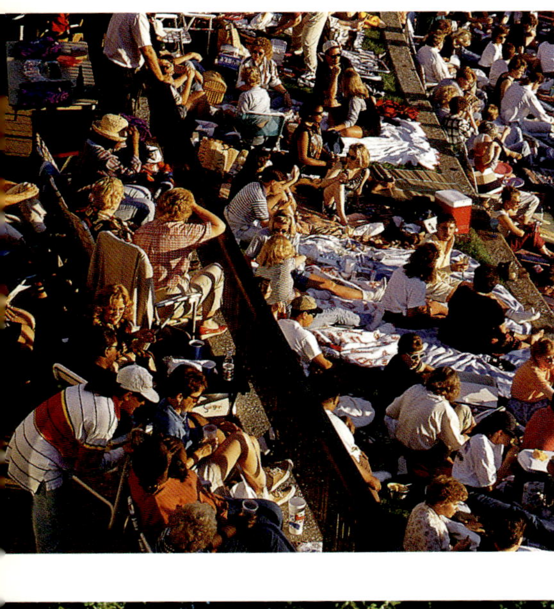
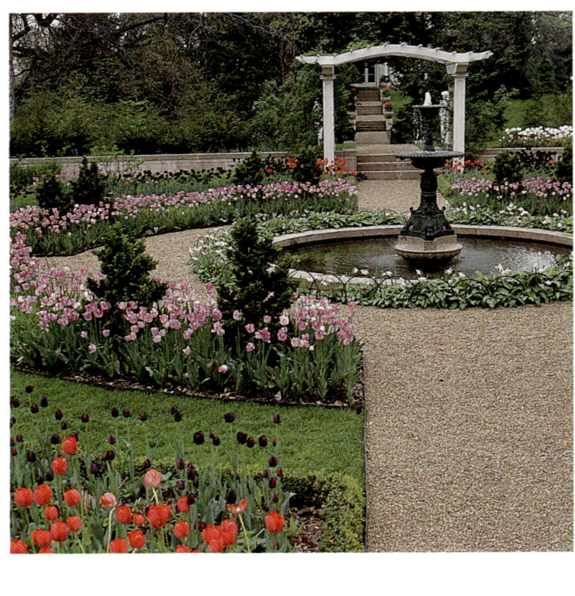
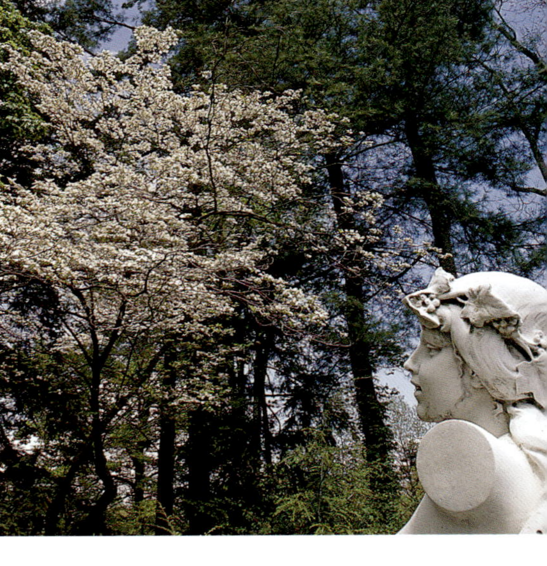
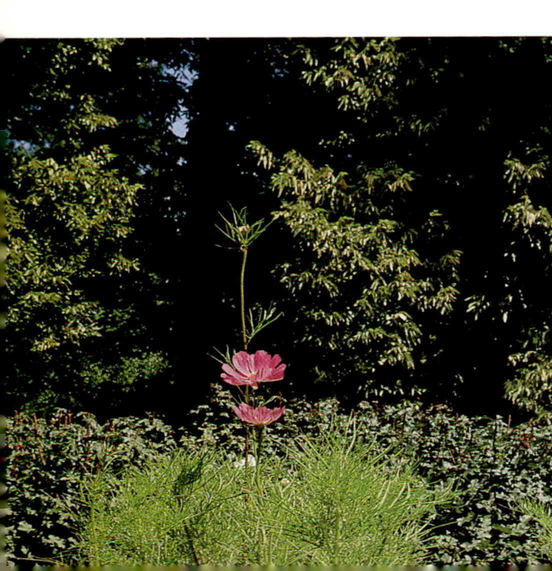
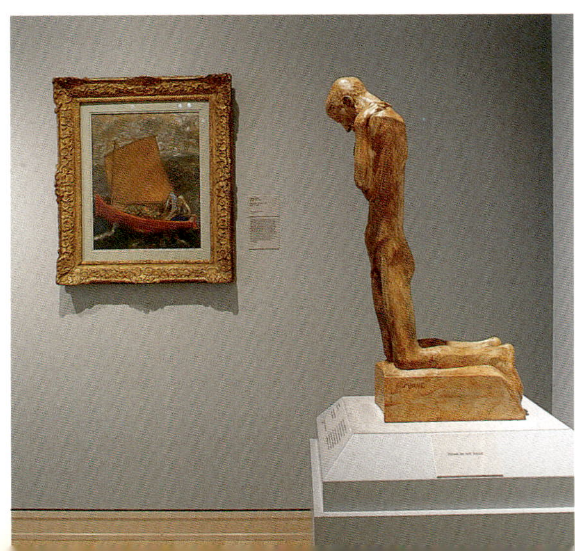
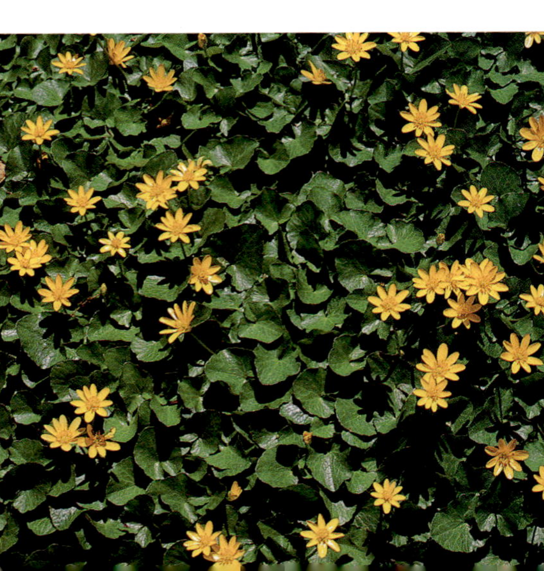

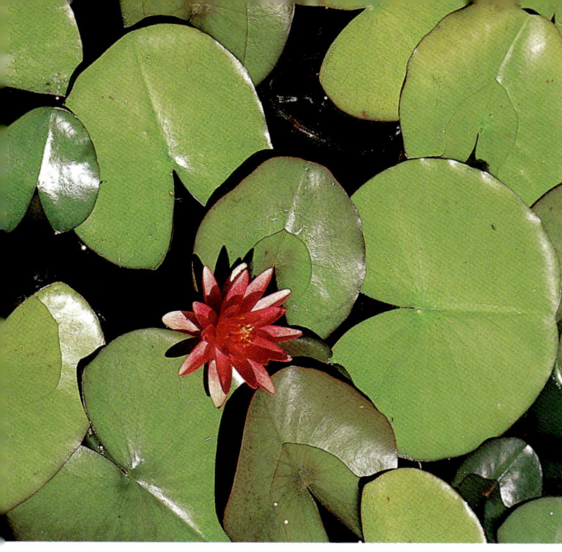
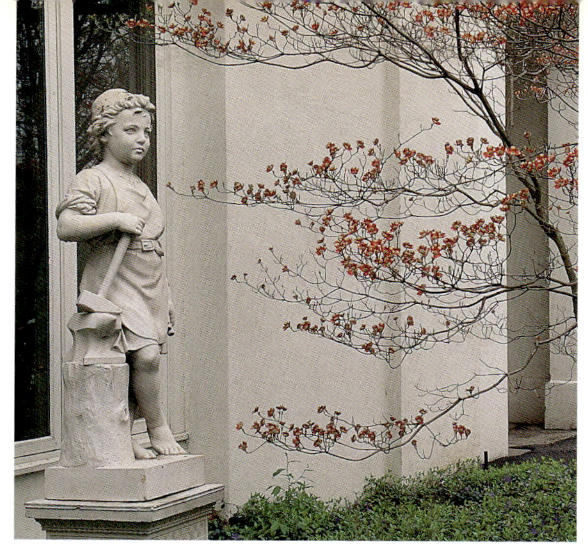
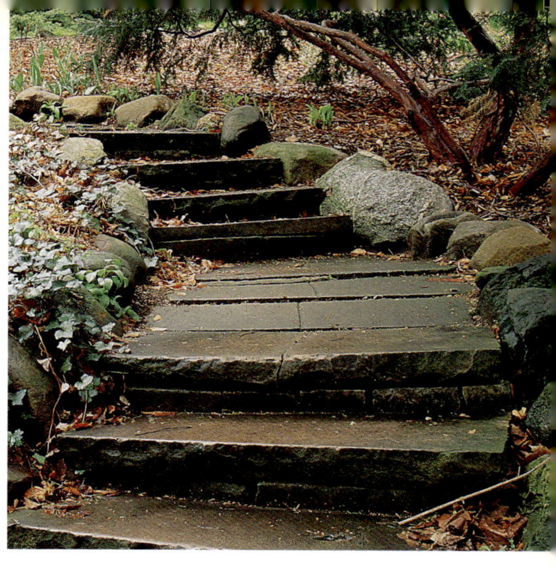
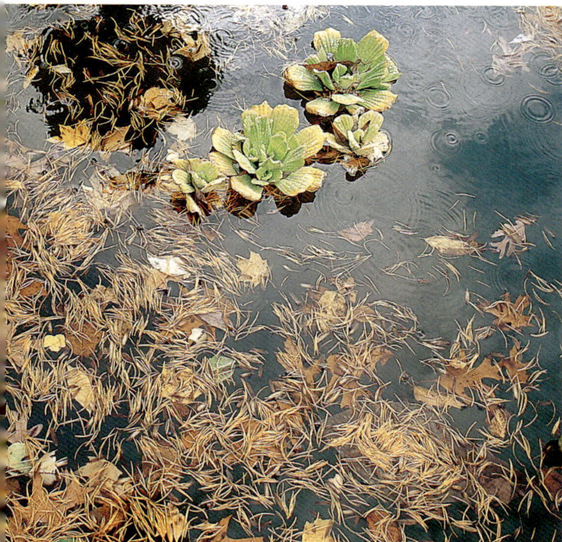
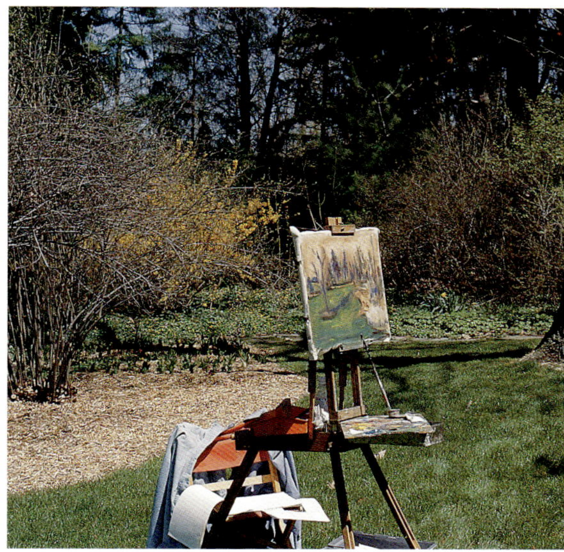
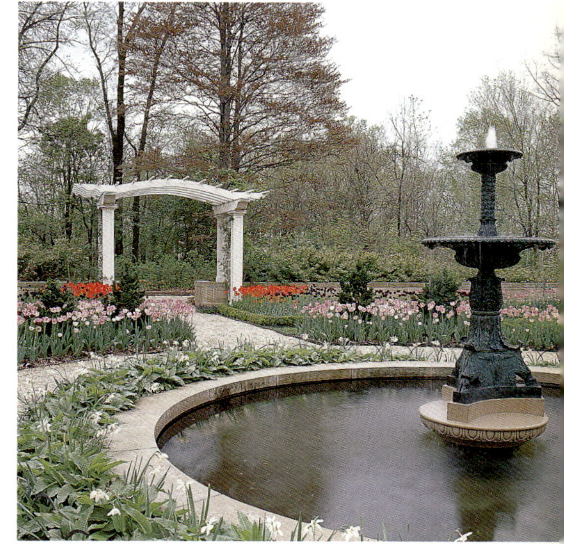
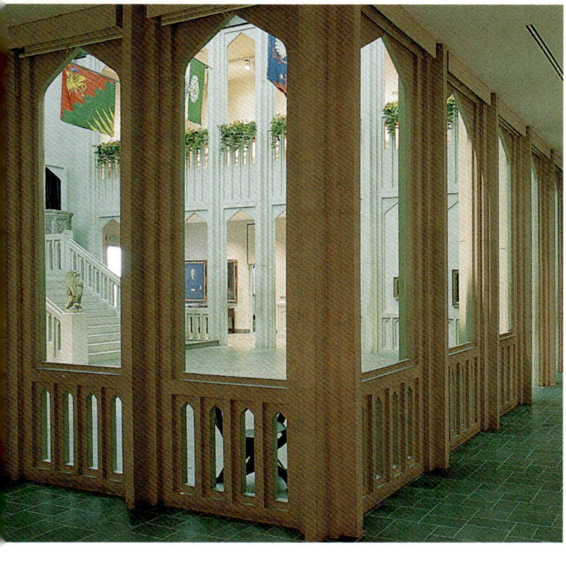
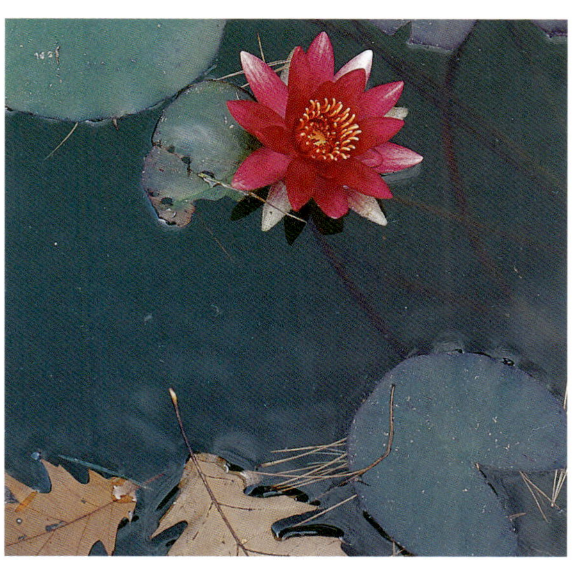
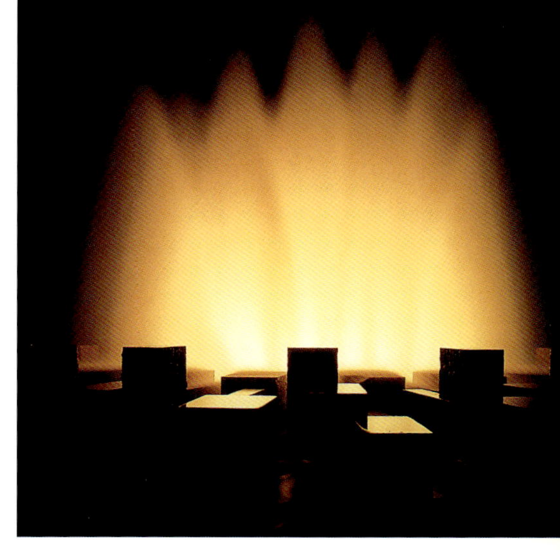
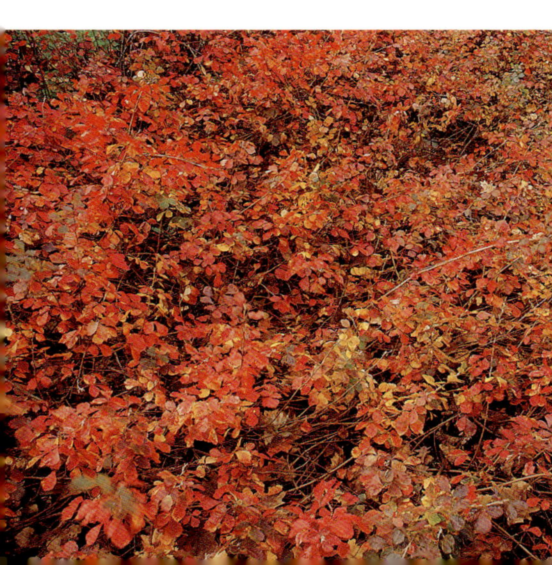
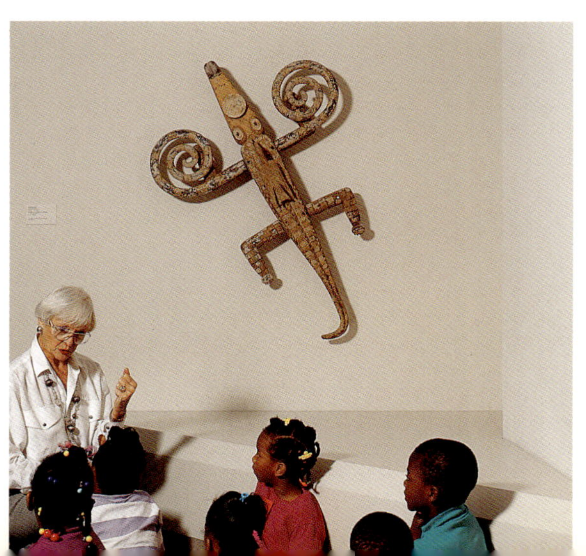
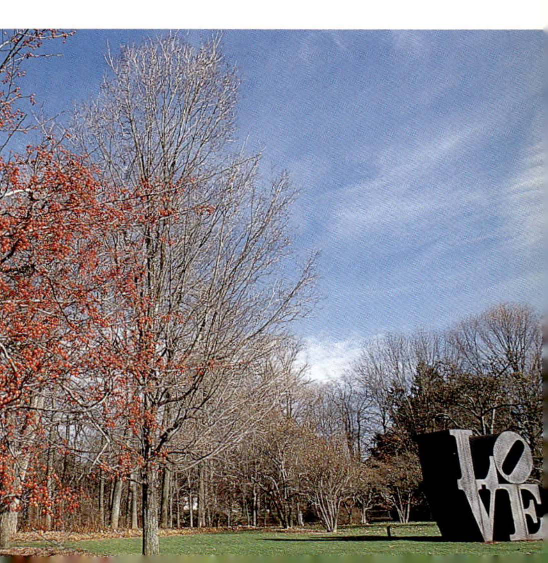

Introduction

With thirteen buildings on its fifty-two-acre parklike campus, the Indianapolis Museum of Art is one of the largest general art museums in the United States. It also is one of the oldest. Founded in 1883 as the Art Association of Indianapolis, the museum now boasts a permanent collection of more than forty thousand works of art distributed among eight curatorial departments. But above and beyond the statistics, the story of the IMA is a story of people, and it begins with the civic-minded men and women who believed that nurturing artists and bringing art to their young city would make life better, richer, and more rewarding for the entire community. That belief has been passed down from one generation to the next, and it continues to inspire the efforts of those who hold the museum in trust today.

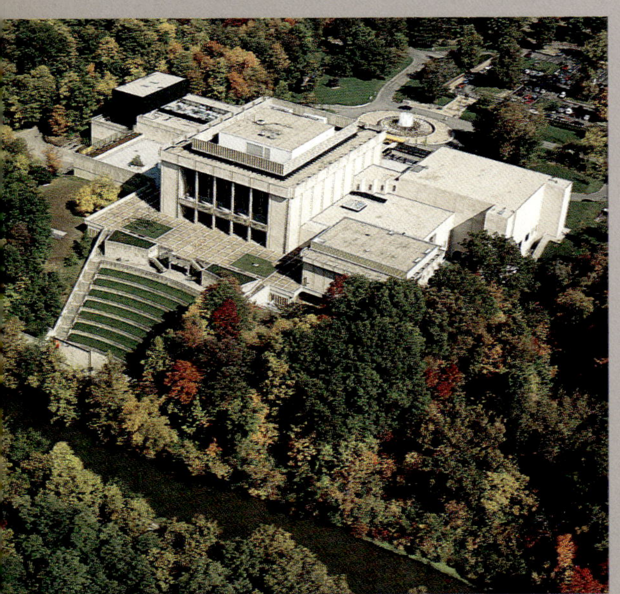

The IMA has been described as a "collection of collections." Over the decades, important private collections formed in this city and state have found a permanent place in the museum, each contributing to the distinctive character of the institution. The Niblack collection of textiles, the Eli Lilly collection of Chinese art, the Kurt F. Pantzer collection of works by British artist J. M. W. Turner, the W. J. Holliday collection of Neo-Impressionist paintings, the Harrison and Sonja Eiteljorg collection of African art, the Marilyn and Eugene Glick collection of contemporary studio glass, and many others have left their imprint on the IMA. The Clowes Collection, owned by the Clowes Fund, has been exhibited for a quarter of a century in the Clowes Pavilion and is the cornerstone of the museum's collection of Old Master paintings. One of the museum's great collector-patrons, Caroline Marmon Fesler set out consciously and systematically to acquire important works of art in a variety of styles and from a variety of periods and schools, not for her private enjoyment, but to enhance the quality of the art holdings the IMA could place before the public. As she wrote to a New York art dealer in 1944, "I will tell you what I am trying to do; to build up our small museum by placing these anonymously—as a memorial to my father and mother, some really good pictures—preferably landscapes." With this aim, she purchased and gave to the IMA paintings by artists ranging from Cézanne, van Gogh, and Picasso, to such seventeenth-century Dutch masters as Hobbema, Cuyp, and Kalf.

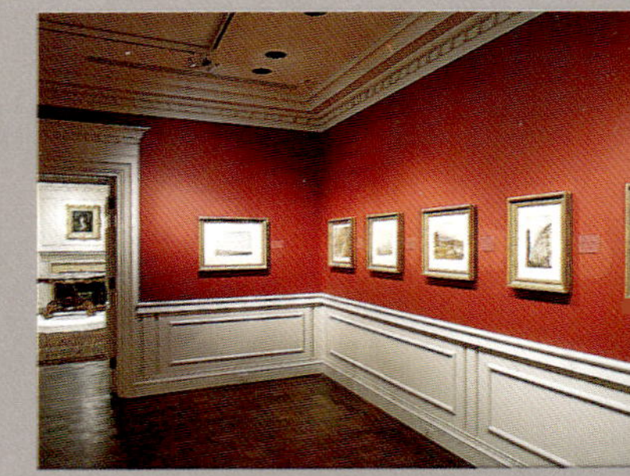

This same generous spirit has long animated the museum's volunteer leaders and professional staff, many of whom have devoted large parts of their lives to serving the community through the IMA. From 1929 until 1965, Wilbur Peat served as the museum's director, steering it safely through years of economic turmoil and international conflict. For nearly as many years—1907 to 1941—Evans Woollen served as president of the museum's governing board. Others have given, and continue to give, their time, their talent, and their treasure to build in Indianapolis one of the nation's great art museums. Each year, volunteers contribute thousands of hours—serving on the governing board, working at information desks and in the shops, guiding visitors through the galleries, organizing events, and raising the funds needed to continue the work of the museum.

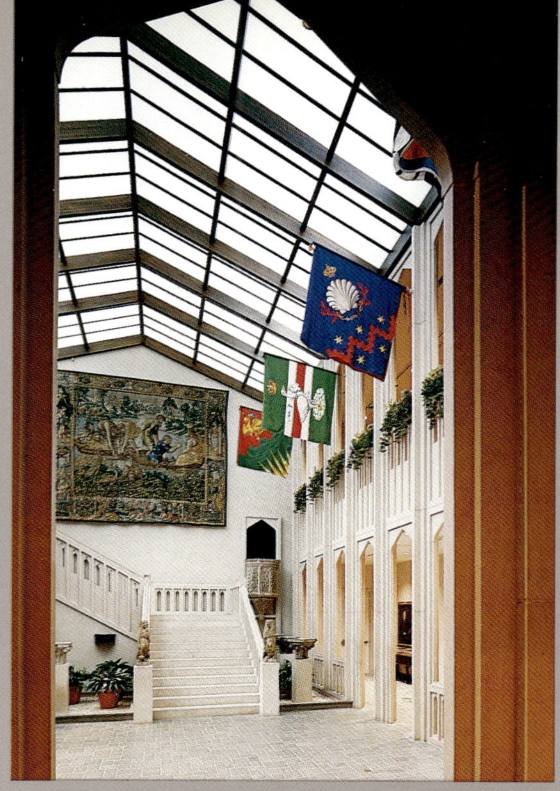

The Annual Report of 1907, which appeared a few months after the museum's first permanent building opened, devoted a page to the organization's early "aims and needs":

> *The Art Association proposes to increase its permanent art collection, to hold frequent exhibitions of the productions of contemporary American and foreign artists, to develop an art library, to add to the facilities for teaching in the Art School in order to keep abreast of the most advanced methods of instruction, to give lectures, receptions, and entertainments of an artistic character, and in every possible way to encourage the study and love of art among the people.*

The Association's founders would be gratified to know that the museum has held true to that early vision and that it continues to collect and preserve art, to exhibit and interpret it, and to make it accessible to a large and diverse audience.

The Association's founders would also find that some challenges remain the same. In the Annual Report dated January 1924, museum president Woollen makes a plea for a permanent endowment fund "for the purpose of bringing the revenues up to the present expenses and for the purpose of enabling the Association to do a more far-reaching work, a work not for art-lovers alone but for all the people of this community." The members of the Art Association rallied. In two years the endowment fund had reached $96,500. By the end of 1928, it was $341,015.36. This story would be repeated many times over the years—when more gallery space or classrooms were needed; when funds for exhibitions and art acquisition were low; in the 1960s, when the Art Association board determined to build a new and more splendid home for the museum, and in the 1980s, when a major building expansion was undertaken.

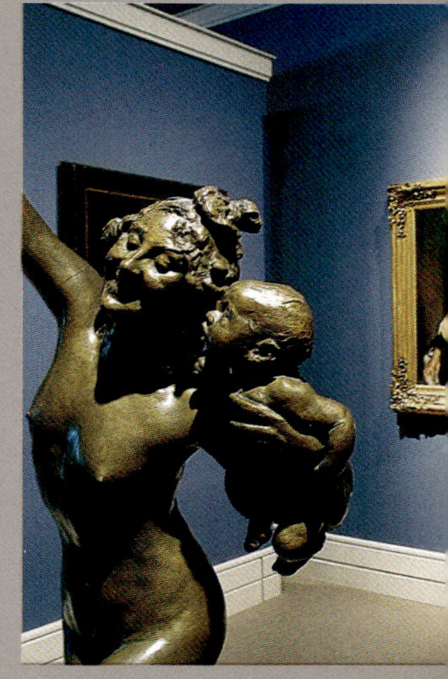

Today, the Indianapolis Museum of Art is a treasure house of art from all over the world, one of the finest collections of art in the country, including ancient bronze vessels from China, masks of power and beauty from Africa, paintings by the great European and American masters, exquisite objects by nineteenth-century metalsmiths and contemporary studio glass artists, superb rugs from Western Asia. The museum has also become a showcase for national and international exhibitions, and paintings and objects in the collection are sought by museums around the world for their special exhibitions.

The IMA is more than a storehouse for art, however. It is a place where people can see and learn about the best of the world's art. It is a community leader in cultural programming and a center of learning for both children and adults. Classes related to the permanent collections and special exhibitions, as well as art survey and studio classes, are offered in the spring and fall; and lectures and symposia are presented throughout the year by distinguished guest speakers on topics as diverse as Japanese woodblock prints, contemporary glass, oriental rugs, and England's greatest landscape painter, J. M. W. Turner.

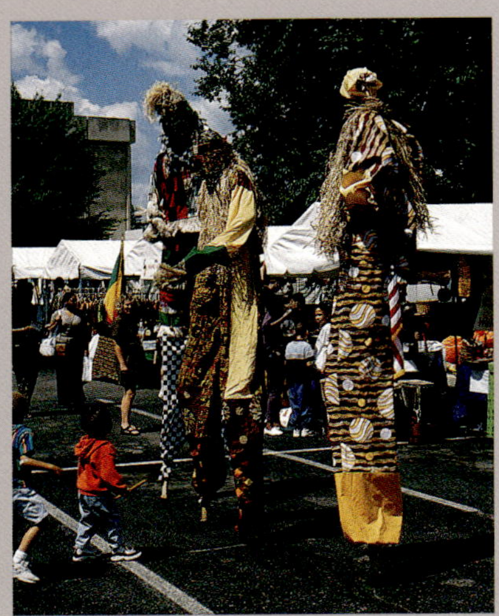

The Education Division of the IMA offers classes, workshops, and tours for children all year, and resource kits about the collections help those who teach art. The more than 30,000 reference books, periodicals, and films housed in the Stout Reference Library and the more than 150,000 slides available in the Jane S. Dutton Educational Resource Center are valuable resources for scholars and others. Special events such as AfricaFest and the recent Chinese New Year Celebration for families provide insight into other cultures, and concerts of classical and contemporary music feature local, regional, and international performers.

The IMA is committed to enriching the lives of the hundreds of thousands of visitors who come each year to see the collections and participate in programs and activities.

Now, the Indianapolis Museum of Art stands at the threshold of a new millennium, poised to make great strides that will establish it firmly in the top tier of American art museums. By continuing to build on the strengths of its existing collections, by enhancing its program of temporary exhibitions, by securing its financial base, and by fully developing its unique outdoor attractions—including restoration of Oldfields, the former J. K. Lilly, Jr., family estate, as a country estate of the early decades of the century—the IMA will give Indianapolis the great art museum this city needs and deserves.

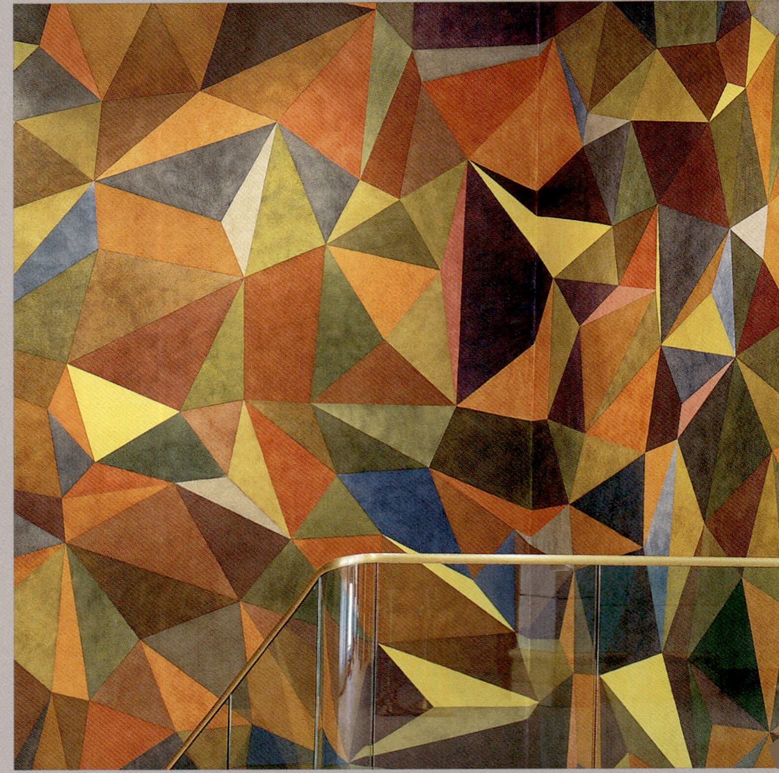

Sol LeWitt
American, b. 1928
Wall Drawing No. 652, on three walls, continuous forms with color ink washes superimposed, 1990
color ink wash
Gift of the Dudley Sutphin Family
1990.40

THE COLLECTIONS OF THE INDIANAPOLIS

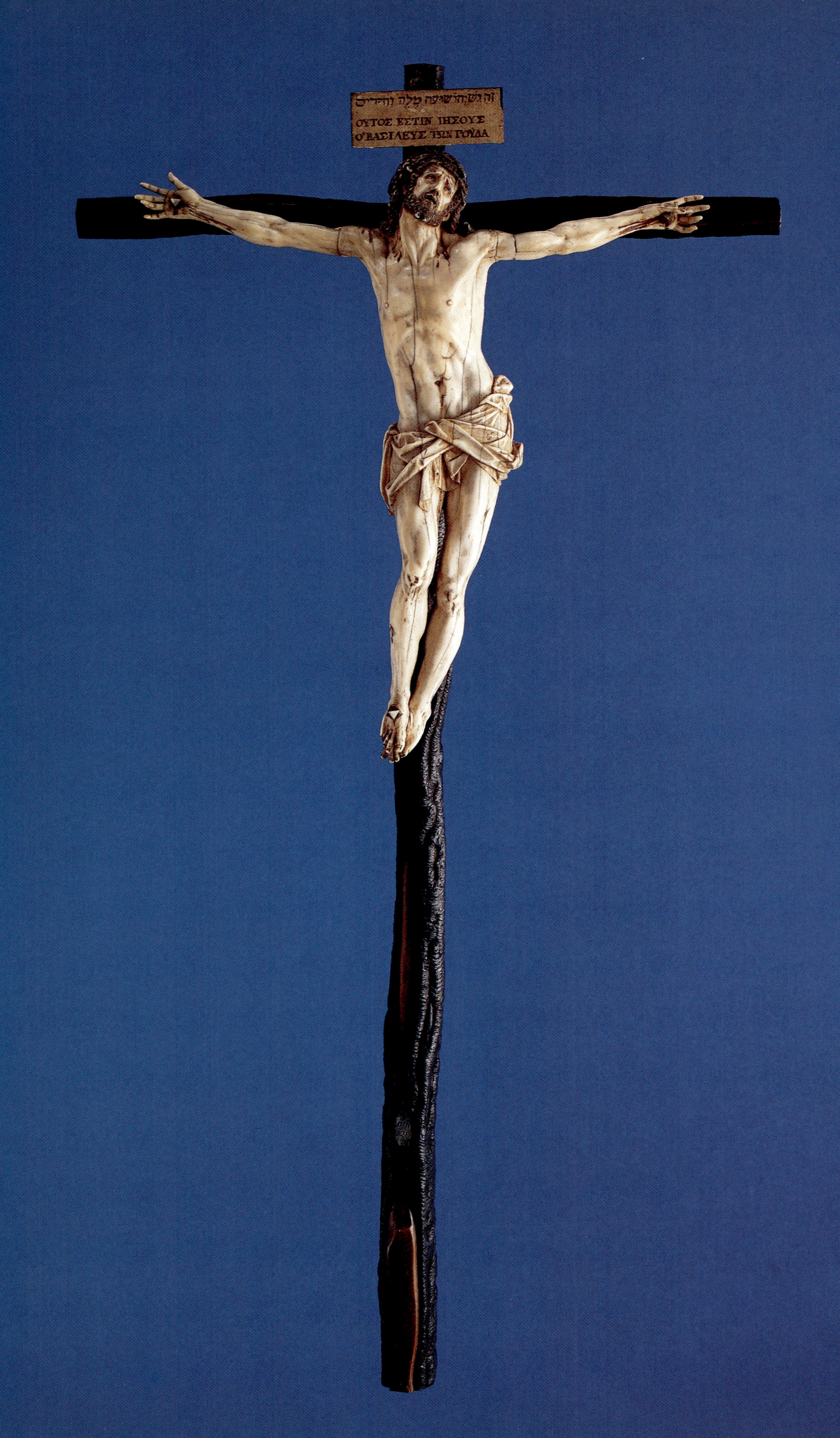
ΟΥΤΟΣ ΕΣΤΙΝ ΙΗΣΟΥΣ
Ο ΒΑΣΙΛΕΥΣ ΤΩΝ ΓΟΥΔΑ

Old Master Painting and Sculpture

The collection of European painting and sculpture from the twelfth through the beginning of the nineteenth century includes many of the museum's finest and most important works of art. There are strong holdings of Italian Renaissance art, an impressive collection of seventeenth-century Dutch and Flemish paintings, and superb examples of eighteenth-century French, Italian, and British painting.

The collection includes rare and important examples of Romanesque fresco painting in two scenes from the life of Christ executed around 1125 for the remote Spanish hermitage of San Baudelio de Berlanga.

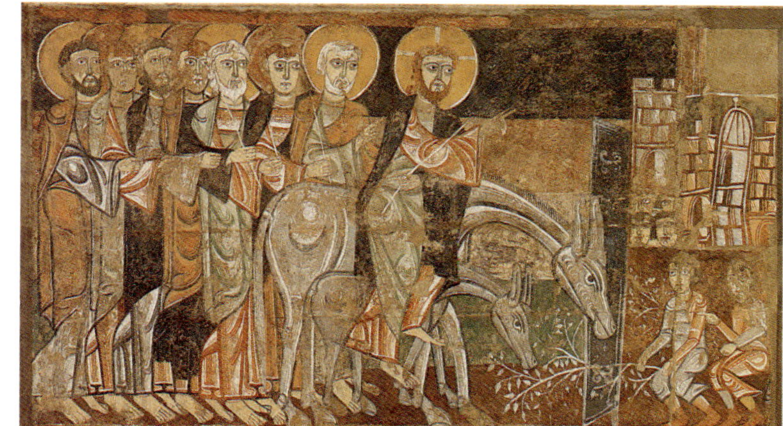

The range of Italian Renaissance painting is suggested in the stylistic distance between Barnaba da Modena's powerfully expressionistic *Crucifixion*, dating from around 1375, and the humanist naturalism of Titian's *Portrait of a Man*, painted about 125 years later. Giuliano Bugiardini's serenely monumental *Virgin and Child with the Infant St. John* is a fine example of the High Renaissance style in Florence. Renaissance artists outside Italy produced works of comparable quality; among the examples in Indianapolis is the beautiful and miraculously well-preserved *Annunciation Triptych,* painted in Bruges around 1483 by the Master of the Legend of St. Ursula.

The museum's outstanding collection of seventeenth-century Dutch and Flemish painting includes a noteworthy group of landscapes by Meindert Hobbema, Jacob van Ruisdael, Jan van Goyen, Jan Both, and Aelbert Cuyp. Cuyp's *Valkof at Nijmegen* is one of the artist's finest works. Dutch marine painting is represented in tempests by Simon de Vlieger and Ludolph Backhuysen. The collection also includes a small but important group of Dutch still life paintings, including fine works by Pieter Claesz and Willem Kalf. Works by seventeenth-century Flemish artists include one of Anthony van Dyck's earliest works, *The Entry of Christ into Jerusalem*, painted in about 1618, and an immense altarpiece painted in 1656 by Erasmus II Quellinus for the "hidden" Jesuit church of St. Francis Xavier in Amsterdam.

The Baroque art of Italy is exemplified by the Caravaggesque naturalism of Valentin de Boulogne's masterful portrayal of Rafaello Menicucci as well as by the stylistically antithetical late Roman classicism of Carlo Maratta's graceful and radiantly colored *Rebecca and Eliezer at the Well.* The advent of the baroque style in Spain is signaled by Gaspar Núñez Delgado's *Crucifixion*, a work characterized by its robust realism and profoundly human expression of anguish. It is among the most important works of Spanish baroque sculpture in America.

ABOVE:
Master of San Baudelio de Berlanga
Spanish, 12th century
Entry of Christ into Jerusalem
about 1125
fresco mounted on canvas
70 3/4 x 121 in.
Gift of Dr. G. H. A. Clowes and Elija B. Martindale
57.151

OPPOSITE:
Gaspar Núñez Delgado
Spanish, active 1581-1606
Crucifix, 1599
ivory with polychromy, ebony, mahogany, and silver
26 3/4 x 14 x 3 1/4 in.
Gift of Walter E. and Tekla B. Wolf by exchange
1995.24

A fine collection of eighteenth-century French paintings by Rococo masters such as Antoine Watteau, François Boucher and Jean Honoré Fragonard complements the museum's holdings of contemporaneous work by Italian and British artists. The art of eighteenth-century Italy is well represented in turbulent landscapes by Alessandro Magnasco and Marco Ricci, a Venetian *vedute* by Canaletto, imaginary Roman views by Panini, and a splendid oil sketch by Corrado Giaquinto. The extravagant and ingenious art of eighteenth-century France can be seen in Watteau's rustic *Country Dance* and Boucher's more refined *Idyllic Landscape with Woman Fishing.* Only slightly later, Richard Wilson's *Apollo and the Seasons (*about 1768) exemplifies the early picturesque landscape in England.

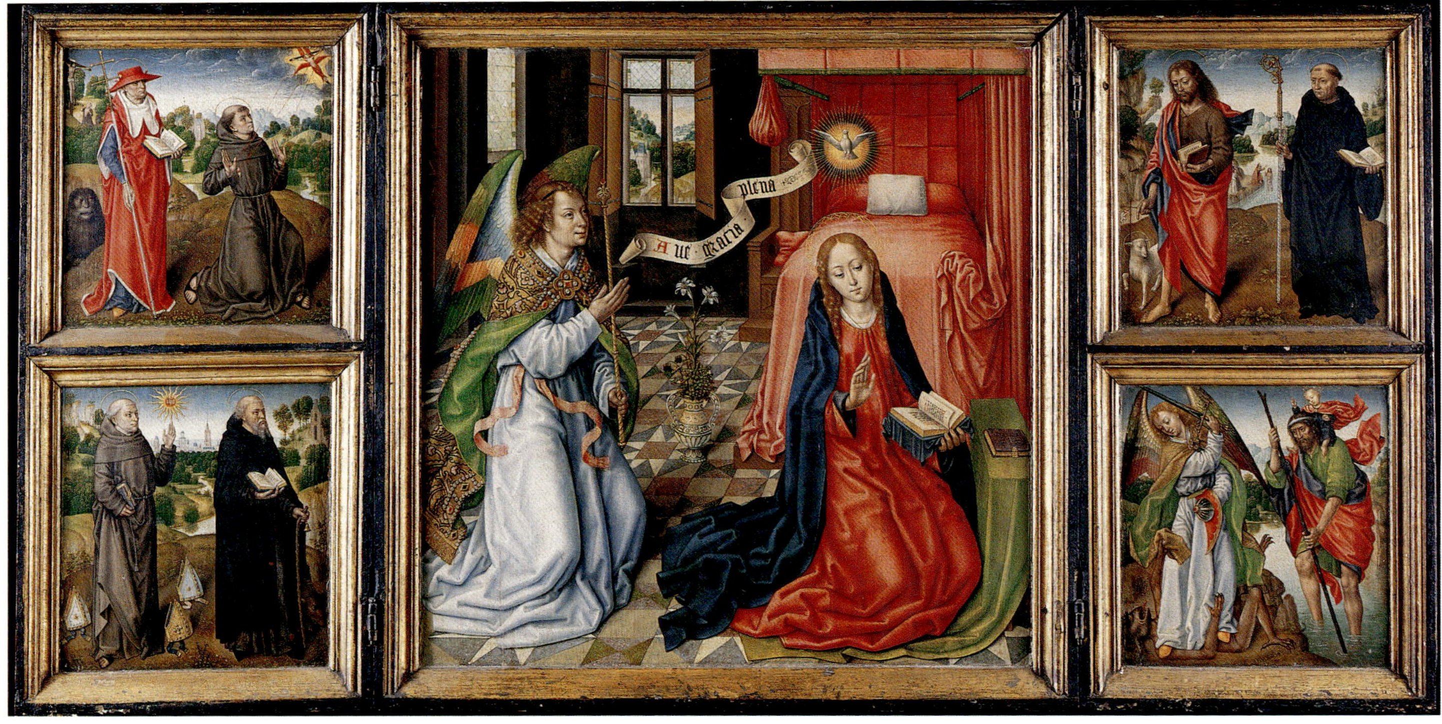

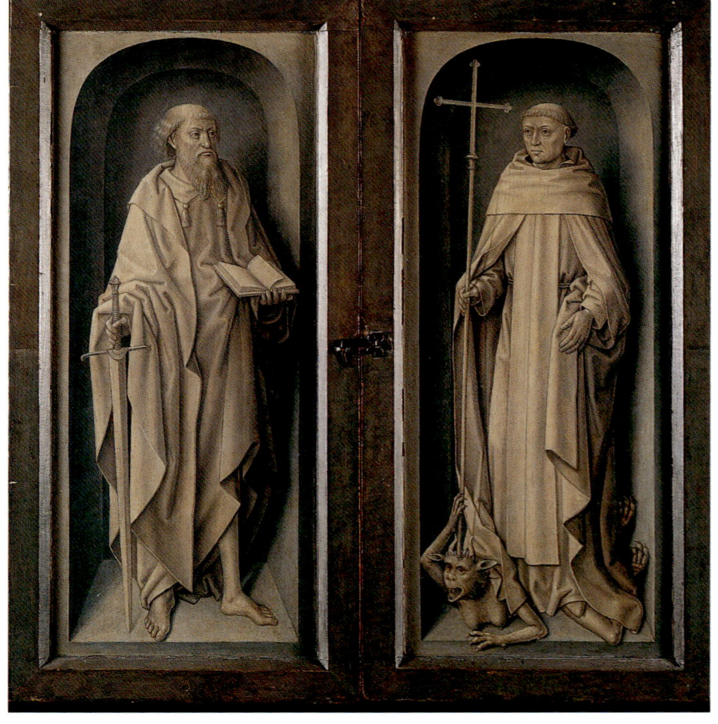

ABOVE AND RIGHT:
Master of the Legend of St. Ursula
Flemish, active last quarter 15th century
Annunciation Triptych, about 1483
oil on panel
(wings open) 23 1/2 x 45 3/4 in.
anonymous gift and Richard A. Fairbanks Fund
1997.138

OPPOSITE:
Willem Kalf
Dutch, 1619-1693
Still Life with a Chinese Blue-and-White Jar, 1669
oil on canvas
30 3/4 x 26 in.
Gift of Mrs. James W. Fesler in memory of Daniel W. and Elizabeth C. Marmon
45.9

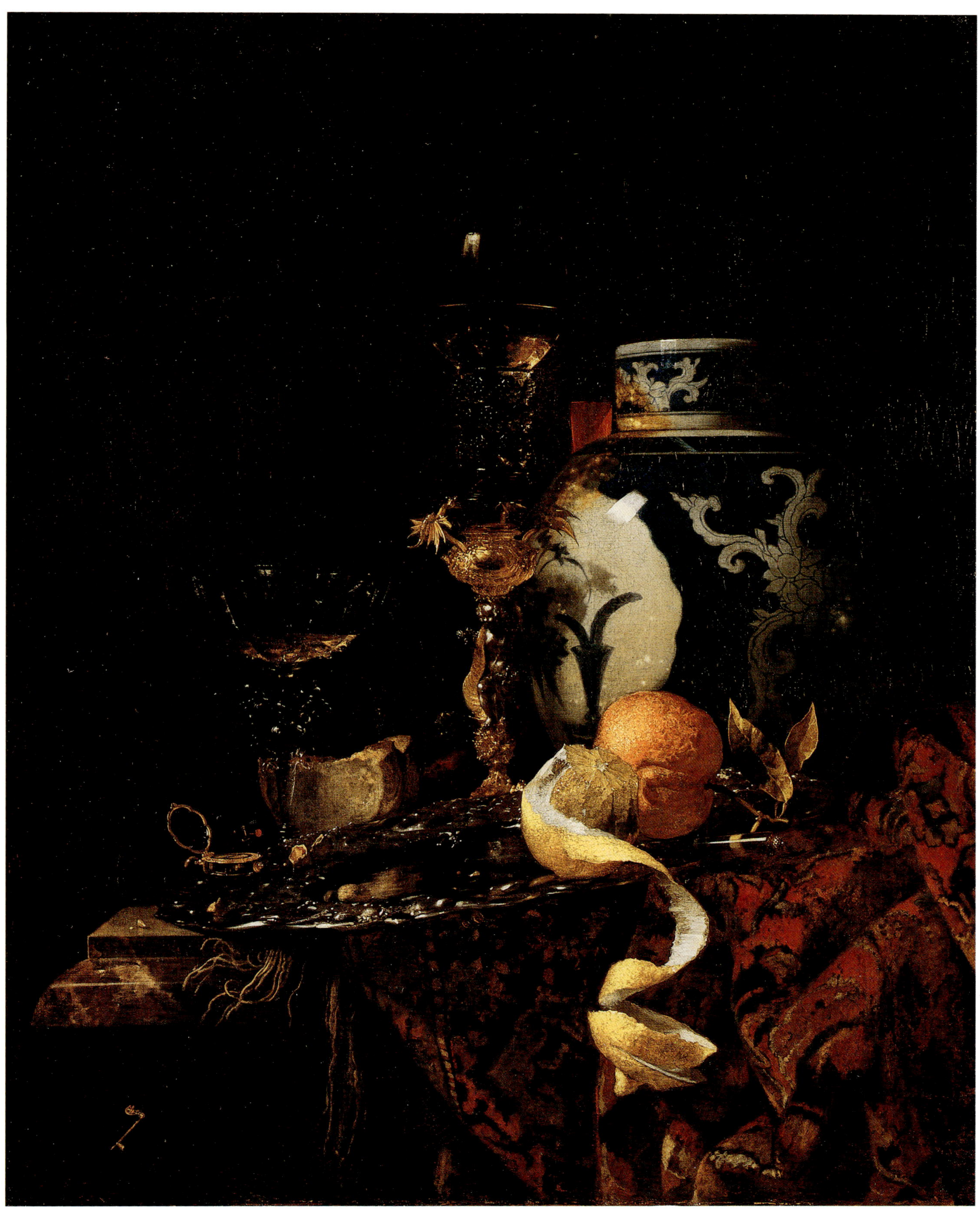

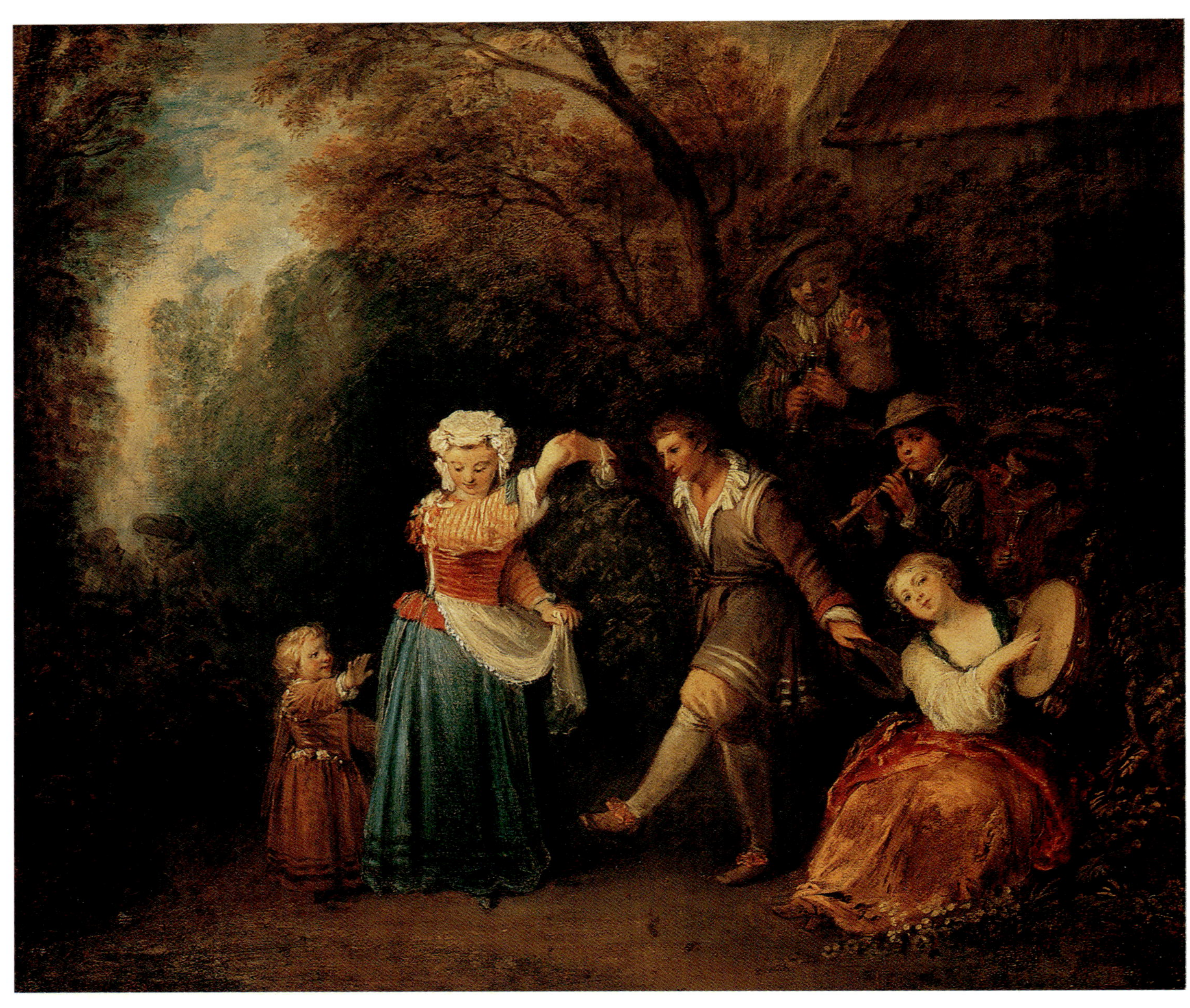

Antoine Watteau
French, 1684-1721
The Country Dance
about 1706-1710
oil on canvas
19 1/2 x 23 5/8 in.
Gift of Mrs. Herman C. Krannert
74.98

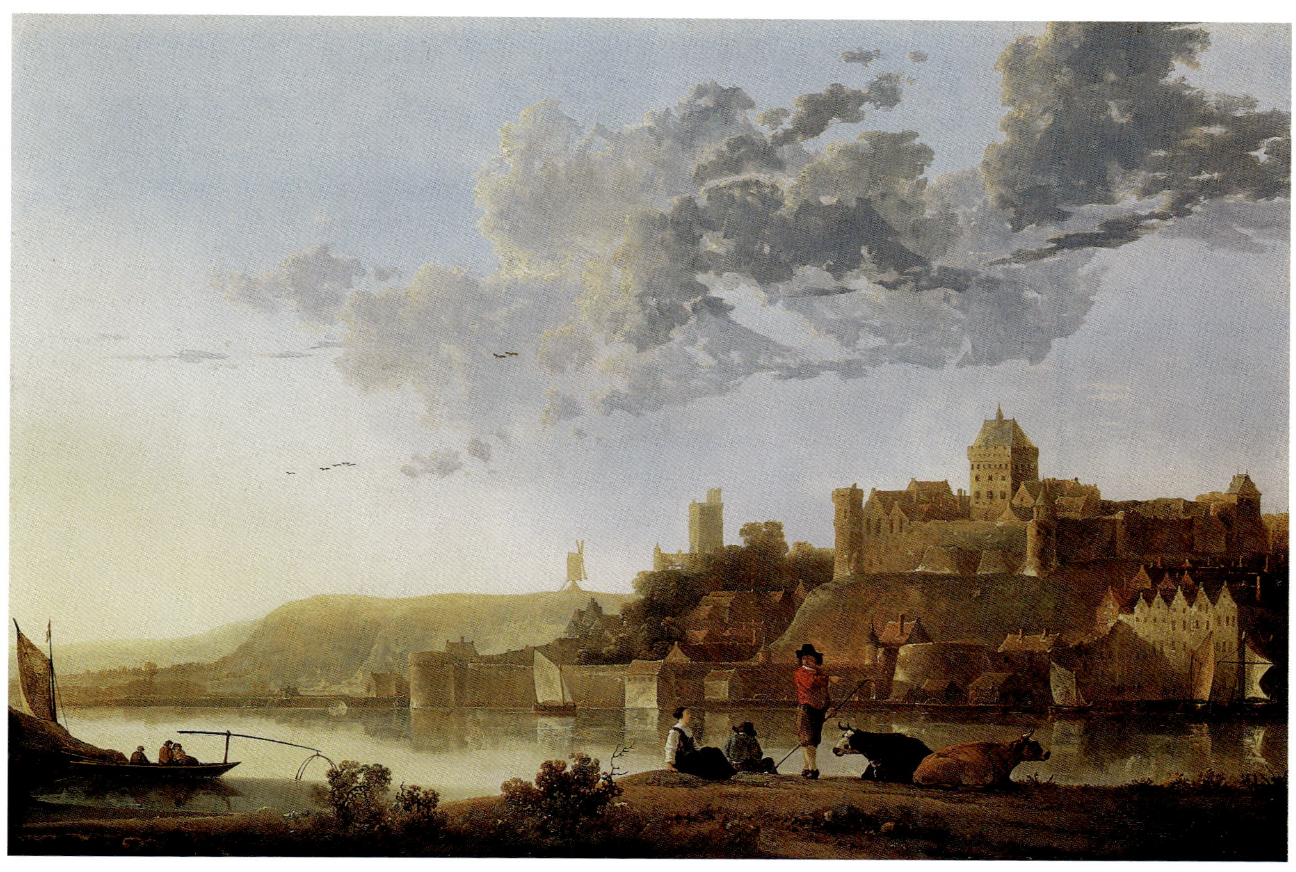

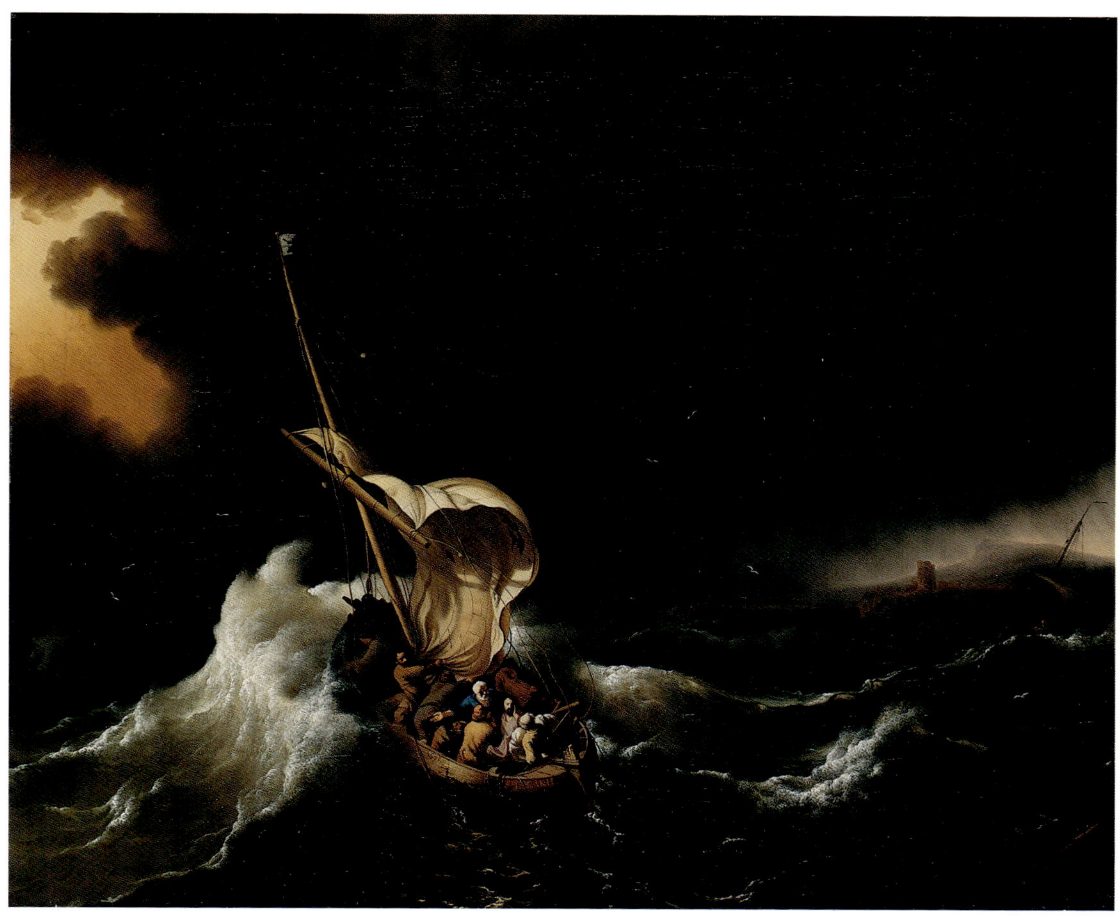

ABOVE:
Aelbert Cuyp
Dutch, 1620-1691
The Valkof at Nijmegen
about 1652-1654
oil on panel, 19 1/4 x 29 in.
Gift in commemoration of the 60th anniversary of the Art Association of Indianapolis in memory of Daniel W. and Elizabeth C. Marmon
43.107

LEFT:
Ludolf Backhuysen
Dutch, 1631-1708
Christ in the Storm on the Sea of Galilee, 1695
oil on canvas, 23 x 28 1/2 in.
Marian and Harold Victor Fund, 1994.117

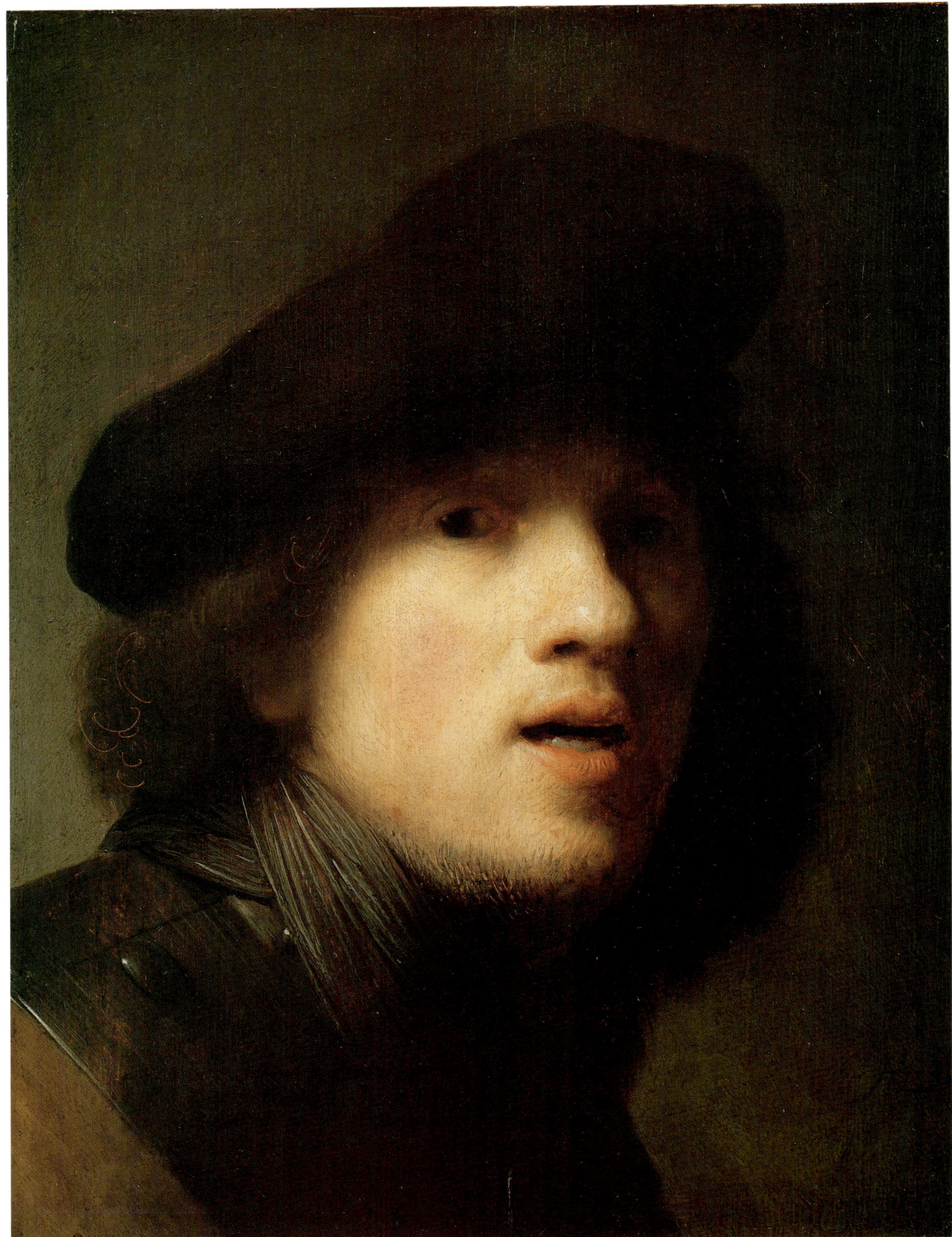

The Clowes Fund Collection

Described as "a collection of Old Masters," the Clowes Fund Collection spans six centuries, from the beginning of the fourteenth to the end of the nineteenth century. Most of the works are small, in keeping with the scale of the setting for which they were originally selected, the home of Dr. George H. A. and Edith Whitehill Clowes.

The Clowes Fund Collection includes works from Italy, Spain, Holland, England, Belgium, France, and Germany, attributed to such well-known artists as Giovanni Bellini, Caravaggio, Goya, El Greco, Rembrandt, Sir Joshua Reynolds, Sir Peter Paul Rubens, and Sir Anthony Van Dyck.

Dr. Clowes, director of research at Eli Lilly and Company until 1946, found himself in the fortunate position of being able to buy fine paintings during the Depression, a time when many of the great European collections were coming onto the market. Gradually, a collection developed at Westerley, the Clowes home, and during the ensuing years, art historians studied a number of the paintings, sometimes providing new information about their origins and history. Following the death of Dr. Clowes in 1958, this collection of paintings and objets d'art became the property of the Clowes Fund, established as a charitable organization. The collection was exhibited in Westerley from 1960 until 1971. In April 1972, the Clowes Pavilion, built to house this fine collection, was dedicated in memory of Edith Whitehill Clowes.

OPPOSITE:
Rembrandt van Rijn
Dutch, 1606-1669
Self-Portrait, about 1629
oil on panel, 17 x 13 in.
The Clowes Fund Collection

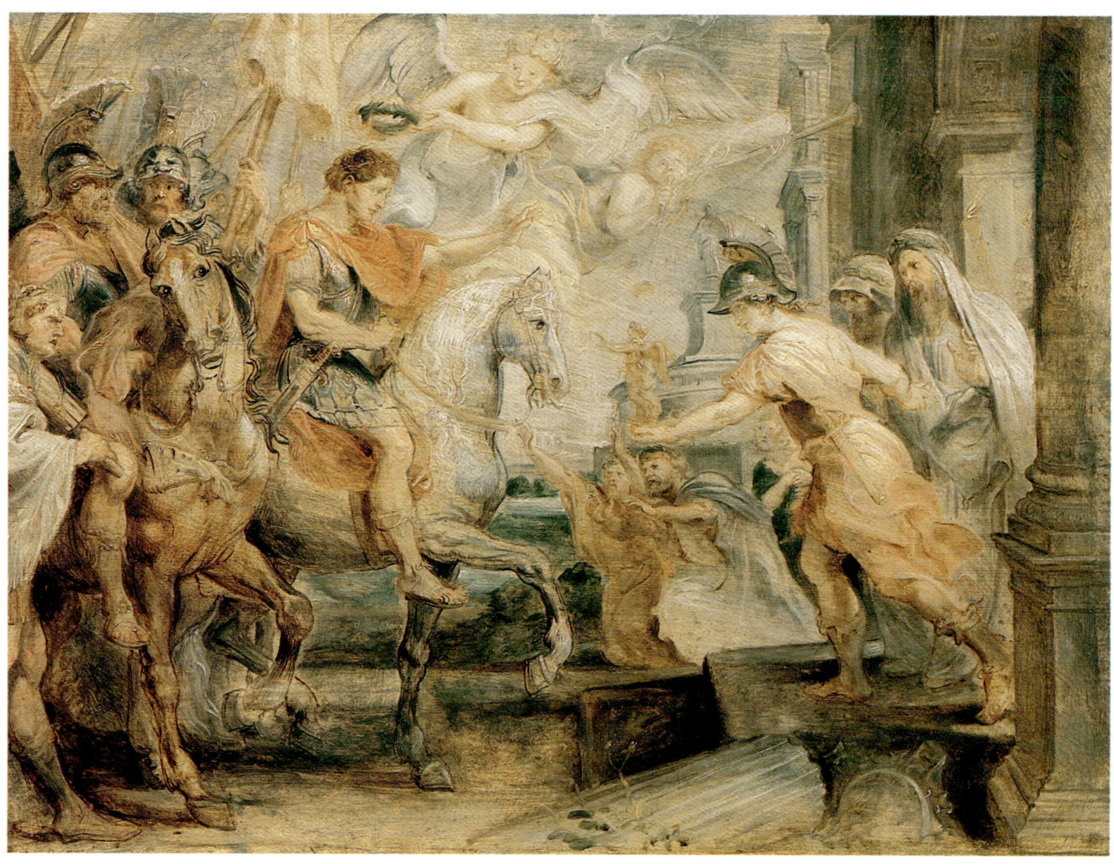

BELOW:
Peter Paul Rubens
Flemish, 1577-1640
Triumphant Entry of Constantine into Rome, about 1622
oil on panel, 19 x 25 1/2 in.
The Clowes Fund Collection

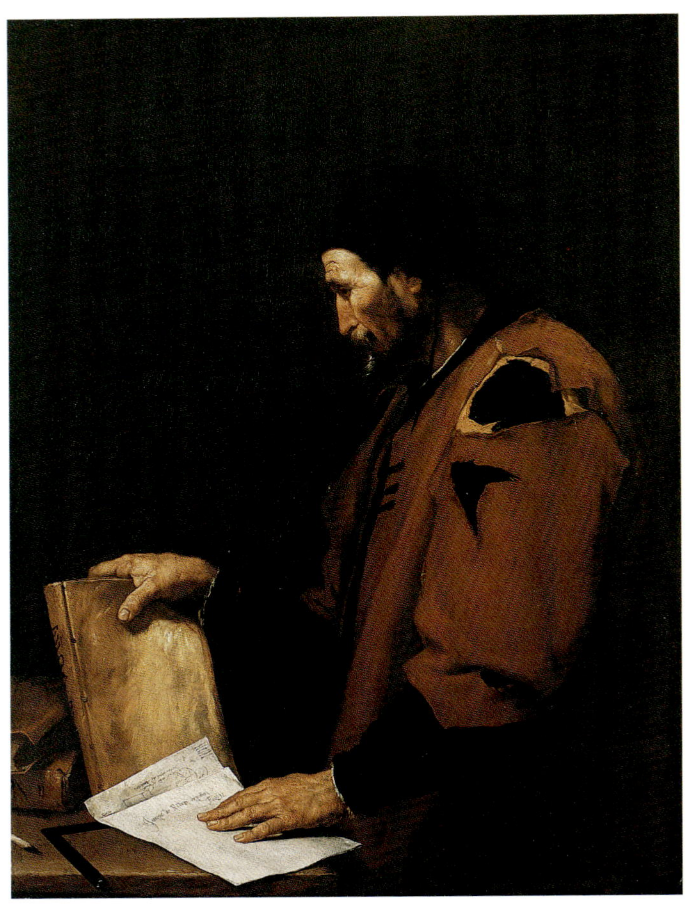

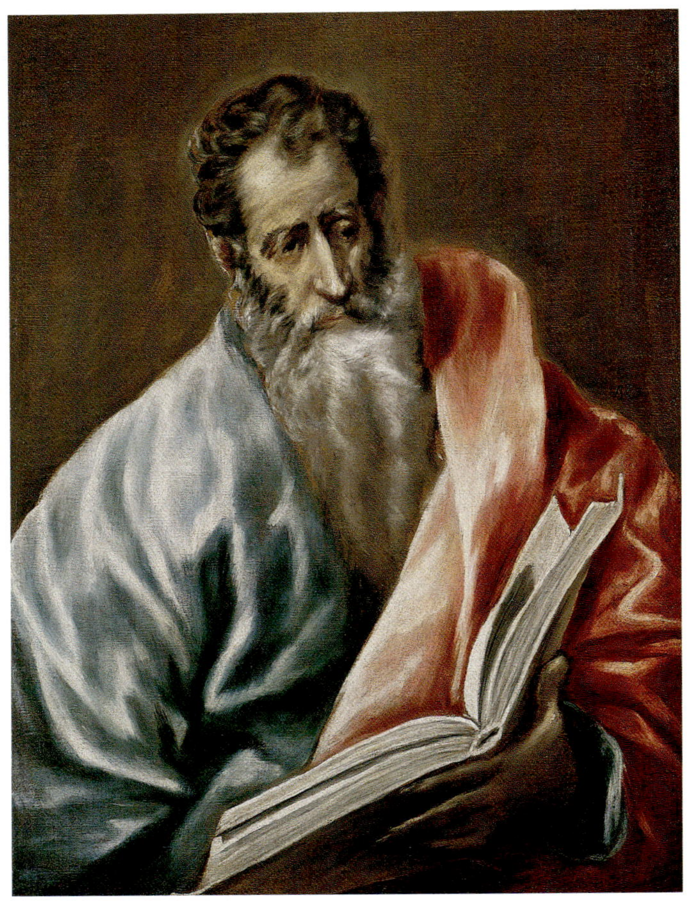

ABOVE:
Jusepe de Ribera
Spanish, 1591-1652
Aristotle, 1637
oil on canvas, 49 x 39 in.
The Clowes Fund Collection

ABOVE RIGHT:
Domenikos Theotokopoulos
called El Greco
Spanish, 1541-1614
St. Matthew, about 1610-1614
oil on canvas
28 3/8 x 21 7/8 in.
The Clowes Fund Collection

RIGHT:
François Clouet
French, about 1522-1572
Marquis de Scepeaux, 1566
oil on panel, 12 1/2 x 9 1/4 in.
The Clowes Fund Collection

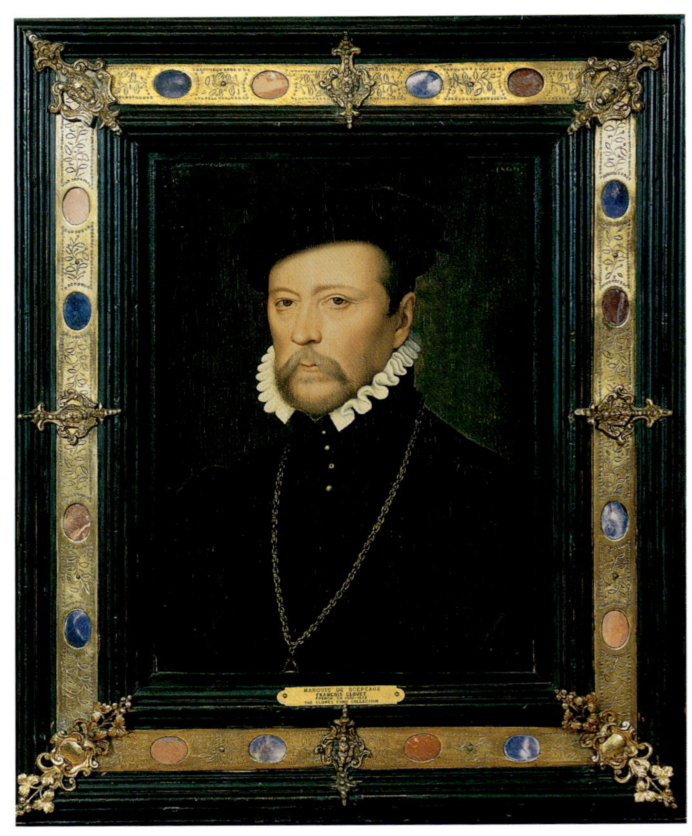

Agnolo Gaddi
Italian, 1369-1396
Saint Mary Magdalene in the Wilderness, St. Benedict, St.Bernard of Clairvaux, and St.Catherine of Alexandria, about 1390
tempera on panel
28 1/2 x 8 in., each panel
The Clowes Fund Collection

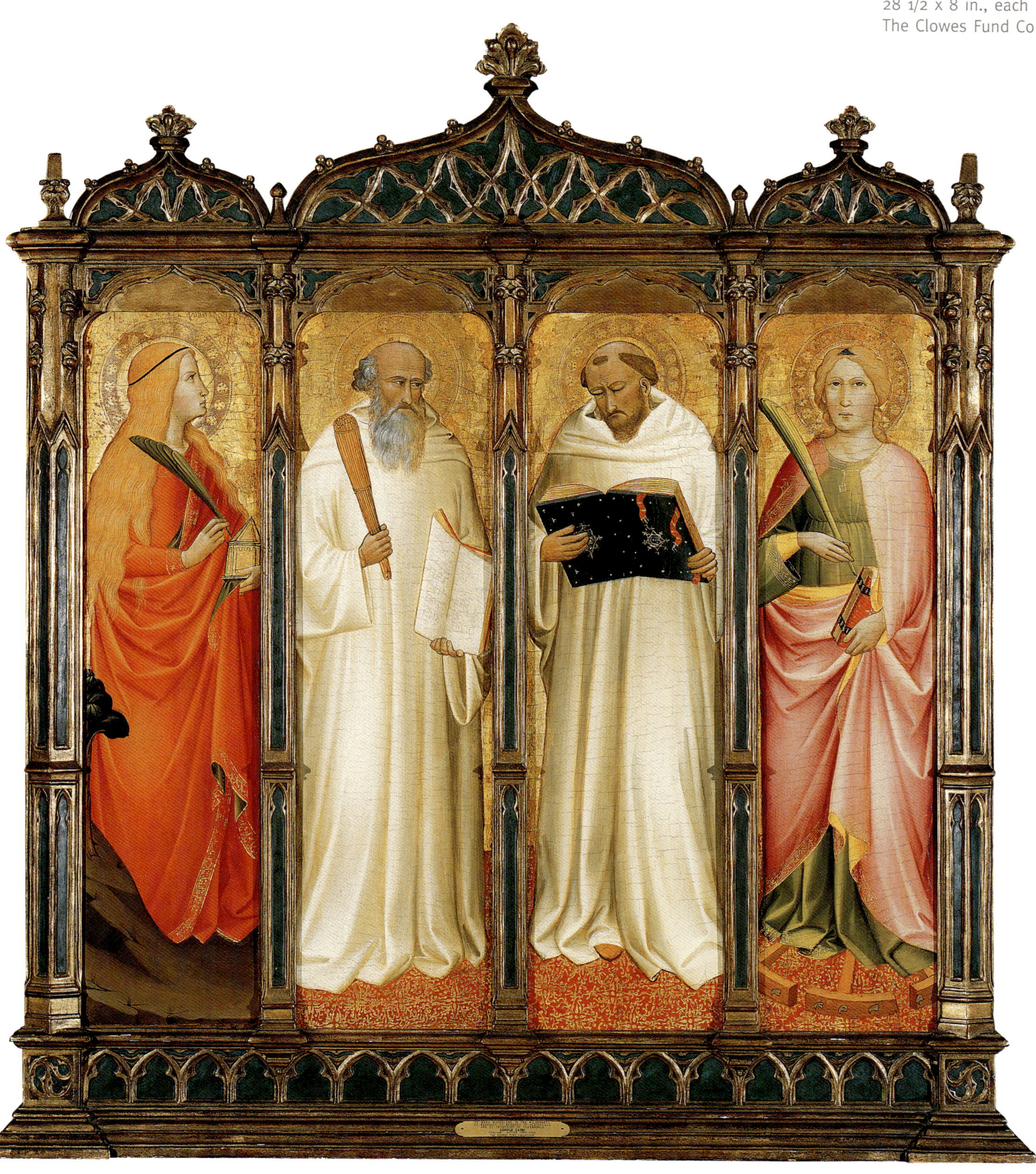

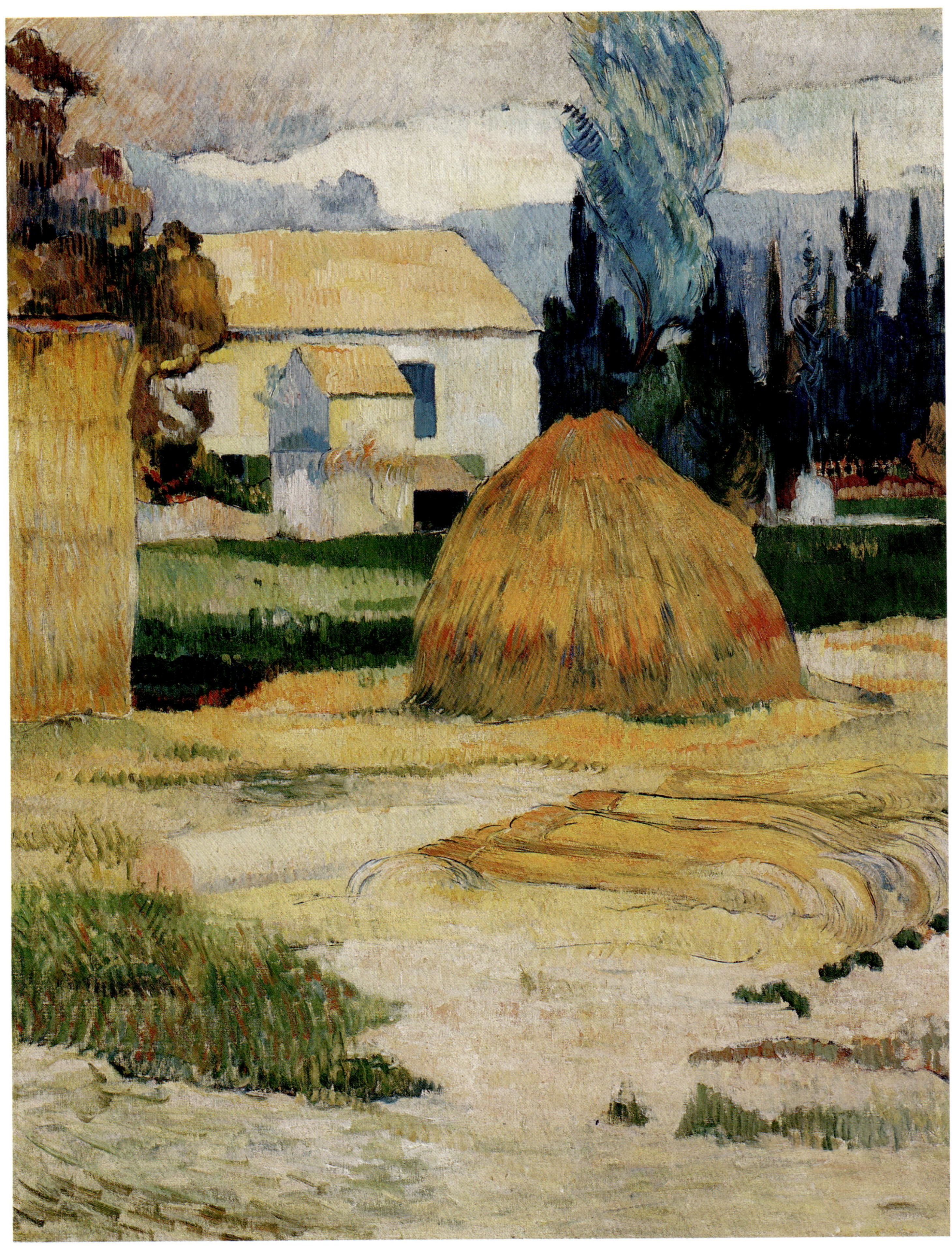

European Painting and Sculpture, 1800-1945

From the dramatic landscapes of J. M. W. Turner to the geometric forms of Fernand Léger's machine age, the nineteenth- and twentieth-century European painting collection includes many of the IMA's best-loved works. The collection's earlier paintings draw upon the harmony and order of the neoclassical movement or the romantic era's fascination with nature. The Barbizon School of mid-nineteenth-century France lives on through the landscapes of Corot, Daubigny, and Millet; while vivid canvases by Renoir and Pissarro exemplify the brilliant color and luminous effects of French Impressionism. Late-career views of London and Venice demonstrate Monet's long-standing commitment to the movement.

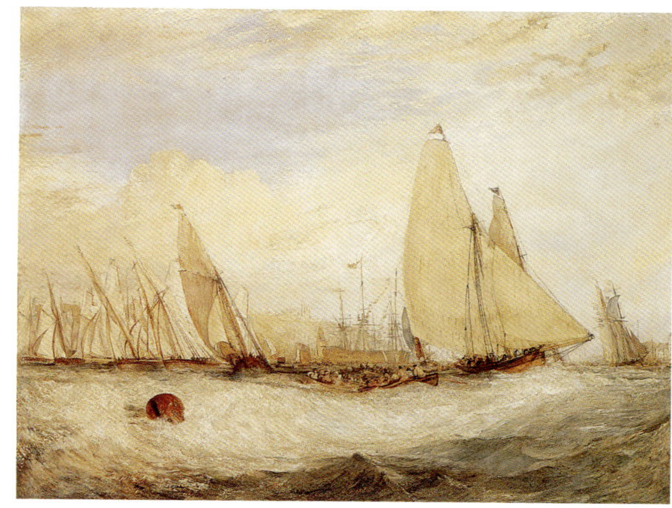

At the heart of the museum's post-impressionist collection are three magnificent canvases by Cézanne, van Gogh, and Seurat, working at the height of their powers. All three paintings were the gifts of Indianapolis connoisseur Caroline Marmon Fesler, who devoted herself to finding great landscapes for the IMA.

With Seurat's radiant harbor scene, and the many works bequeathed to the museum by Indianapolis industrialist W. J. Holliday in 1979, the IMA possesses the finest group of Neo-Impressionist, or pointillist, paintings in America. This unique collection, featuring pictures by Signac, van Rysselberghe, Luce, and van de Velde, documents the development and impact of the Neo-Impressionist movement from the 1880s through the early years of the twentieth century. Drawing upon a wide variety of artists, it reflects the allure of Seurat's theories and methods for artists in Belgium, Holland, and Germany, as well as France. In recent years, the collection has been embellished by the addition of paintings by Lucien Pissarro, H. P. Bremmer, and Willy Finch.

Paul Gauguin, the other towering figure of late nineteenth-century French painting, is represented by a majestic landscape given in memory of William Ray Adams. Works by his followers, related to the broad artistic movement known as Symbolism, have a distinct presence in the European galleries. A small interior by Vuillard exemplifies the Nabi artists' penchant for pattern, while Redon's mystical images and Lacombe's powerful vistas reflect vastly different attempts to bridge the physical and spiritual realms.

While the IMA's nineteenth-century sculpture collection is not large, it is indicative of the era's major themes. The collection features *animalier* bronzes by Barye and other French sculptors, a caricature by Daumier, and neoclassical and romantic mythological subjects in marble, bronze, and terra cotta. Later in the century, the restrained dignity of Jules Dalou's sculpture contrasts with expressive, tormented figures by Rodin. Finally, an angular,

OPPOSITE:
Paul Gauguin
French, 1848–1903
Landscape near Arles, 1888
oil on canvas, 36 x 28 1/2 in.
Gift in memory of William Ray Adams, 44.10

ABOVE:
Joseph Mallord William Turner
English, 1775–1851
East Cowes Castle, the Seat of J. Nash Esq., The Regatta Beating to Windward, 1828
oil on canvas
35 1/2 x 47 1/2 in.
Gift of Mr. and Mrs. Nicholas Noyes, 71.32

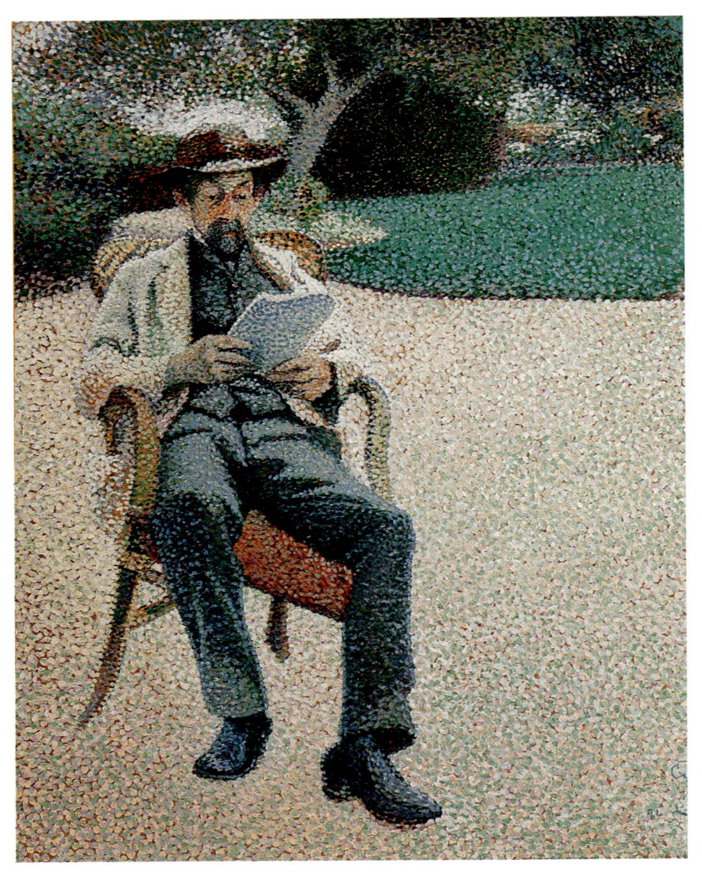

introspective figure by George Minne embodies the mood of the Belgian Symbolist movement.

Cubism, one of the first really pivotal movements of the twentieth century, is represented at the IMA by the canvases of Picasso and Braque. Figural and landscape paintings by Modigliani, Utrillo, and Dufy exemplify the artists affiliated with the School of Paris, when the French capital was the center of the Western art world. While a signature Léger canvas assumes the machine-like forms of the modern era, works by Rouault and Chagall turn to whimsical or spiritual themes.

Twentieth-century three-dimensional works are largely confined to representational images and include a small nude by Maillol, a wistful terra cotta bust by Lehmbruck, and a full-figure sculpture by Joseph Bernard that suggests the stylized approach of the Art Deco era. A strategic recent addition to the collection is an elegant female form by Archipenko.

ABOVE:
Henry van de Velde
Belgian, 1863–1957
Père Biart Reading in the Garden
1890 or 1891
oil on brown paper
mounted to canvas
24 7/16 x 20 7/16 in.
The Holliday Collection
79.320

RIGHT:
Lucien Pissarro
French, 1863–1944
Interior of the Studio, 1887
oil on canvas
25 1/4 x 31 1/2 in.
Gift in memory of Robert
S. Ashby by his family and
friends, 1995.100

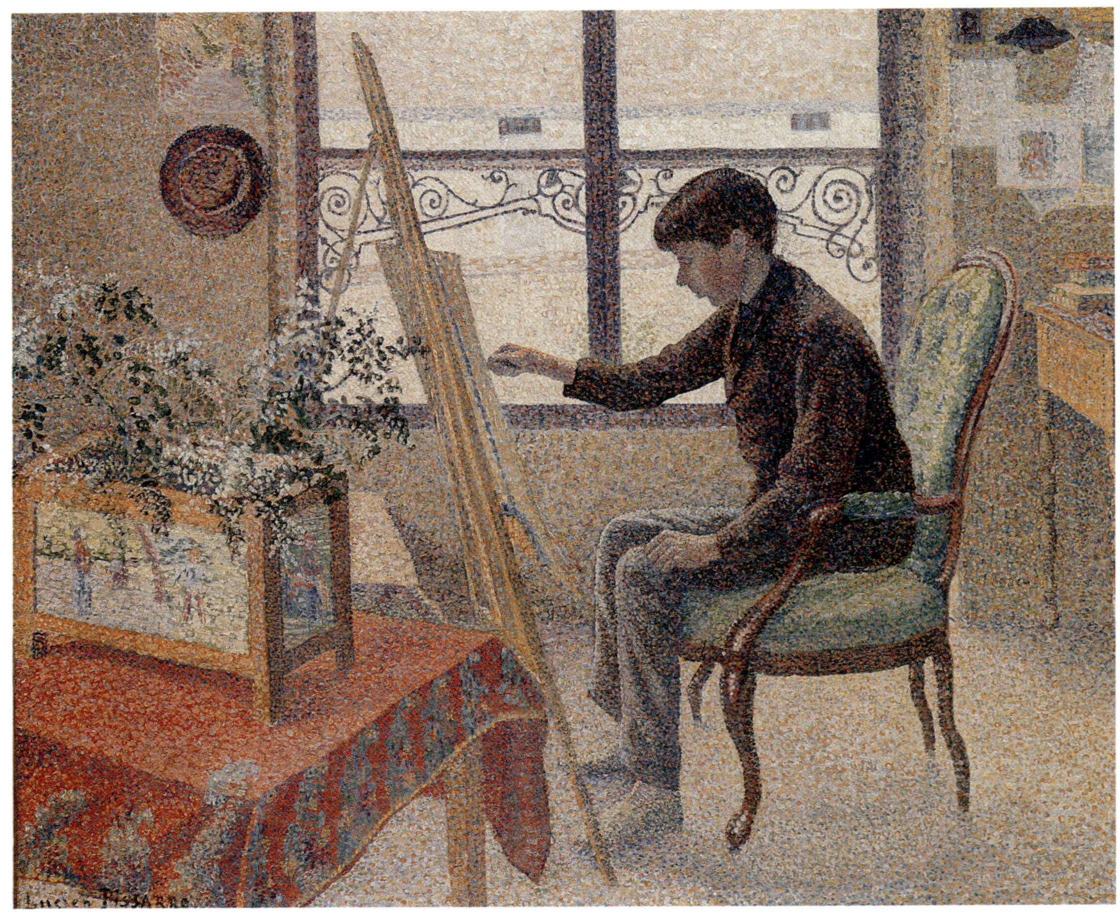

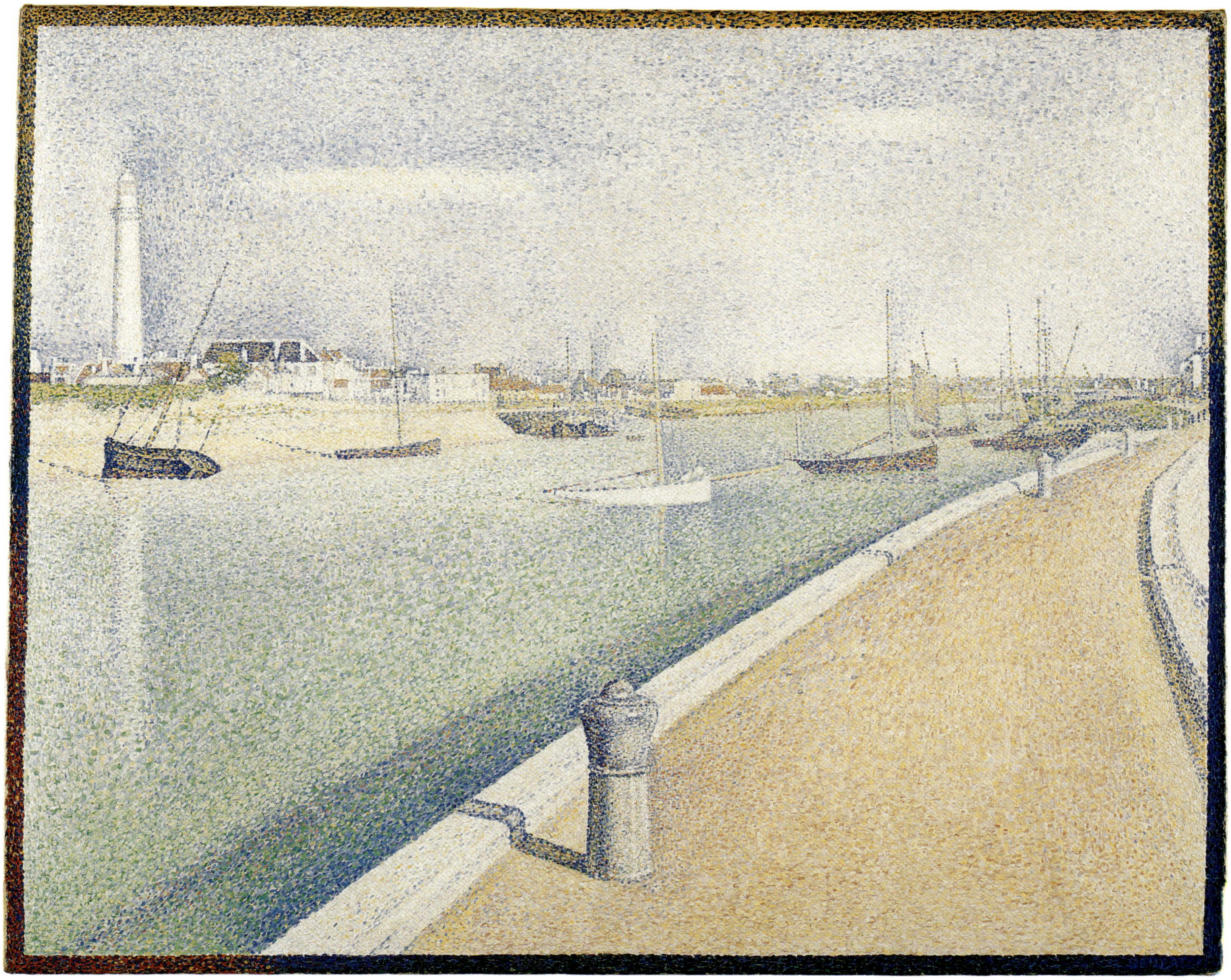

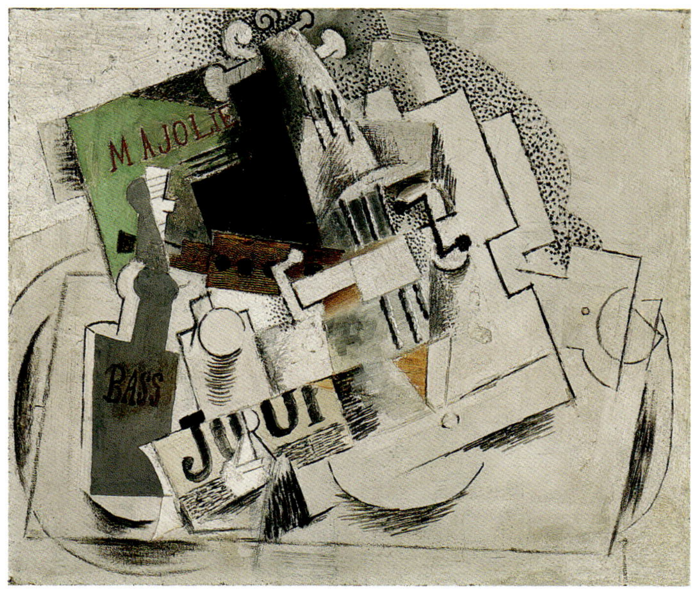

ABOVE:
Georges Seurat
French, 1859–1891
The Channel of Gravelines, Petit Fort Philippe, 1890
oil on canvas
28 7/8 x 36 1/2 in.
Gift of Mrs. James W. Fesler in memory of Daniel W. and Elizabeth C. Marmon
45.195

LEFT:
Pablo Picasso
Spanish, 1881–1973
Ma Jolie, 1913-14
oil on canvas
21 3/8 x 25 1/2 in.
Bequest of Mrs. James W. Fesler, 61.36

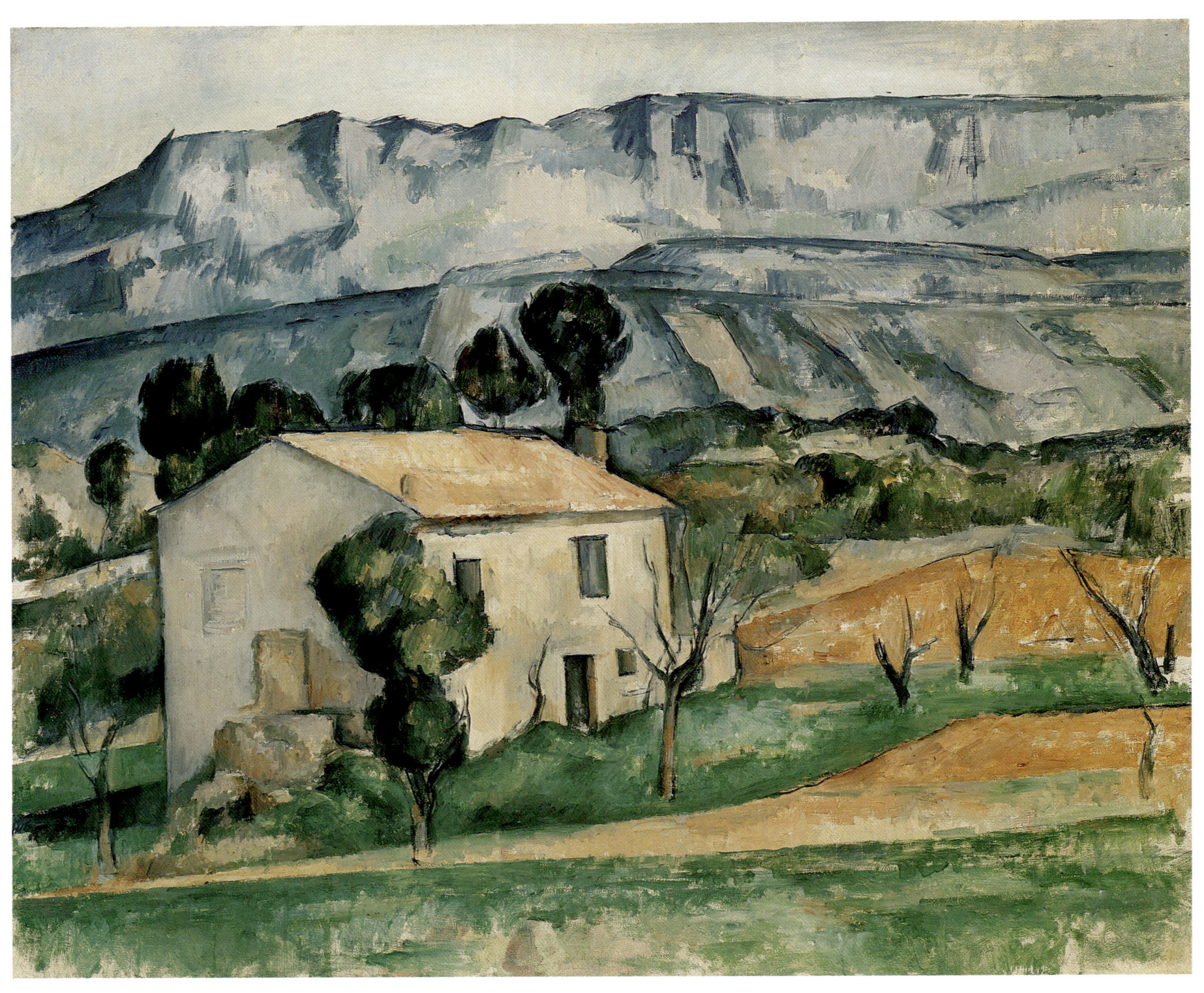

Paul Cézanne
French, 1839–1906
House in Provence, about 1885
oil on canvas, 25 1/2 x 32 in.
Gift of Mrs. James W. Fesler
in memory of Daniel W. and
Elizabeth C. Marmon
45.194

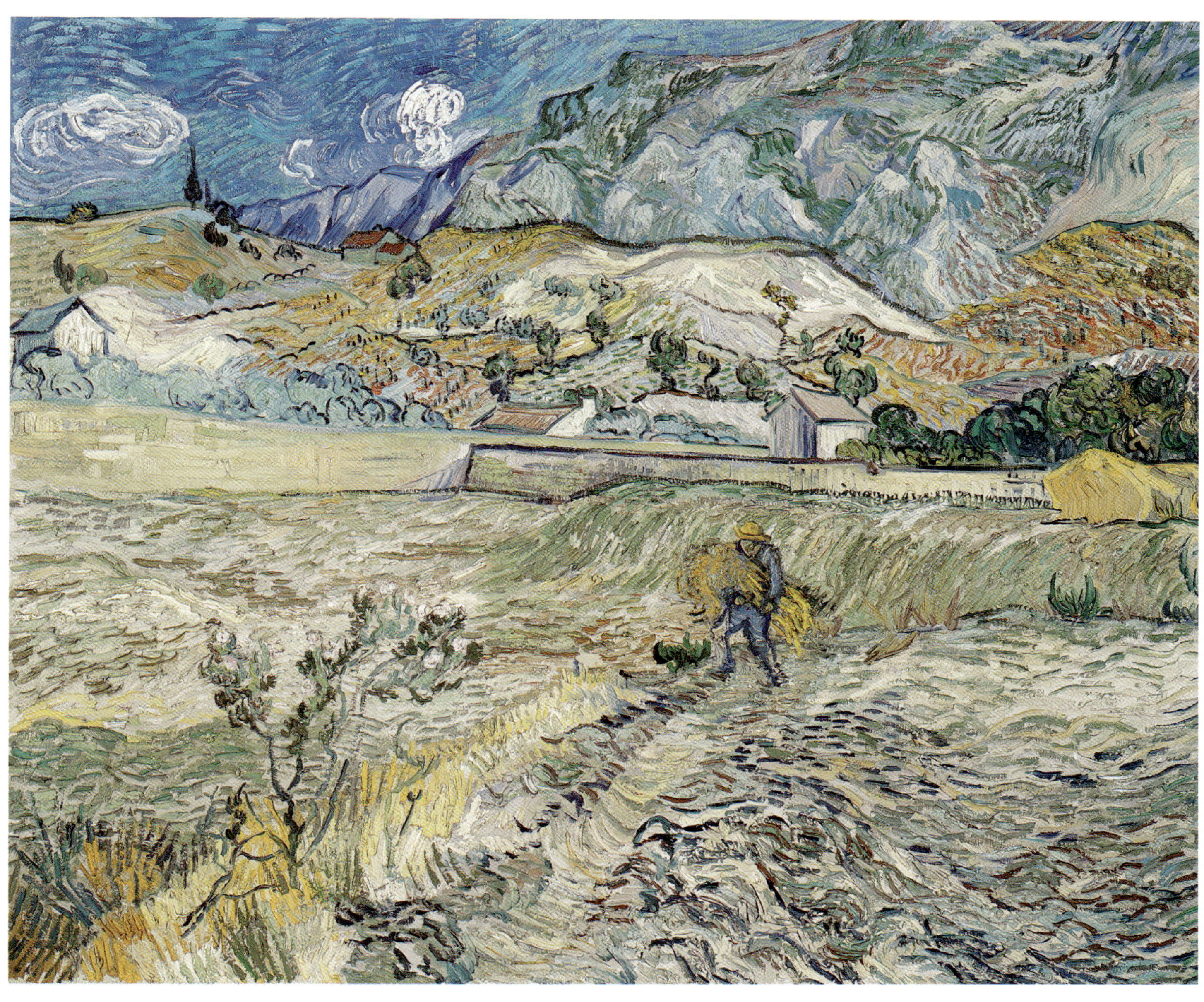

Vincent van Gogh
Dutch, 1853–1890
Landscape at Saint-Rémy (The Ploughed Field), 1889
oil on canvas, 29 x 36 1/4 in.
Gift of Mrs. James W. Fesler in memory of Daniel W. and Elizabeth C. Marmon
44.74

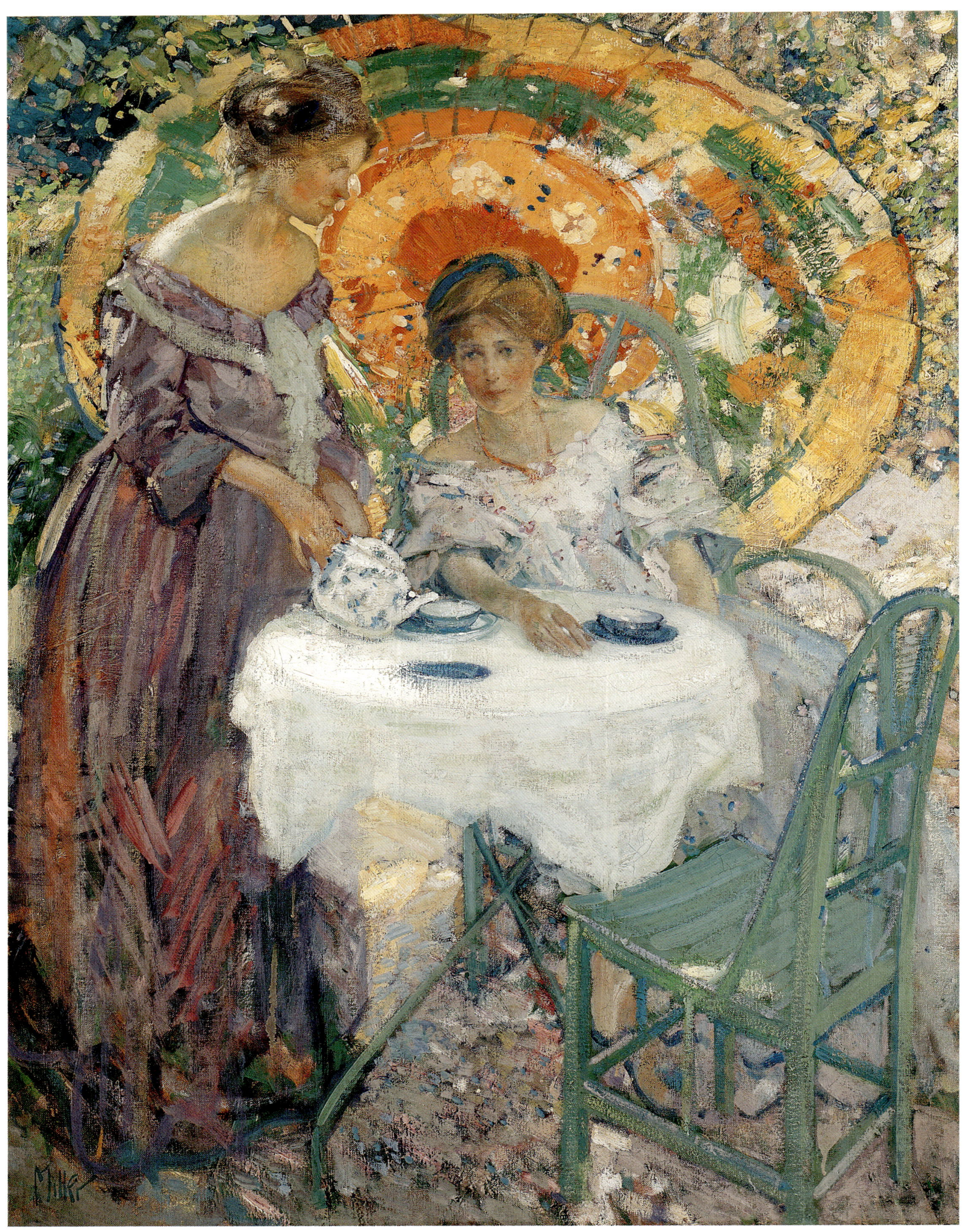
Miller

American Painting and Sculpture, 1800-1945

Throughout the IMA's history, the American Collection has played a prominent role in the life of the museum. American works were among the museum's first acquisitions, and the steady commitment of IMA donors and curators over the years has produced a collection of great range and depth.

The painting and sculpture collection reveals the IMA's dedication to high quality and the richness of America's artistic heritage. Portraits by Gilbert Stuart and the Peale family reflect the faces of colonial and Federal America, while likenesses by Thomas Eakins, John Singer Sargent, and William Merritt Chase document turn-of-the-century realism. The grandeur of the American landscape is exemplified in the Hudson River School's panoramic views juxtaposed to the brilliance of Luminism and the mystic reveries of George Inness and the Tonalists. Works by Winslow Homer, George Lambdin, and Seymour Guy record the styles and sentiments of genre painting as it developed in the Civil War era. While the collection lacks early still-life pictures, late nineteenth- to early twentieth-century examples range from the precise approach of Emil and Dines Carlsen to the broadly brushed *tours de force* of William Merritt Chase.

OPPOSITE:
Richard Edward Miller
1875-1943
Afternoon Tea, 1910
oil on canvas, 40 x 32 in.
Promised gift of Jane and Andrew Paine, 1997.139

BELOW:
Asher B. Durand, 1796-1886
Landscape with Covered Wagon
1847, oil on canvas
26 x 36 3/8 in.
Gift of Mrs. Lydia G. Millard
12.17

One of the collection's best-developed areas is that of American Impressionism. With canvases by Childe Hassam, J. H. Twachtman, Robert Vonnoh, J. Alden Weir, William McGregor Paxton, Edmund Charles Tarbell, Robert Reid, Richard Miller, Louis Ritman, and Frederick Frieseke, the IMA can feature both the *plein air* landscape tradition and the more academically grounded figural and genre scenes.

The Realist, Social Realist, and Regionalist schools active in America during the 1930s and 1940s are represented by Edward Hopper, Thomas Hart Benton, Jacob Lawrence, and Reginald Marsh, while the modernist movement of the same era includes paintings by Georgia O'Keeffe, Marsden Hartley and John Marin.

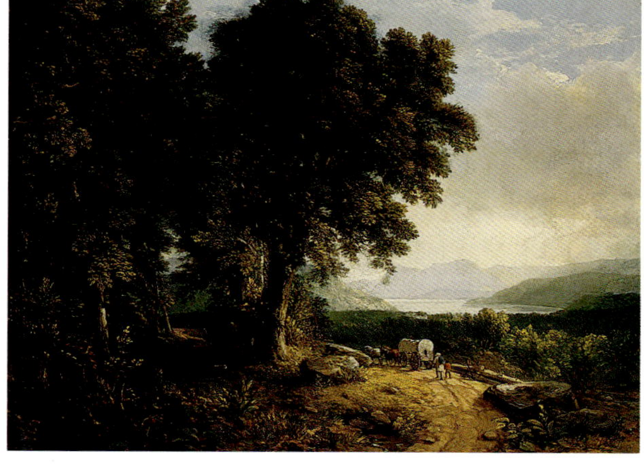

The IMA has a special interest in Indiana's artists. Among the museum's extensive collection of regional art are canvases by the pioneer painters Jacob Cox, Barton Hays, and George Winter, excellent paintings by Hoosier Group artists T. C. Steele, J. Ottis Adams, William Forsyth, R. B. Gruelle, and Otto Stark, and numerous portraits and landscapes by twentieth-century Indiana artists.

The nineteenth-century sculpture collection ranges from the sober dignity of neoclassical marble to the frivolity and naturalism of bronzes by Frederick MacMonnies and Augustus Saint-Gaudens. A surprisingly strong group of pieces by Paul Manship, John Storrs, and Gaston Lachaise creates a fascinating blend of classical themes and modernist symbols, all crafted in the midst of the Roaring Twenties.

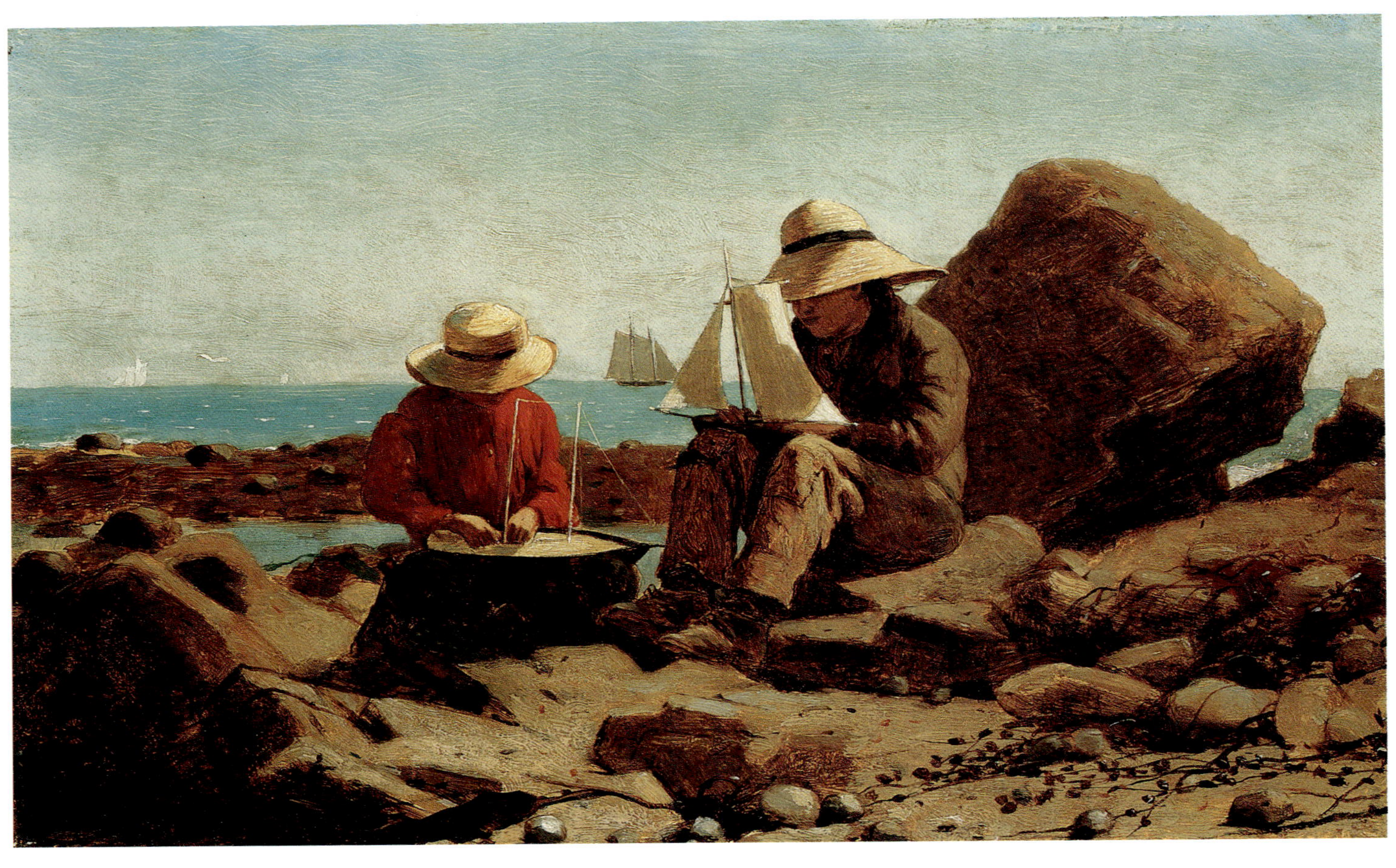

ABOVE:
Winslow Homer, 1836-1910
The Boat Builders, 1873
oil on panel, 6 x 10 1/4 in.
Martha Delzell Memorial Fund, 54.10

RIGHT:
Gilbert Stuart, 1755-1828
Marianne Ashley Walker, 1799
oil on canvas
29 1/8 x 24 1/8 in.
Gift of Mrs. Nicholas W. Noyes, 52.6

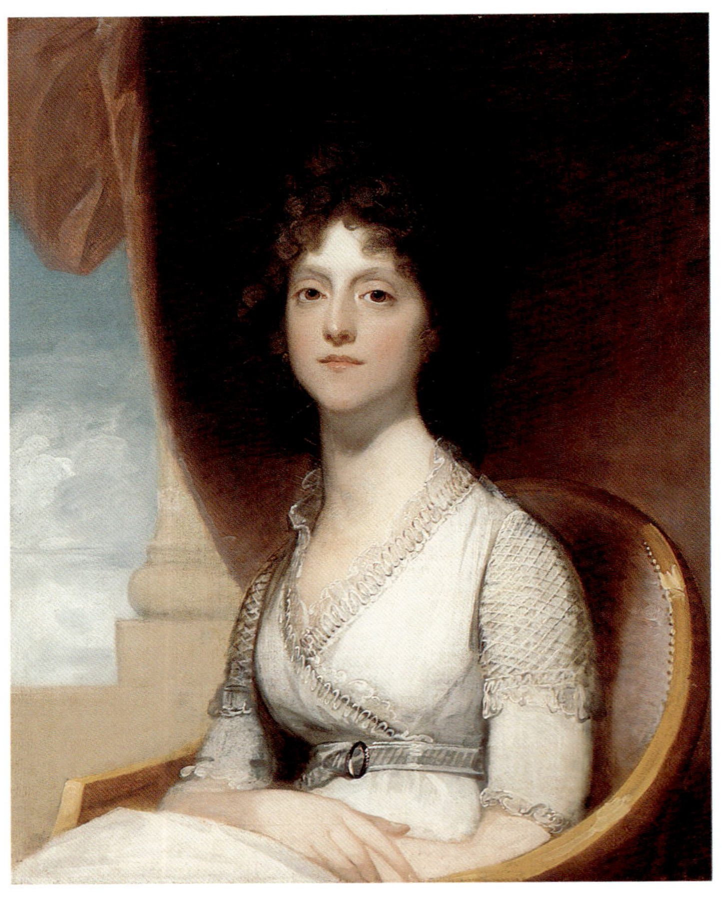

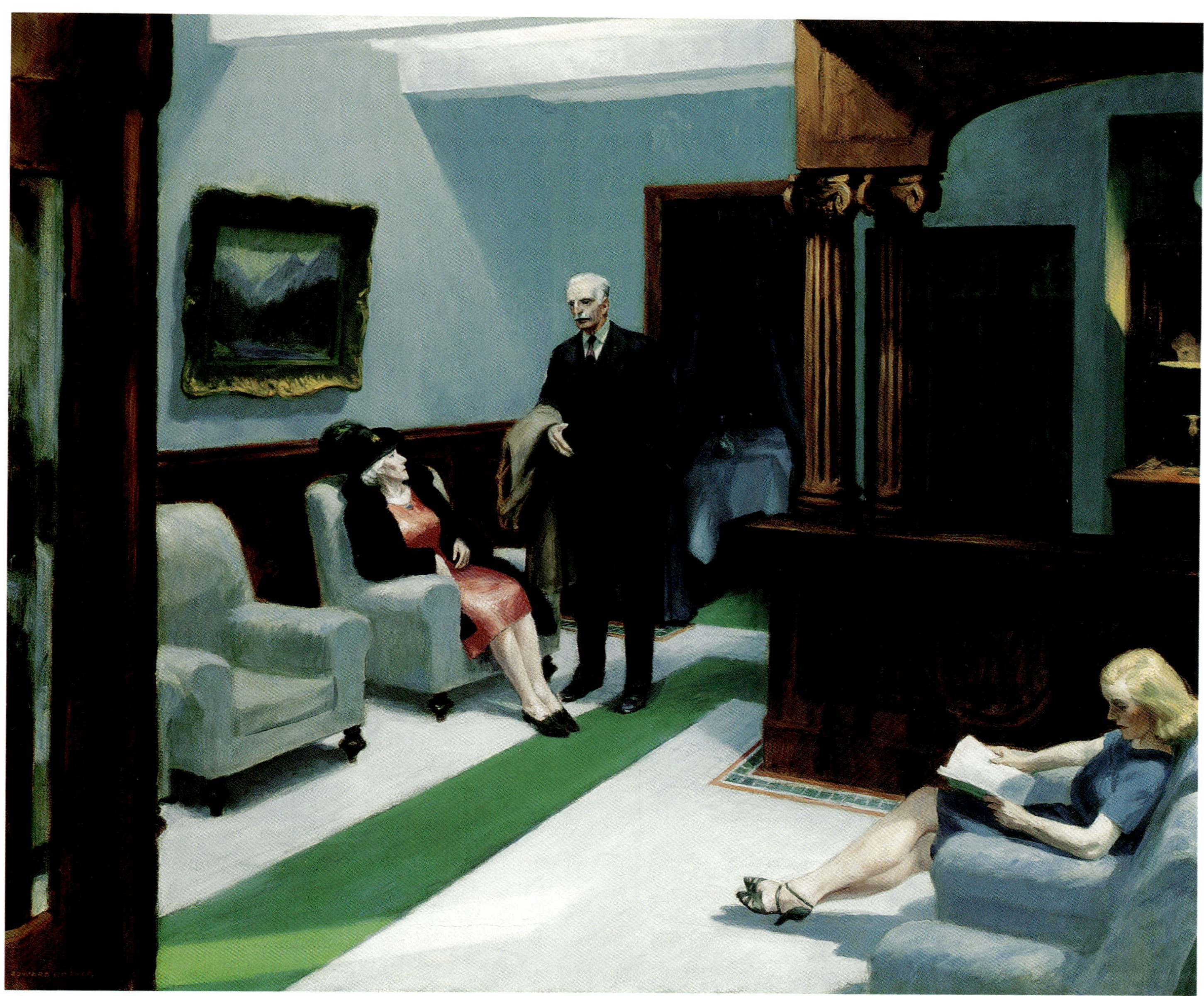

Edward Hopper, 1882-1967
Hotel Lobby
oil on canvas
32 1/4 x 40 3/4 in.
William Ray Adams Memorial
Collection, 47.4

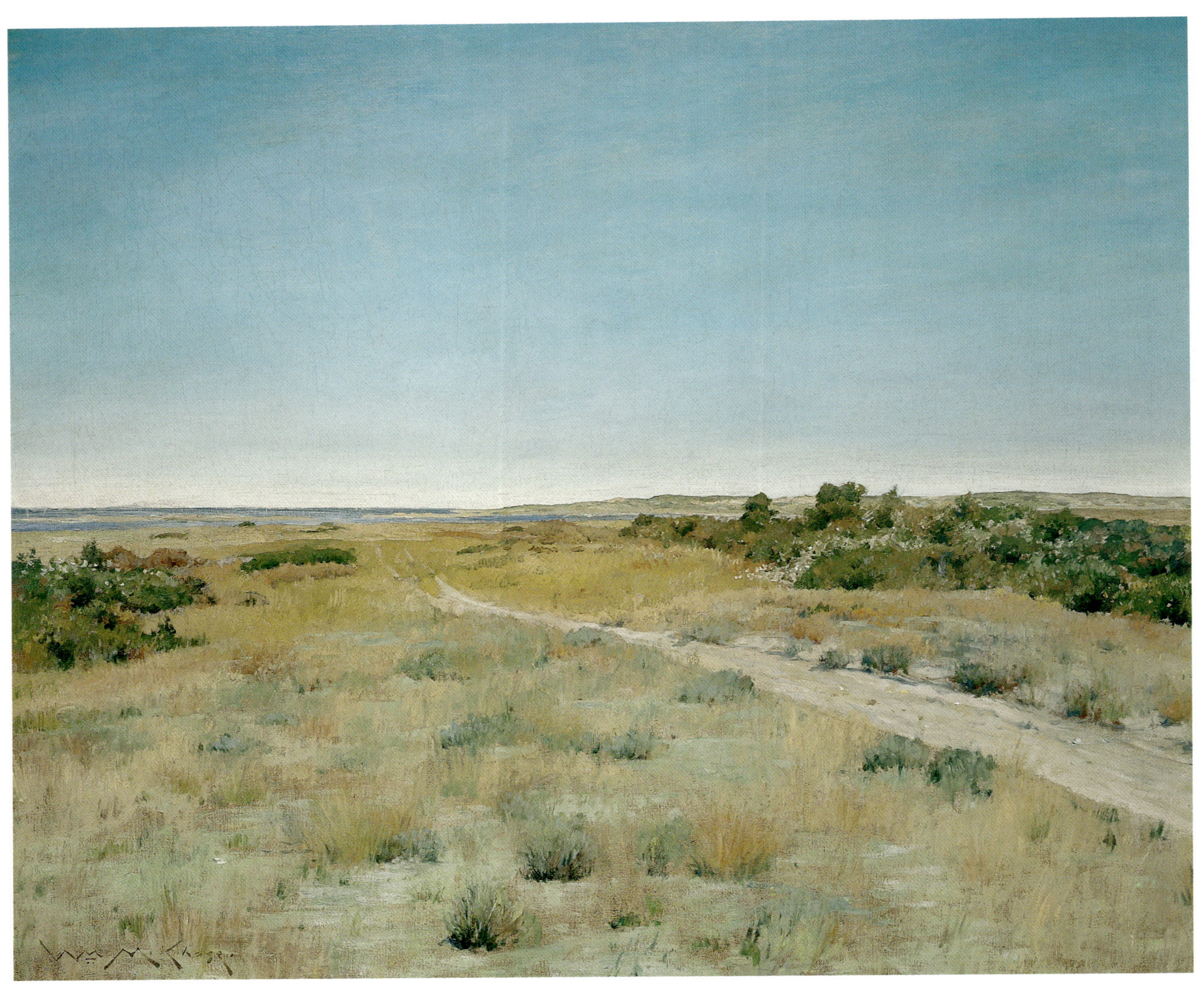

William Merritt Chase
1849-1916
First Touch of Autumn
oil on fabric, 40 x 50 in.
Gift of Peter C. Reilly and
Dr. Jeanette P. Reilly
1997.183

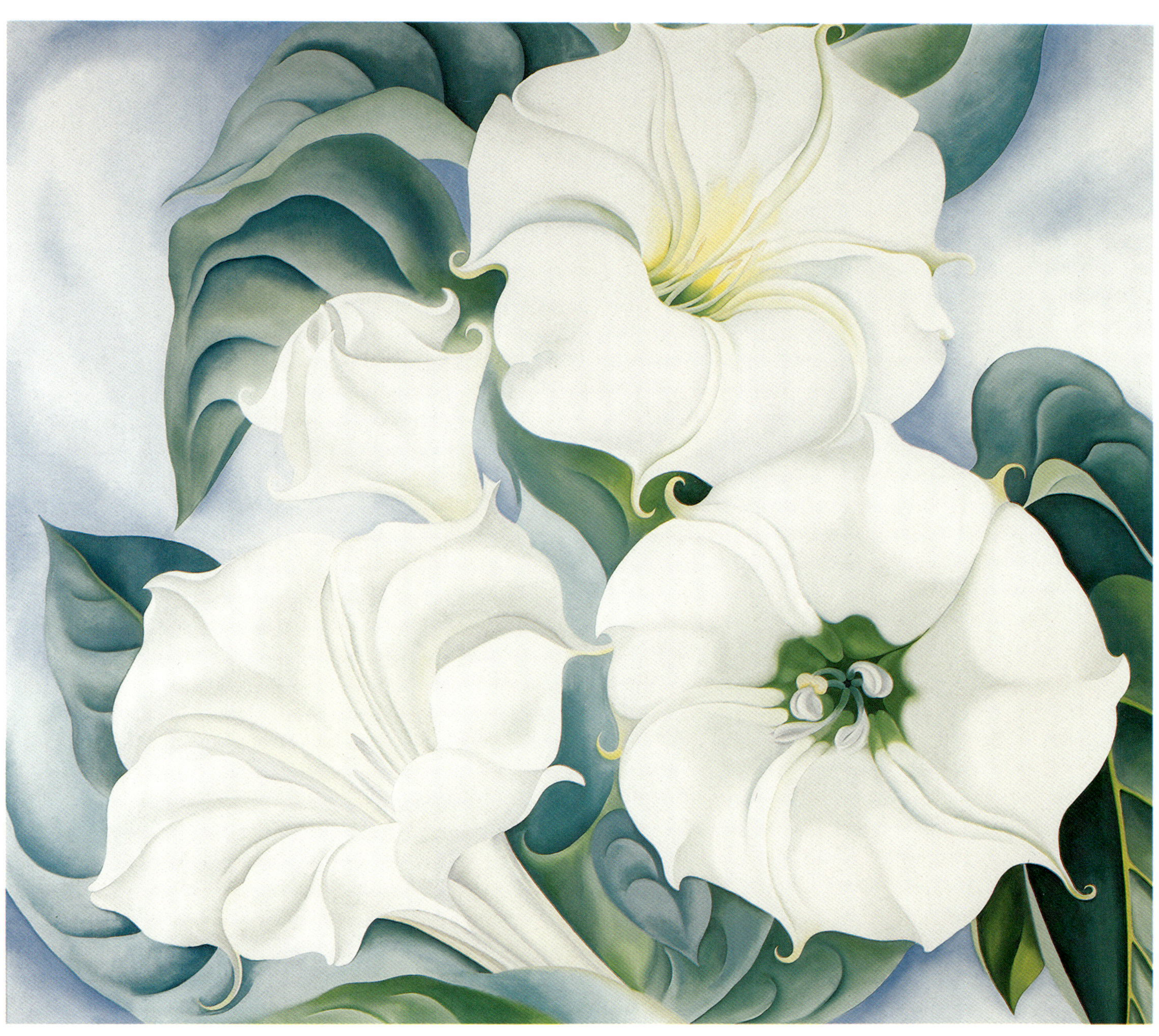

Georgia O'Keeffe, 1887-1986
Jimson Weed, 1936-37
oil on linen, 70 x 83 1/2 in.
Gift of Eli Lilly and Company
1997.131

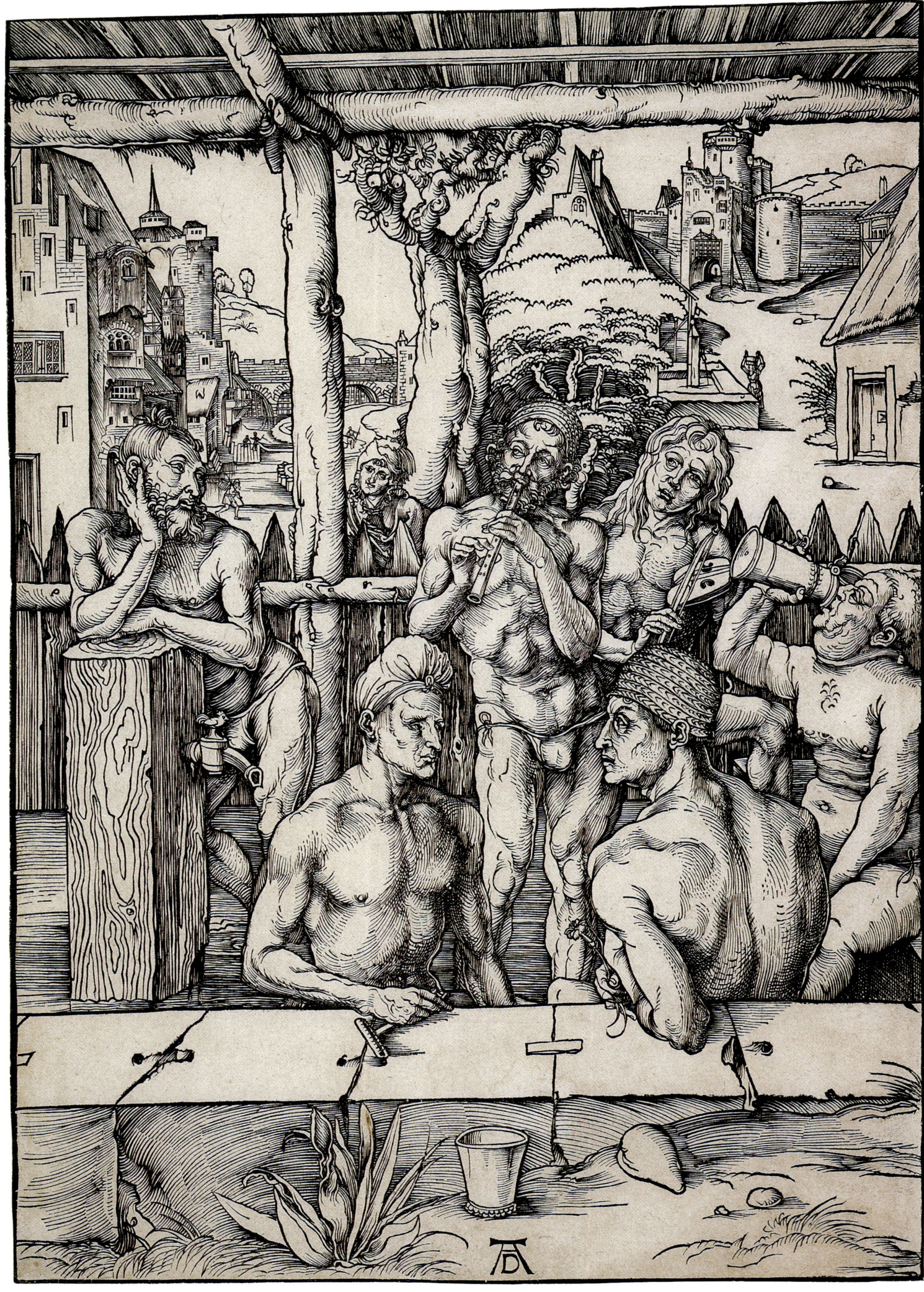

Works on Paper

The IMA's largest collection, consisting of more than 25,000 prints, drawings, and photographs, includes manuscripts and early printed books, Old Master prints (1450-1800), Old Master drawings, nineteenth-century prints and drawings, modern prints (1900-1945) and contemporary prints and drawings. Prints include those by such well-known artists as Albrecht Dürer, Rembrandt, Canaletto, William Hogarth, Francisco Goya, Henri de Toulouse-Lautrec, Pablo Picasso, Henri Matisse, Marc Chagall, Joan Miró, Andy Warhol, Jim Dine, and Jasper Johns. Examples of draughtsmanship include works by Giambattista Tiepolo, Antoine Watteau, Henry Fuseli, William Blake, Jean-Auguste Dominique Ingres, Eugène Delacroix, Edgar Degas, Odilon Redon, Mary Cassatt, John Singer Sargent, Winslow Homer, William Merritt Chase, Childe Hassam, Isamu Noguchi, Man Ray, Charles Burchfield, Fernand Léger, and Chagall. The recently founded photography collection is highlighted by vintage prints by William Henry Fox Talbot, Julia Margaret Cameron, Peter Henry Emerson, Charles Sheeler, Brassai, Robert Frank, and Diane Arbus.

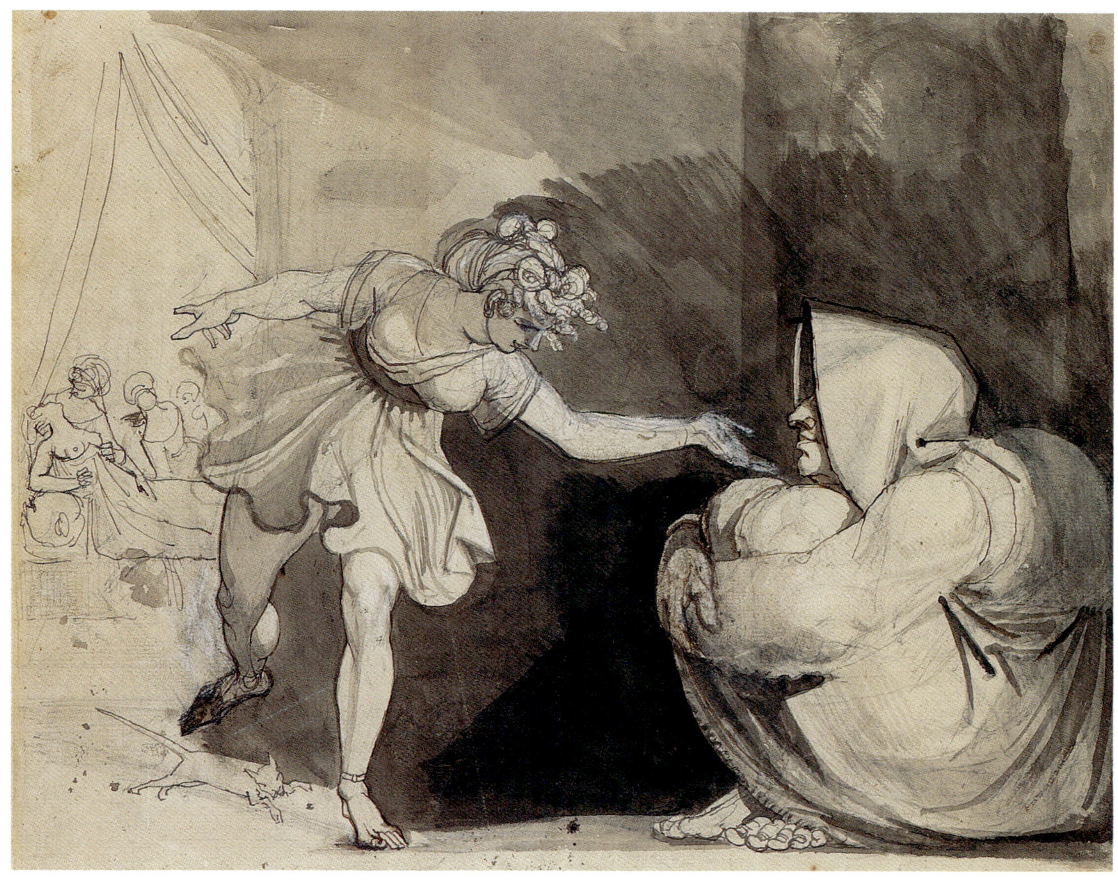

OPPOSITE:
Albrecht Dürer
German, 1471-1528
The Men's Bath, 1496-97
woodblock print
15 1/2 x 11 1/8 in.
Alliance Income Fund
1992.355

LEFT:
Henry Fuseli
English (b. Switzerland)
1741-1825
Galinthias Outwits Eileithyia by Announcing the Birth of Heracles, 1791
pencil and gray ink washes on white laid paper
12 1/4 x 15 5/8 in.
Gift of Mr. and Mrs. J. Irwin Miller, 1993.172

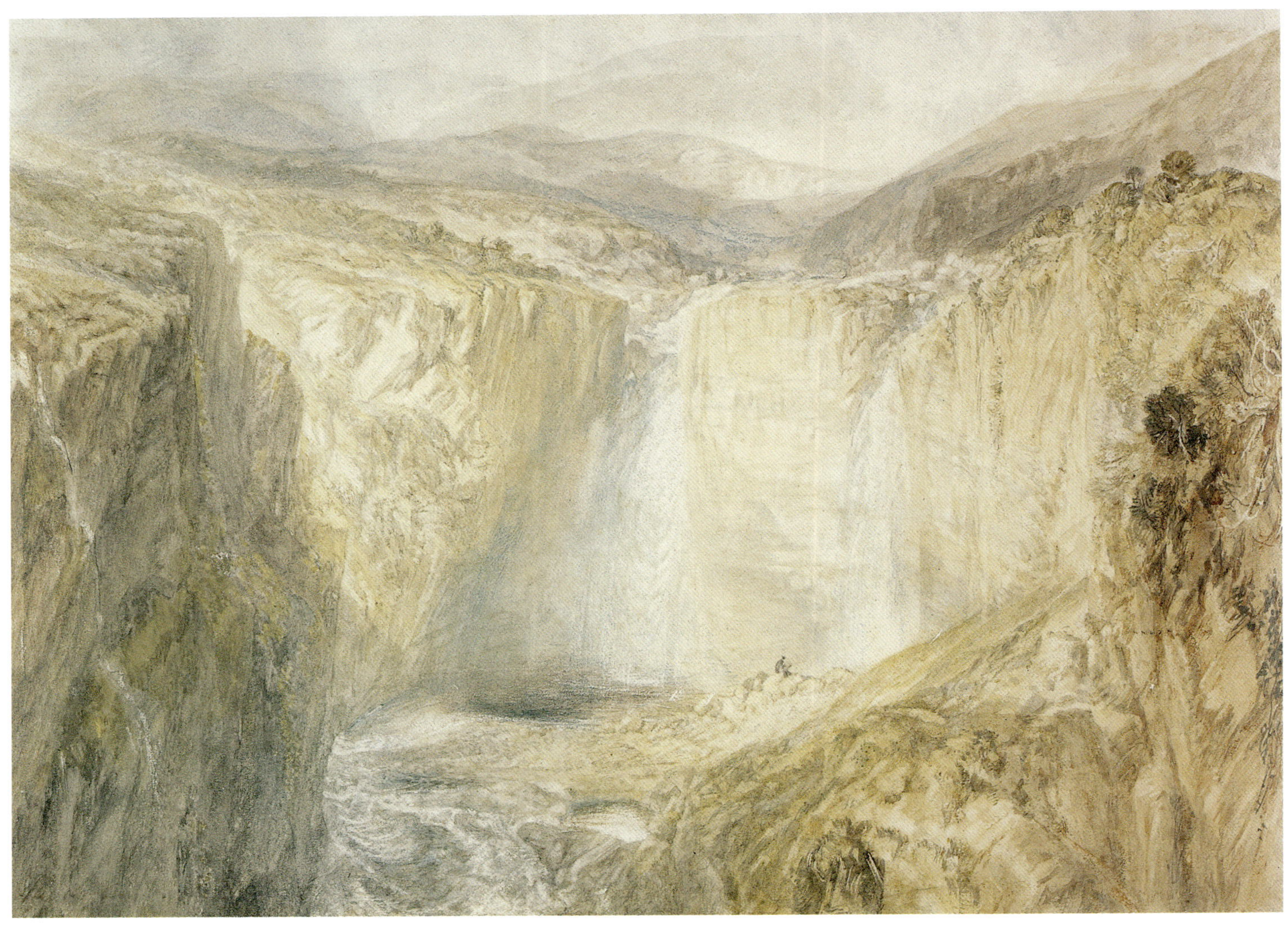

The Works of J. M. W. Turner

Joseph Mallord William Turner
English, 1775-1851
Fall of the Tees, Yorkshire
1825-26
watercolor on white wove paper
11 1/16 x 15 1/16 in.
Gift in memory of Dr. and Mrs. Hugo O. Pantzer by their Children (by exchange), Bequest of Evelyn Bartlett, the Alliance Income Fund, the Nicholas H. Noyes Fund, the James E. Roberts Fund, and the E. Hardy Adriance Fund
1997.141

The IMA owns one of the world's largest and most comprehensive collections of watercolors by the English artist Joseph Mallord William Turner. The collection, consisting primarily of prints and drawings, spans more than fifty years, from 1790 through the late 1840s. Recognized in his own time as the greatest landscape painter of the age, Turner is also considered the father of watercolor painting and a forerunner of modern art in the impressionistic style. Always maintaining a close identity with nature, Turner emphasized light, atmosphere, and color in his work.

The collection comprises two major oil paintings, forty-three drawings and watercolors, eight portraits of Turner between the ages of sixteen and seventy-six, and more than 3,000 impressions of prints either made by Turner or under his supervision. References for the collection include first editions of books illustrated by Turner; sales catalogues dating from the nineteenth century; a complete library of books on the artist; a rare copy of the published collection of Turner's patron Walter Fawkes, issued privately in 1864 with early photographs of the collection, and many other rare books of the period. It also includes watercolors by such Turner contemporaries as John Robert Cozens, Thomas Girtin, Samuel Prout, Thomas Shotter Boys, Anthony Vandyke Copley Fielding, Clarkson Stanfield, Samuel Palmer, and John Ruskin.

The Turner collection was established in 1913 with the purchase of five Turner drawings. It was immeasurably enriched by the donations of Kurt F. Pantzer, a local attorney, who was, in the 1950s and 1960s, the world's most active collector of Turner's works. Since the opening of the Clowes Pavilion in 1972, the Turner Collection has been housed on the second floor in a three-room gallery designed for its display and study. One room houses the books illustrated by Turner and selections from the library of more than 500 volumes on Turner, letters from the artist, and various manuscripts relating to his life and work. The second room is devoted to Turner's drawings and watercolors, and the third displays his prints. Selections from these extensive collections are on view at all times.

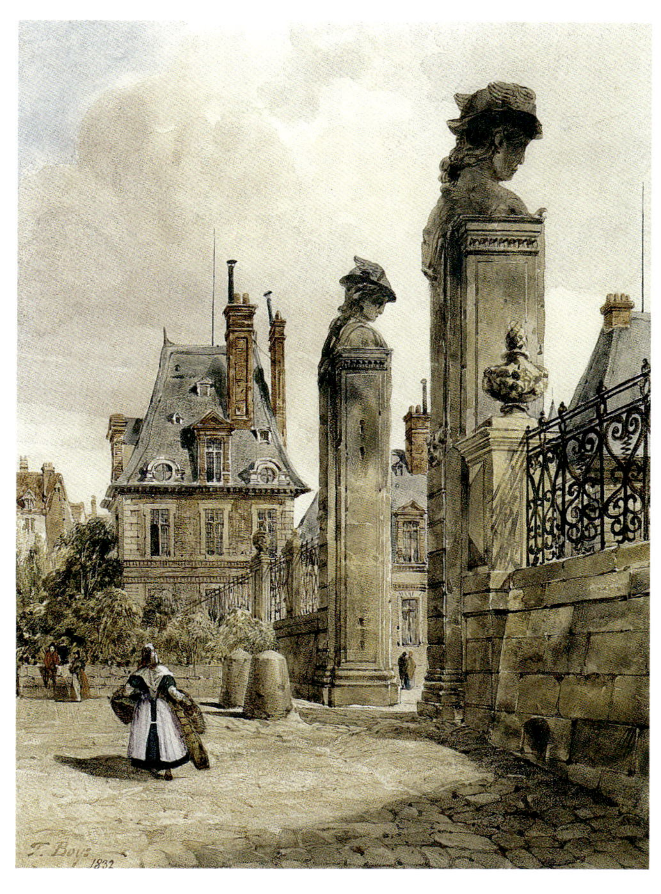

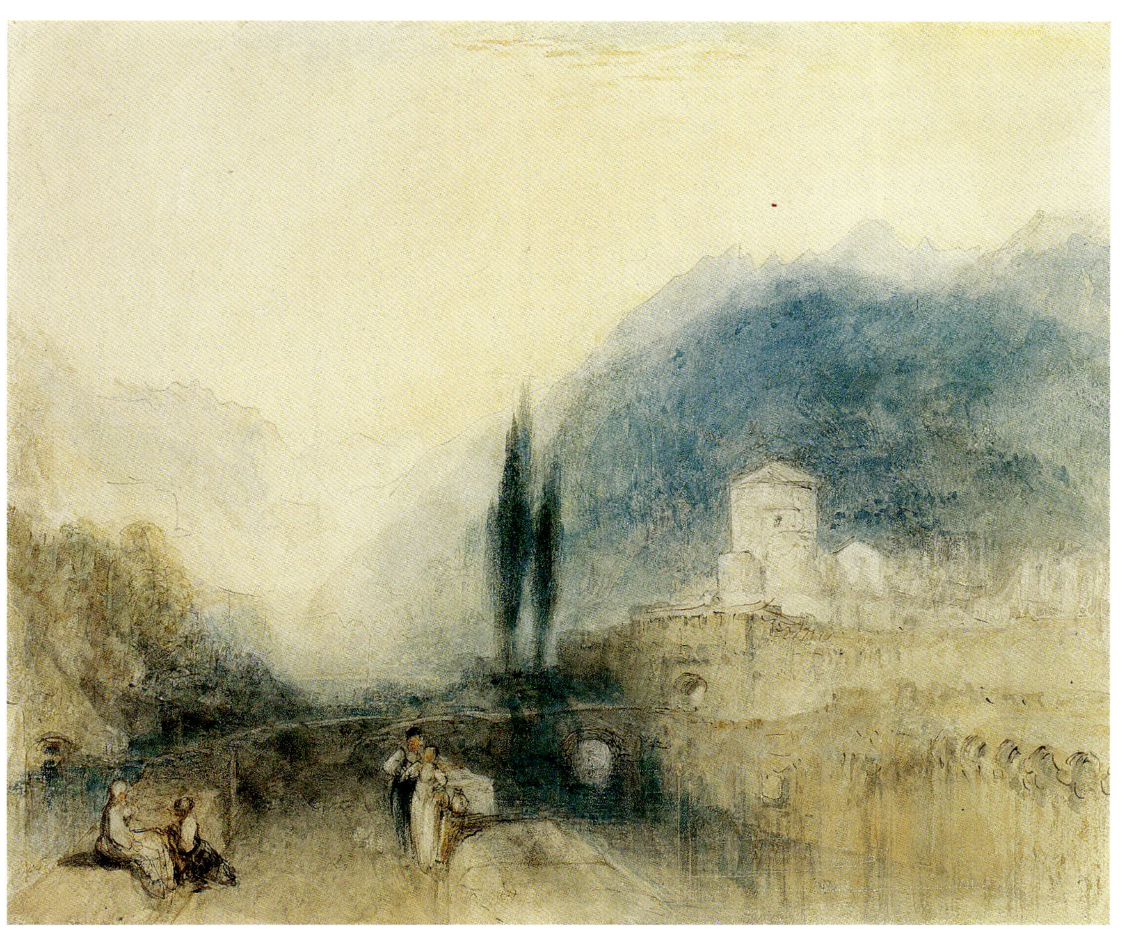

ABOVE:
Thomas Shotter Boys
English, 1803-1874
Grille des Hermès, Porte Dauphine, Palace of Fontainebleau, 1832
watercolor with touches of gum arabic over pencil on white wove paper
14 x 10 1/4 in.
William B. Spurlock Fund
1996.186

LEFT:
Joseph Mallord William Turner
English, 1775-1851
Bellinzona, 1842
watercolor over pencil strengthened with pen and sepia ink on white wove paper, 9 x 11 1/4 in.
Gift in memory of Dr. and Mrs. Hugo O. Pantzer by their Children, 72.209

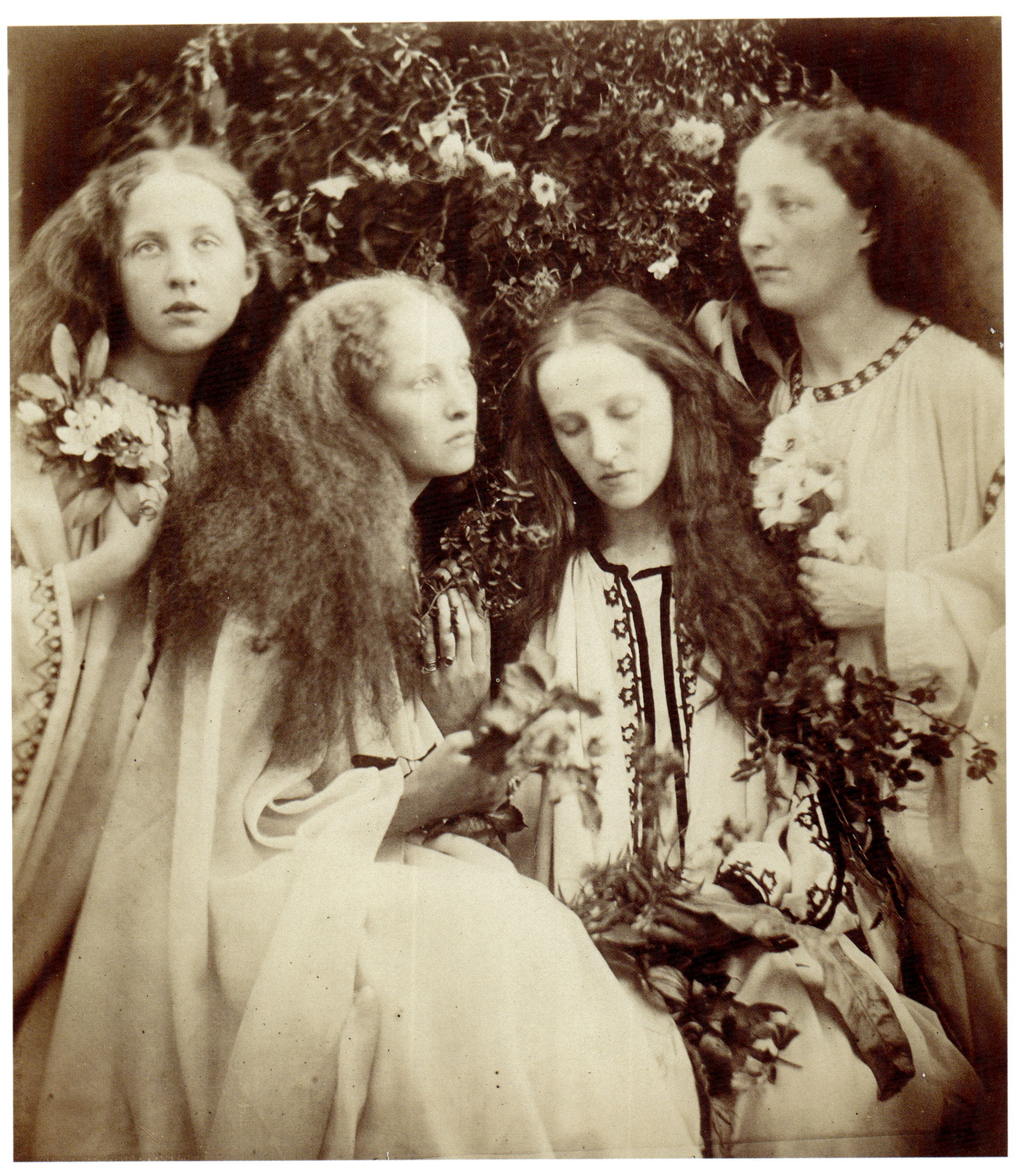

Julia Margaret Cameron
English, 1815-1879
The Rose Bud Garden of Girls, 1868
albumen print, 12 1/16 x 10 5/8 in.
Allen Whitehill Clowes Fund
1993.16

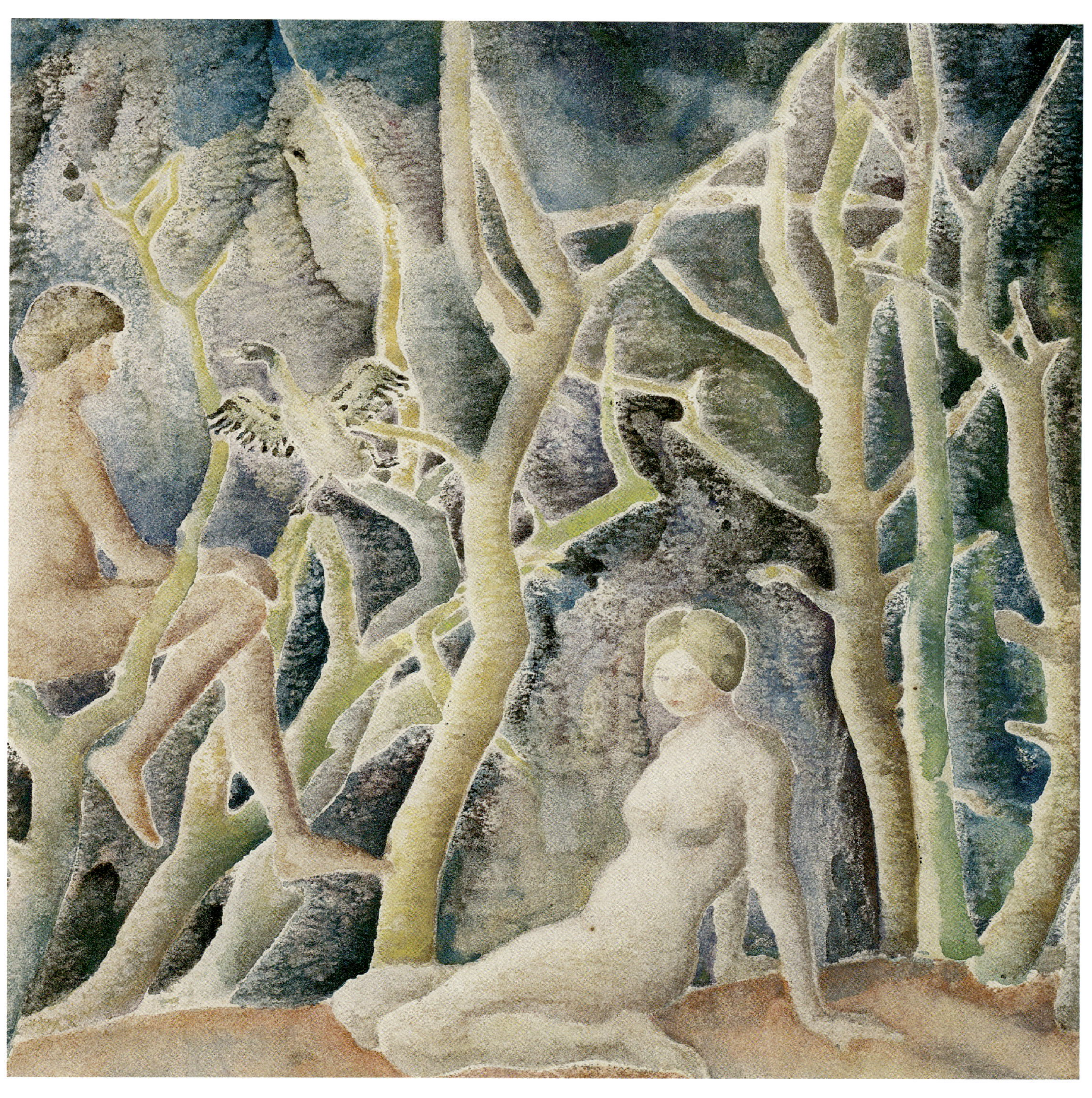

Ada Gilmore
American, 1882-1955
The Wild Goose, 1923
color woodblock print
11 7/8 x 12 1/8 in.
Gift of Dr. Steven Conant in
honor of Mrs. H. L. Conant and
Miss Joan D. Weisenberger
1991.97

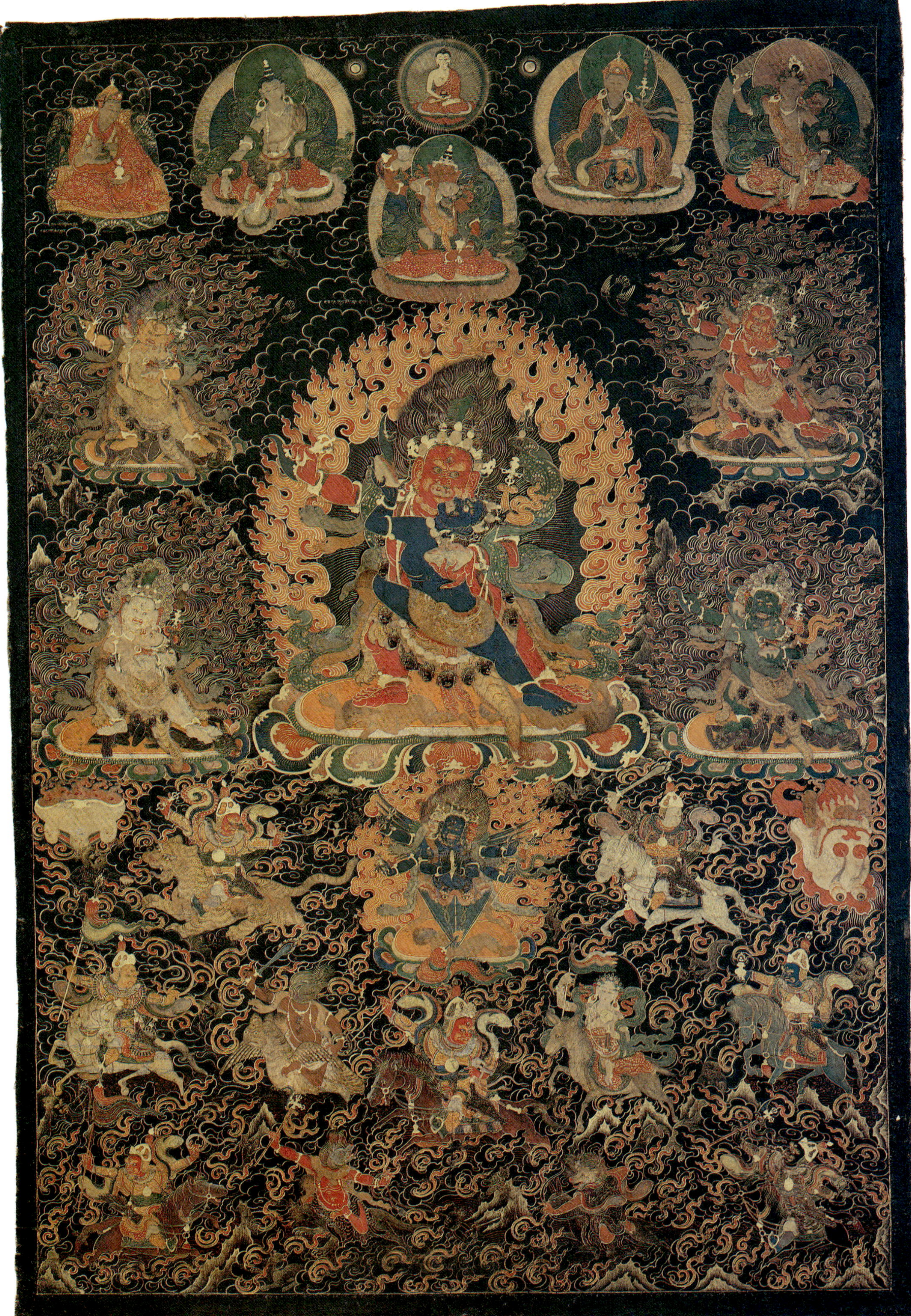

Asian Art

From its beginning in the late-nineteenth century, the Indianapolis Museum of Art has collected the art of Asia. Early in the twentieth century, Charles Freer, founder of the Freer Gallery in Washington, D.C., gave Japanese tea ceremony ceramics, an eleventh-century Chinese "pilgrim flask," and other Asian objects to the collection of the IMA. Since those early days, generous donors—in this city and elsewhere—have continued to enrich the museum's holdings of Asian art. Today, the Chinese collection in particular is internationally recognized for its outstanding breadth and quality.

Among the works of art collected by the IMA from cultures other than Chinese, Japan is best represented. Major achievements in Japanese ceramics, painting, and sculpture, from prehistoric times to the present, are documented by the collection. Virtually all types of Japanese art are available for display, from the religious to the secular, from minute boxes and toggles (*inro* and *netsuke*) to large-scale Buddhist statues, from refined and subtle objects used in the tea ceremony to those for sumptuous display. Hiroshige and Kunisada are particularly well represented in the substantial collection of *ukiyo-e* woodblock prints and books that so accurately capture the pleasures of daily life in the Edo period (1600–1868). Paintings in both screen and scroll formats illustrate the variety and richness of that art in Japan, from examples in the purely native style to the decorative and those influenced by Chinese and European painting.

Representative examples of ceramics, metalwork, painting, sculpture, and textiles in the Asian collection illustrate the grand artistic achievements of Indian, Korean, Tibetan, Southeast Asian, and West Asian artists in both the religious and secular spheres.

The ancient sculptural traditions of Asia are represented by objects in metal, stone, stucco, and wood. They reveal the spread of the pan-Asian Buddhist faith across the silk roads of Asia from Pakistan, India, Nepal, and Tibet eastward through China to Korea and Japan.

Asia's unparalleled ceramic heritage from all quarters of that vast continent is well illustrated. There are examples from more than three thousand years ago, including a bull-shaped vessel that rivals modern sculpture, from West Asia, near the Caspian Sea; jars from Ban Chiang, Thailand, in southeast Asia; and relics from the Jomon and Yayoi periods of Japan, in the far east of Asia. Glazed ceramics also come from all parts of the continent. Among the best are a bowl with a charming elephant design under turquoise glaze made in the Kashan region of Iran; inlaid celadons, a high point of the Korean tradition; and Japanese tea ceremony vessels. All were made about 1200 and exemplify the richness of art and culture from opposite ends of Asia.

OPPOSITE:
Tibet, 18th century
Hayagriva
gouache on cloth
26 1/2 x 18 1/2 in.
Gift from the collection of Louis Herlands and James E. Roberts Fund, 1989.36

BELOW:
Iran, Gilan (Amlash)
bull-shaped vessel
about 1000 B.C.
earthenware
9 1/2 x 12 1/2 in.
Gift of Grain Dealers Mutual Insurance Co., 75.301

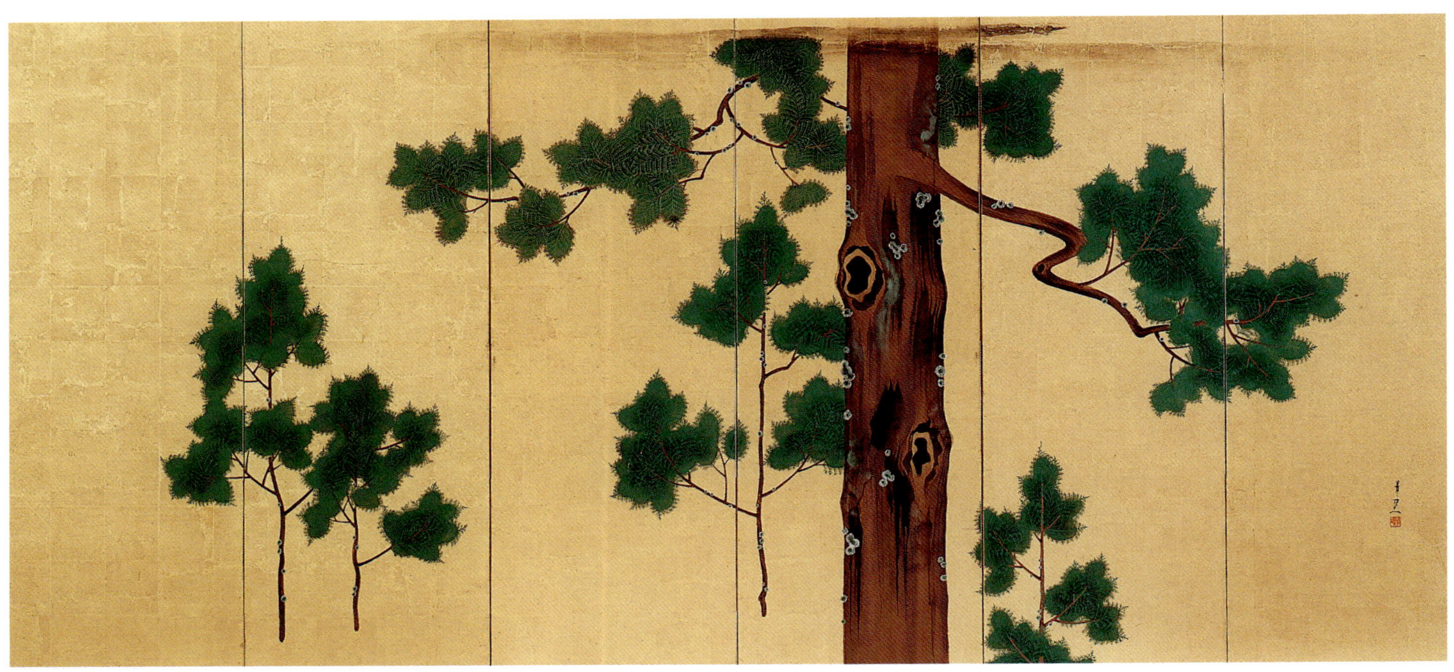

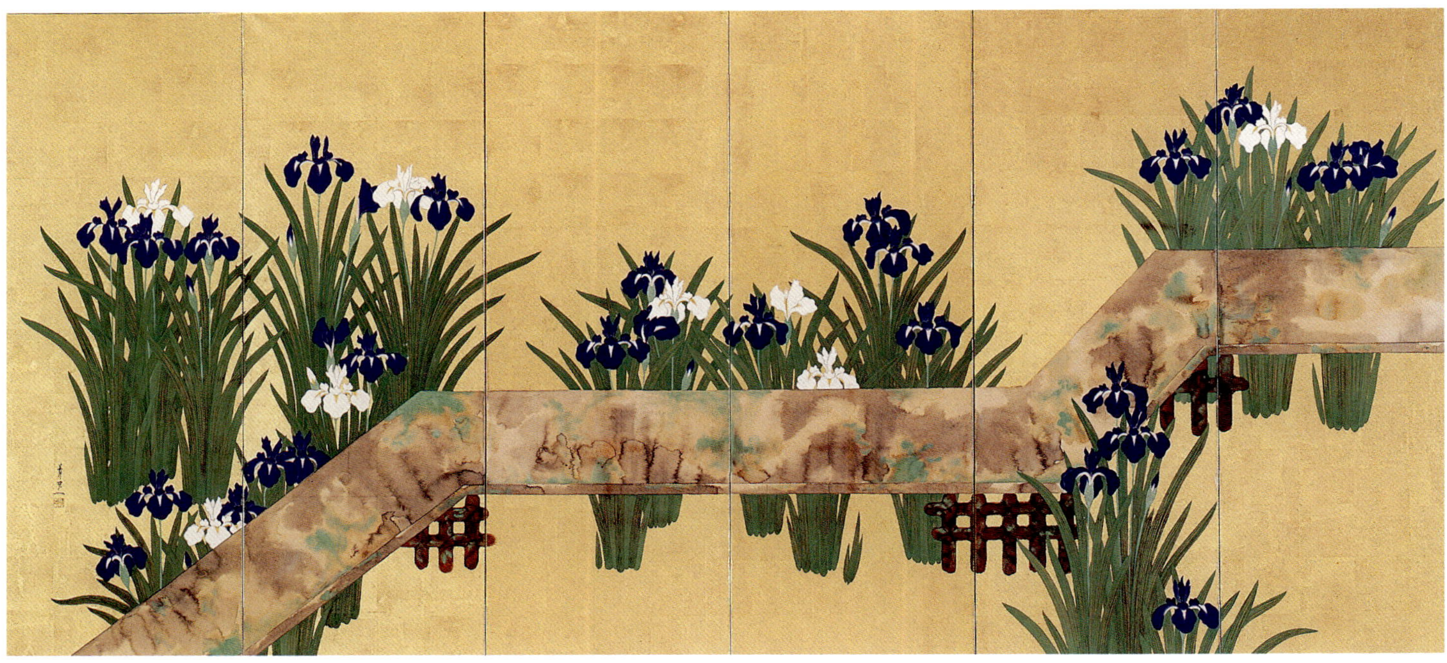

ABOVE:
Kiitsu, Suzuki Montonaga,1796–1858
Japanese, Edo period, 1600–1868
Bridge over Iris Pond and *Cypress Trees*
ink and color on gold paper
12 panels, 50 x 17 1/2 in. each
Mr. and Mrs. William R. Spurlock Fund
1987.43–44

OPPOSITE:
Pakistan, Gandhara period
1st-5th century
head of Buddha, 3rd-4th century
stucco with paint, h: 15 3/4 in.
Alliance Income Fund, 1994.1

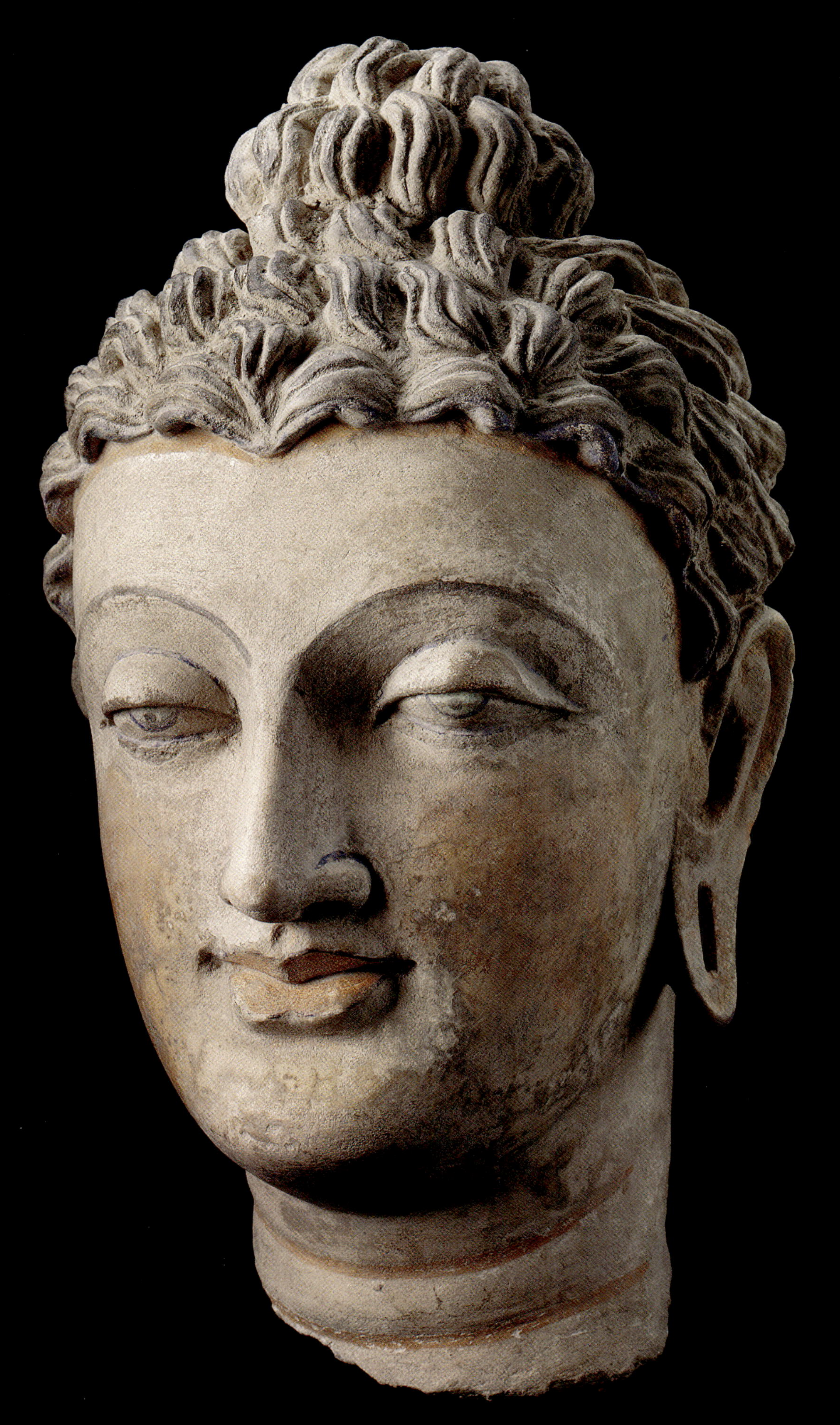

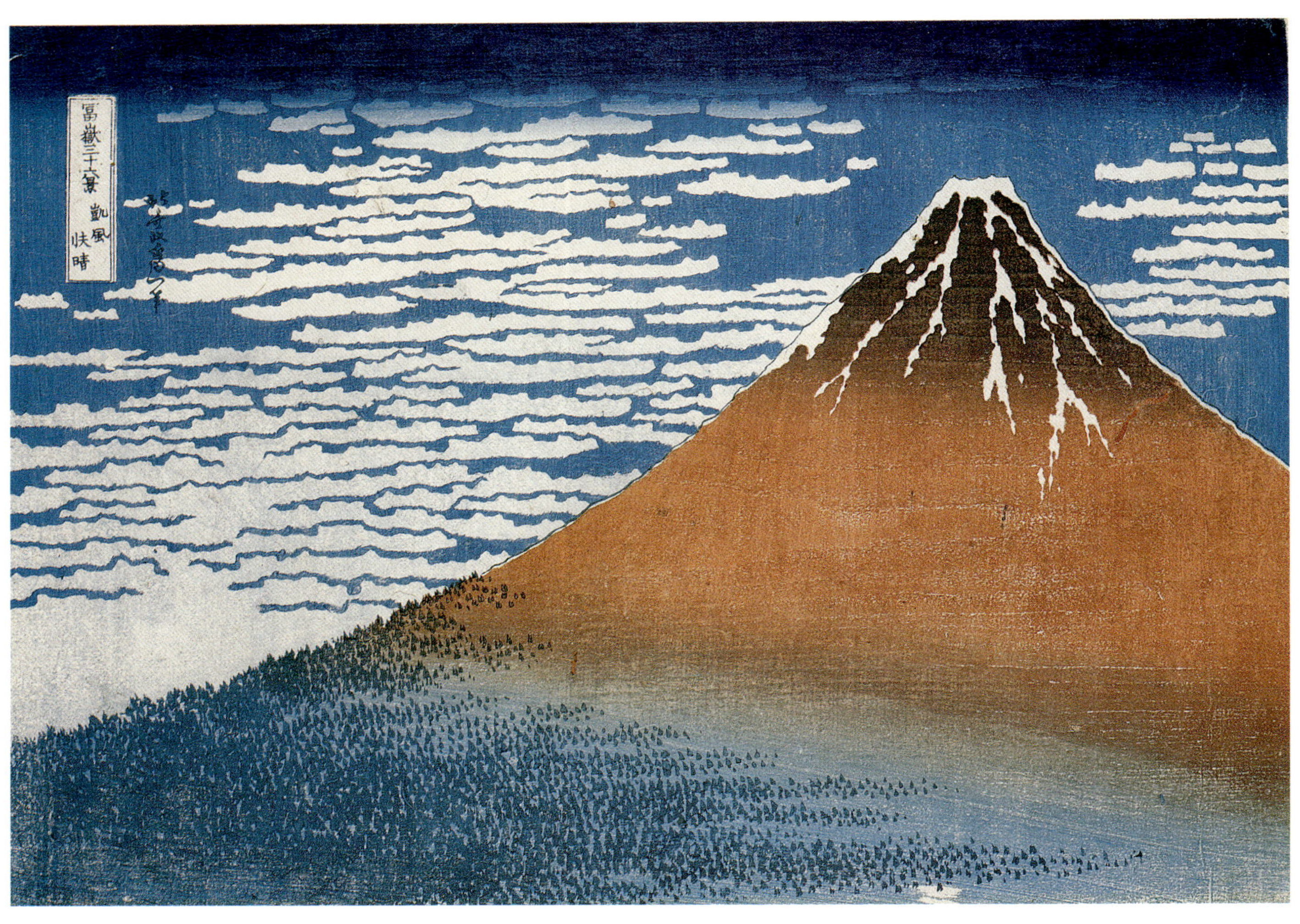
冨嶽三十六景
凱風快晴

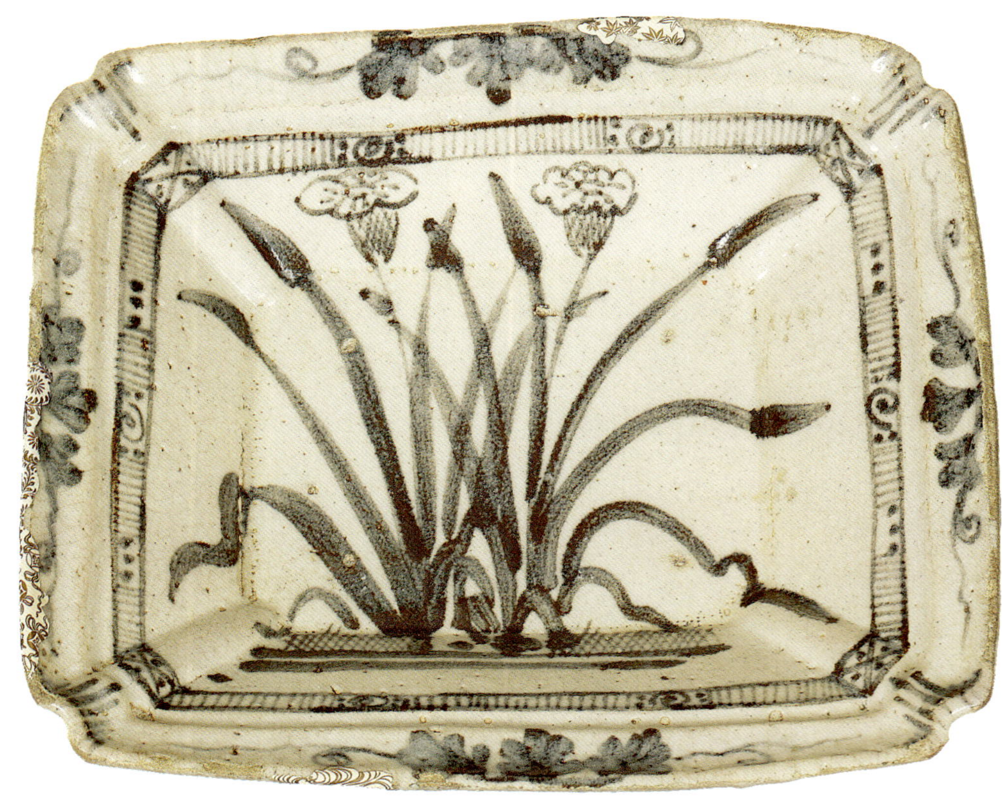

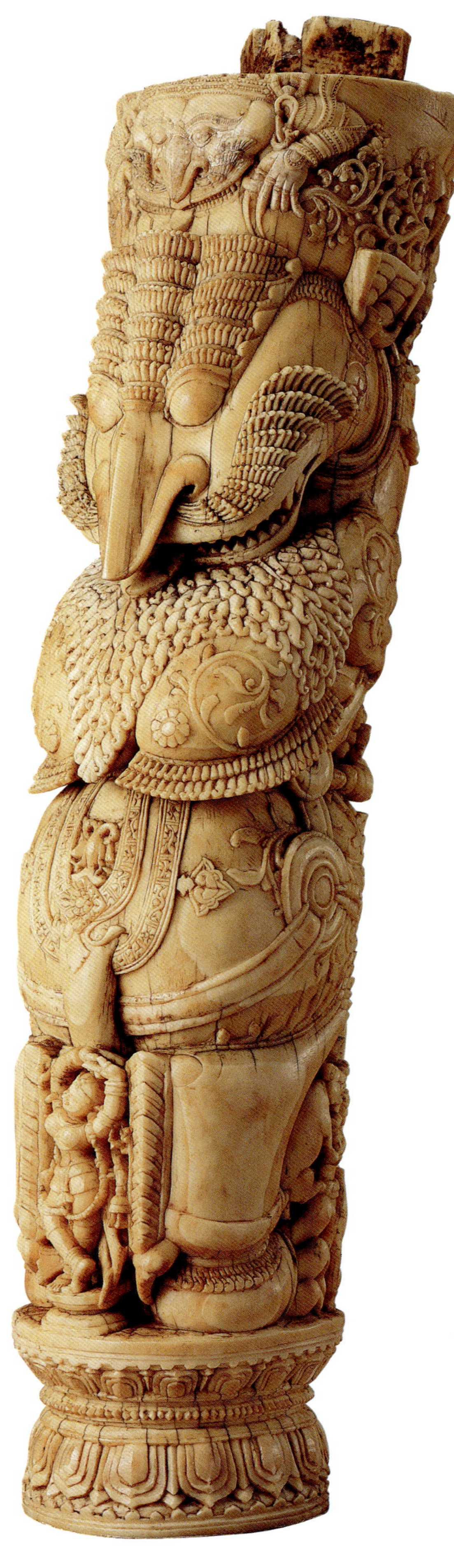

LEFT:
India, Ganga dynasty
1076-1586
throne leg, 16th century
ivory, h: 16 1/4 in.
Gift of Walter E. and Tekla
B. Wolf by exchange
1993.170

OPPOSITE:
Hokusai
Japanese, 1760-1849
South Wind and Fair Weather,
from the series
The Thirty-Six Views of Fuji, 1823
color woodblock print
10 1/8 x 15 in.
Carl H. Lieber Fund, 60.12

OPPOSITE BELOW:
Japan, Momoyama period
1568-1598
rectangular dish with
flower design
Mino ware, Shino type
stoneware with white and
iron glaze, 9 9/16 x 8 1/8 in.
Gift of the Alliance of the
Indianapolis Museum of Art
1983.1

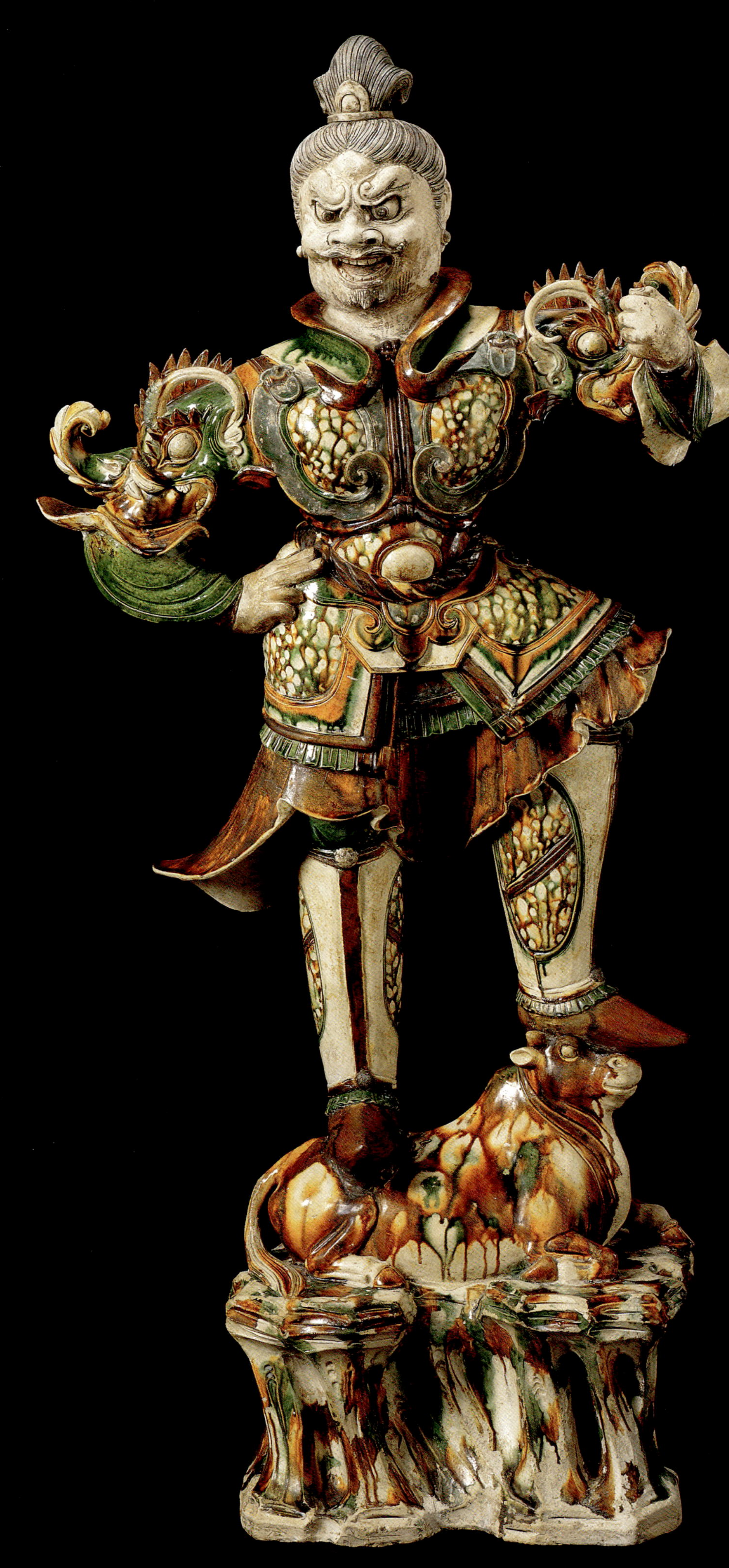

Asian Art:
The Chinese Collection

Many donors have generously added to the museum's collection of Chinese art over the last hundred years. Notable among them is Eli Lilly, who purchased many objects for the museum that may be counted among the finest of their types in the world. Working with museum director Wilbur Peat, beginning in the 1940s, Mr. Lilly assembled one of the finest comprehensive collections of Chinese art built by an individual in this country.

China, about the same size as Europe and with as many regional styles, can boast a continuous artistic production spanning more than 6,000 years. The museum has exquisite examples that represent the finest traditions in all materials. The bronzes include intricately cast ritual vessels of the Shang and Zhou dynasties (seventeenth–third centuries B.C.), mirrors, utilitarian objects, and miniature Buddhist figures, many of which were donated by James W. Alsdorf. The collection of Professor and Mrs. Norris Shreve greatly contributed to the museum's holdings of archaic and archaistic jades.

The strongest area of the collection is ceramics, for it includes excellent examples from all periods of Chinese history. Beginning with the middle of the Neolithic (about 4500 B.C.), the encyclopedic collection displays the wonderful achievements of past masters. Tomb figures and vessels capture the diversity of forms and shapes. From the bold, powerful forms and tri-color glazes of the Tang dynasty (618-907), to the elegant and delicate wares of the Song dynasty (960–1279) and the brilliant porcelains of the Ming and Qing dynasties (1368–1911), the accomplishments and changing tastes of regions and times are available for all to enjoy.

The painting collection is rich with important works that document the wide variety of styles and traditions in Chinese art. Particularly noteworthy are works from the academic traditions of the Southern Song dynasty (1127–1279); early artists of the Yuan dynasty (1279–1368), such as Li Kan and Wang Meng, who helped establish the great scholar-painter tradition; later masters such as Shen Zhou and the eccentric Wu Wei of the Ming dynasty (1368–1644); and academic and orthodox artists, such as "the Four Wangs" of the Qing dynasty (1644-1911).

Crystal, glass, and ivory objects, lacquer ware, furniture, prints, textiles and sculptures of stone and wood are also part of the collection. Constant rotation of the art between storage and exhibition in the Asian galleries insures that many works from this extensive collection are displayed throughout the year.

ABOVE:
China, Shang dynasty
about 1700-1045 B.C.
ritual vessel *(guang)*
about 1200 B.C.
bronze, h: 8 1/4 in.
Gift of Mr. and Mrs. Eli Lilly
60.43

OPPOSITE:
China, Tang dynasty, 618-907
tomb guardian, 8th century
earthenware with lead glaze,
ink and gold, h: 42 in.
Richard A. Fairbanks Fund
1997.1

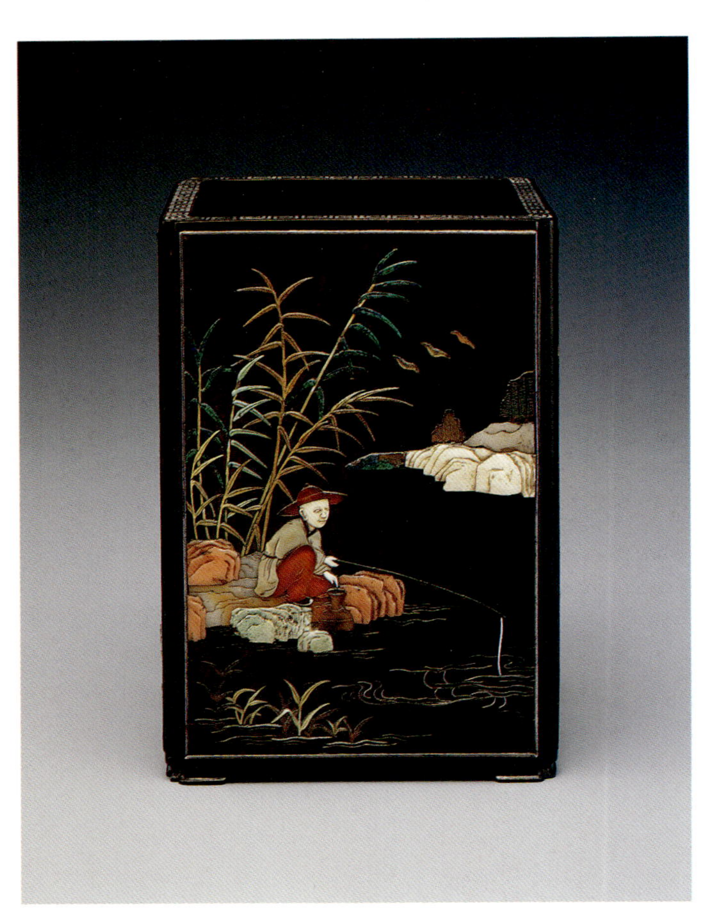

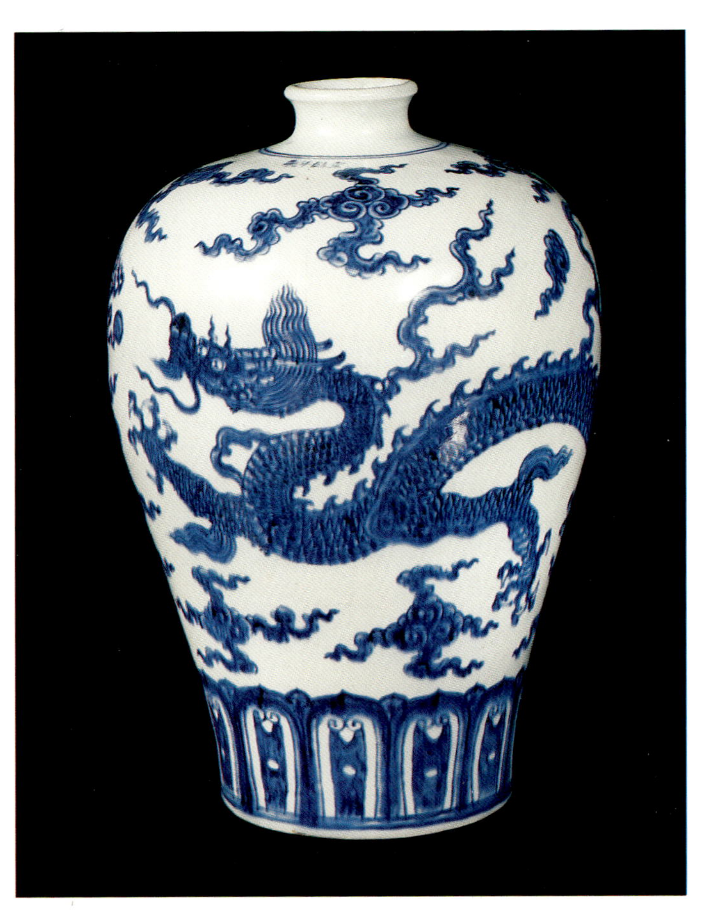

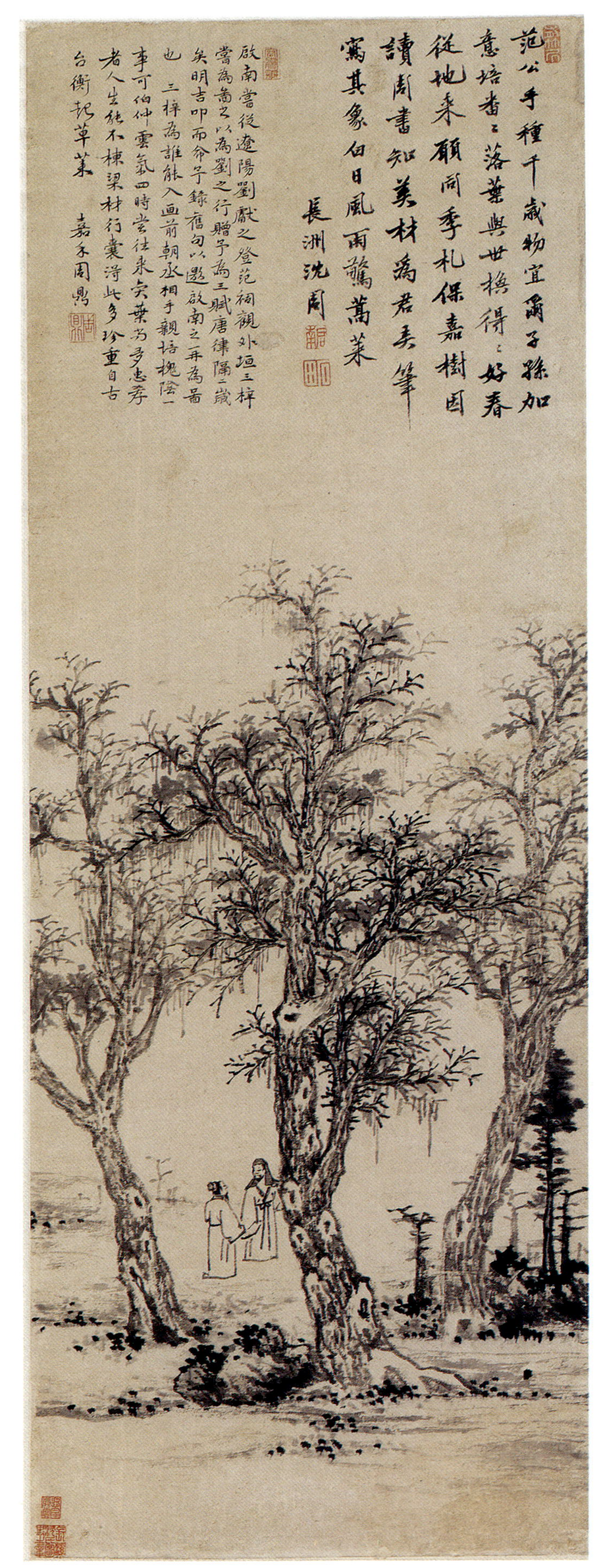
范公手種千歲物宜爾子孫加
意培者々落葉與世換得々好春
從地來顧向季札保嘉樹因
讀周書知美材爲君美筆
寫其象他日風雨驚萬萊
長洲沈周
啟南嘗從遼陽劉獻之登范祠觀外垣三梓
嘗爲畫之以爲劉之行贈予爲三賦唐律隔二歲
矣明吉叩而命予錄舊句以遐啟南之年爲耆
也三梓爲誰能入画前朝丞相手親培槐陰一
事可伯仲雲氣四時嘗往來实葉为予忠孝
者人生能不棟梁材行囊得此多珍重自古
台衡起草萊
嘉禾周鼎

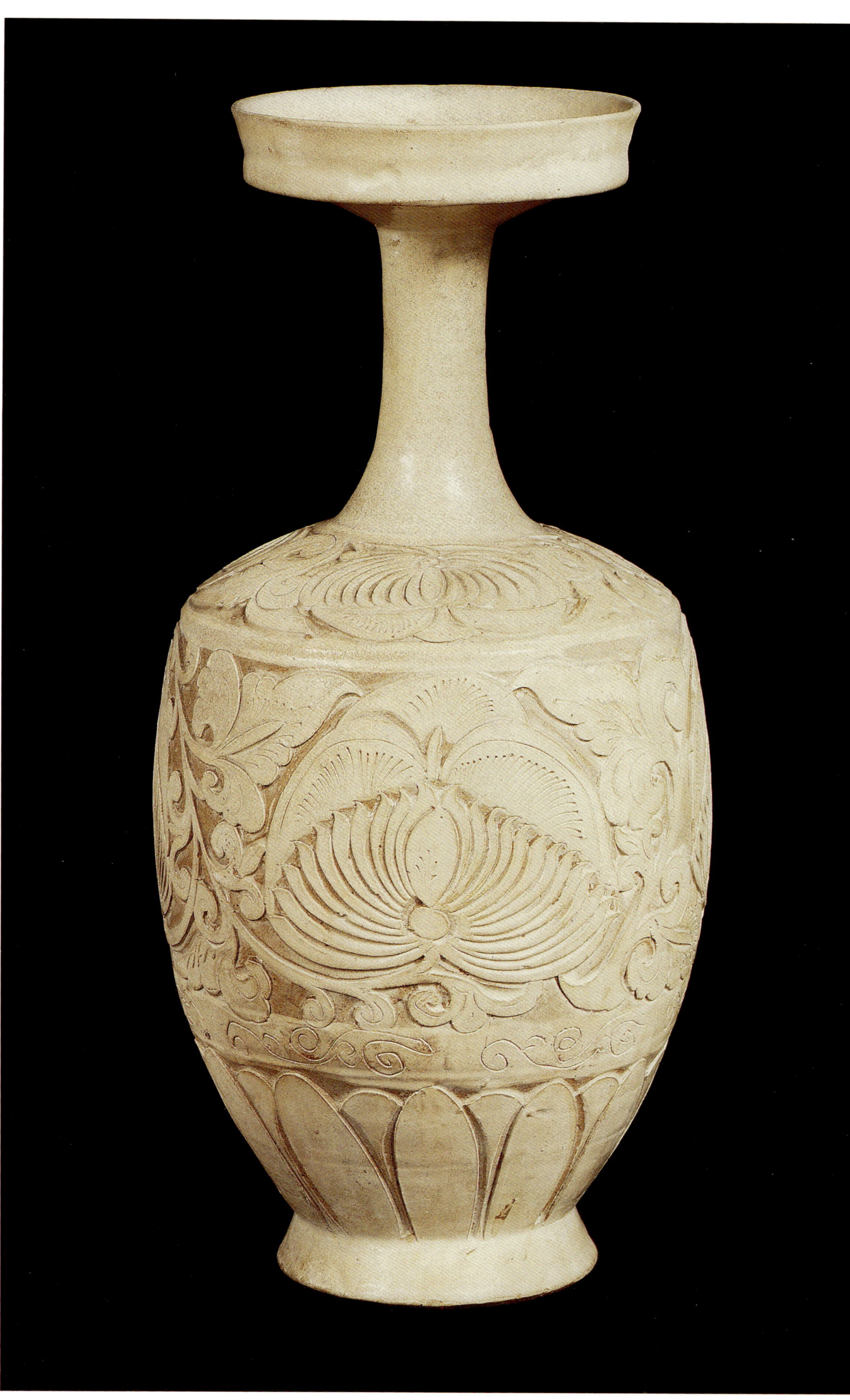

LEFT:
China, Northern Song dynasty, 960-1127
saucer-mouth vase
about 1000
stoneware with slip and clear glaze, Cizhou-type ware
h: 17 in.
Gift of Mr. and Mrs. Eli Lilly
47.153

OPPOSITE TOP LEFT:
China, Qing dynasty 1644-1911
brushpot with scenes of country pursuits, about 1700
various inlays in purple sandalwood (*zitan*)
5 1/4 x 3 3/4 x 3 3/4 in.
Gift of Professor and Mrs. R. Norris Shreve and the Krannert Charitable Trust by exchange, 1997.45

OPPOSITE LOWER LEFT:
China, Ming dynasty 1368-1644
vase with dragon design
Xuande period, 1426-1435
porcelain with underglaze blue, h: 13 1/2 in.
Gift of Mr. and Mrs. Eli Lilly
60.82

OPPOSITE RIGHT:
Shen Zhou, 1427-1509
Chinese, Ming dynasty 1368-1644
Three Catalpa Trees, about 1480
ink on paper, 41 1/2 x 16 in.
Gift of Mr. and Mrs. Eli Lilly
60.140

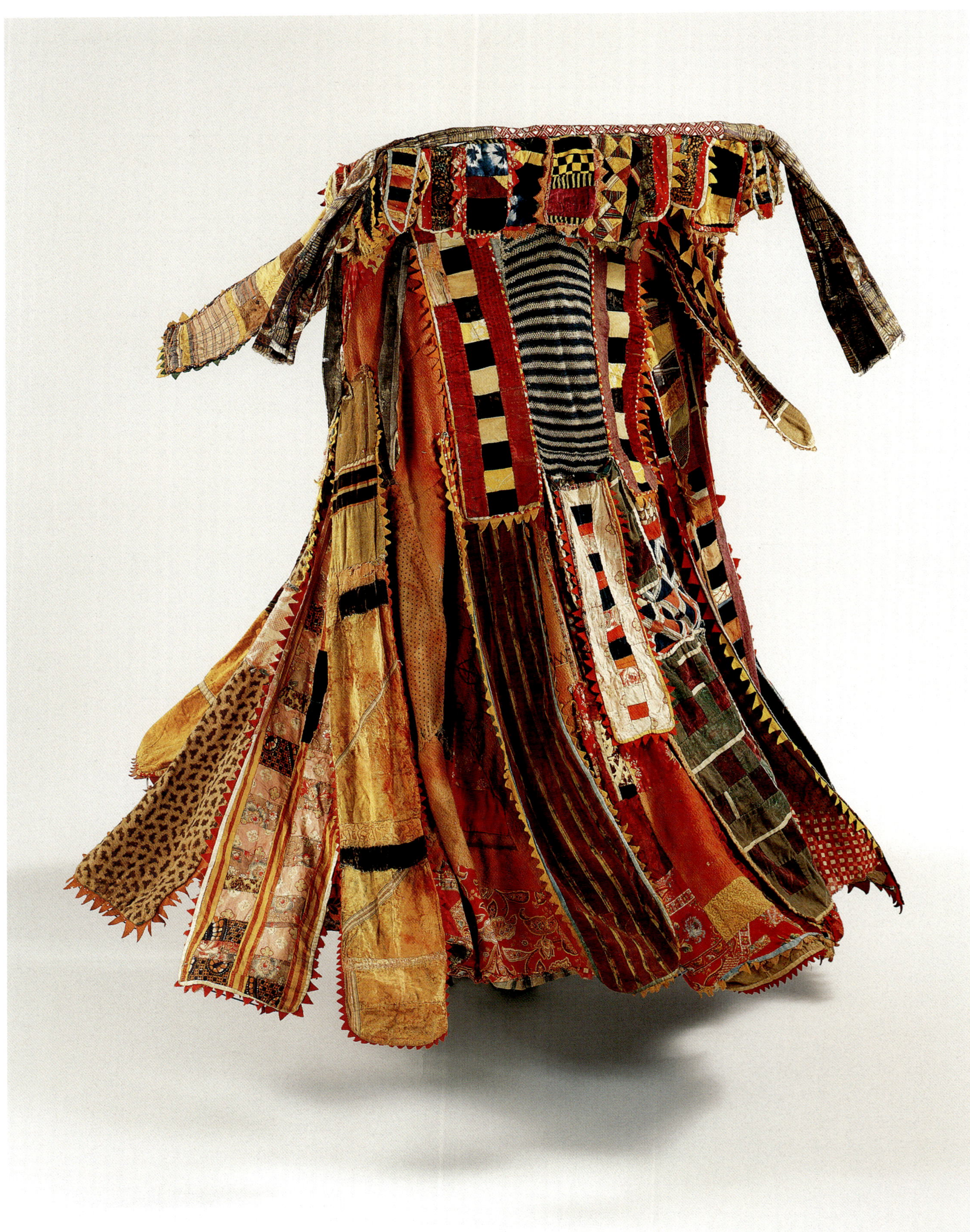

Textiles and Costumes Collection

The IMA was one of the first art institutions in the United States to collect textiles. This 6,000-piece collection, established in 1888 with the purchase of an embroidered piece, represents virtually all of the world's traditions in fabrics and reveals the dissemination of style and technique among many different cultures. In 1906, over 100 Chinese textiles and costumes were purchased by the museum through the John Herron Fund. By 1915, as a result of a number of generous donations and purchases, the collection had grown rapidly in the areas of Chinese, Japanese, European, Persian, and Indian textiles and costumes. In 1916, the first of many generous gifts from the Niblack family of Indianapolis was received. Vice Admiral Albert Niblack and his sisters, Eliza M. and Sarah L. Niblack, were all avid textile collectors and world travelers, and by 1933, they had donated approximately 3,000 pieces to the collection. These superb gifts included North African, Southeast Asian, and European textiles, which form the nucleus of the present collection.

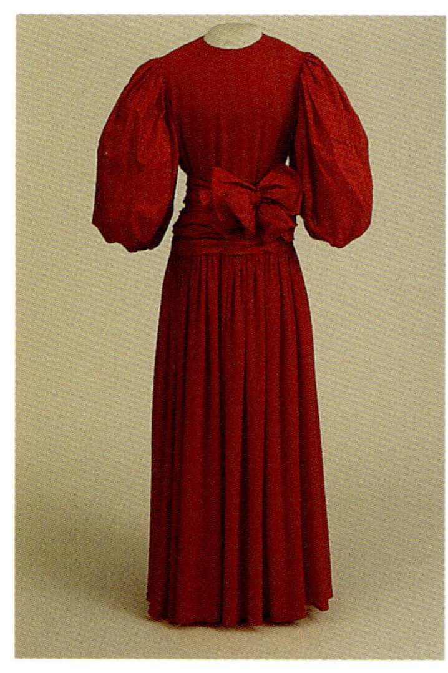

The core of the carpet collection came to the museum through the Delavan Smith Bequest in 1925, and Mrs. Charles Crosley donated her collection of nineteenth-century lace in 1936.

Significant West African and Moroccan textiles and rugs have been added to the collection in recent years, completing the representation of the diverse African cultures. The various cultures of Asia are represented by many important pieces dating from the fourteenth to the early twentieth century. Other recent and important acquisitions include a rare and exquisite Chinese embroidered votive panel dating from the fourteenth century. In 1996, the IMA received the prestigious collection of the late Colonel Jeff W. Boucher, consisting of sixty-five Baluchi rugs from Iran and Afghanistan.

OPPOSITE:
Yoruba people
Nigeria, Western Africa
Egungun masquerade costume
20th century
cotton, cloth, and glass beads
l: 61 in.
Peggy S. Gilfoy Memorial Fund
1990.2

LEFT:
Bill Blass
American, b. 1922
evening dress, 1981
silk, chiffon, and taffeta
Gift of Mrs. Ronald Reagan
and Bill Blass, 82.50

The American and European collections are constantly expanding. Silks from the late sixteenth to nineteenth centuries, a lace collection spanning 500 years, a large and impressive group of nineteenth-century paisley shawls from England, a large collection of costumes dating from the eighteenth through the twentieth centuries, and many fine Indiana quilts and coverlets are part of these outstanding holdings.

Another important area of the collection is twentieth-century fashion. In 1973 a gift of five pieces from the estate of Norman Norell established the Indiana Fashion Design collection. Since that time, the museum's holdings have been enriched by gifts of contemporary costumes by Norell, Bill Blass and Halston—all Indiana natives—as well as other American and European high-fashion designers.

The museum has recently developed a state-of-the-art storage and study area for textiles and costumes, making these collections more accessible to scholars, students, and the general public.

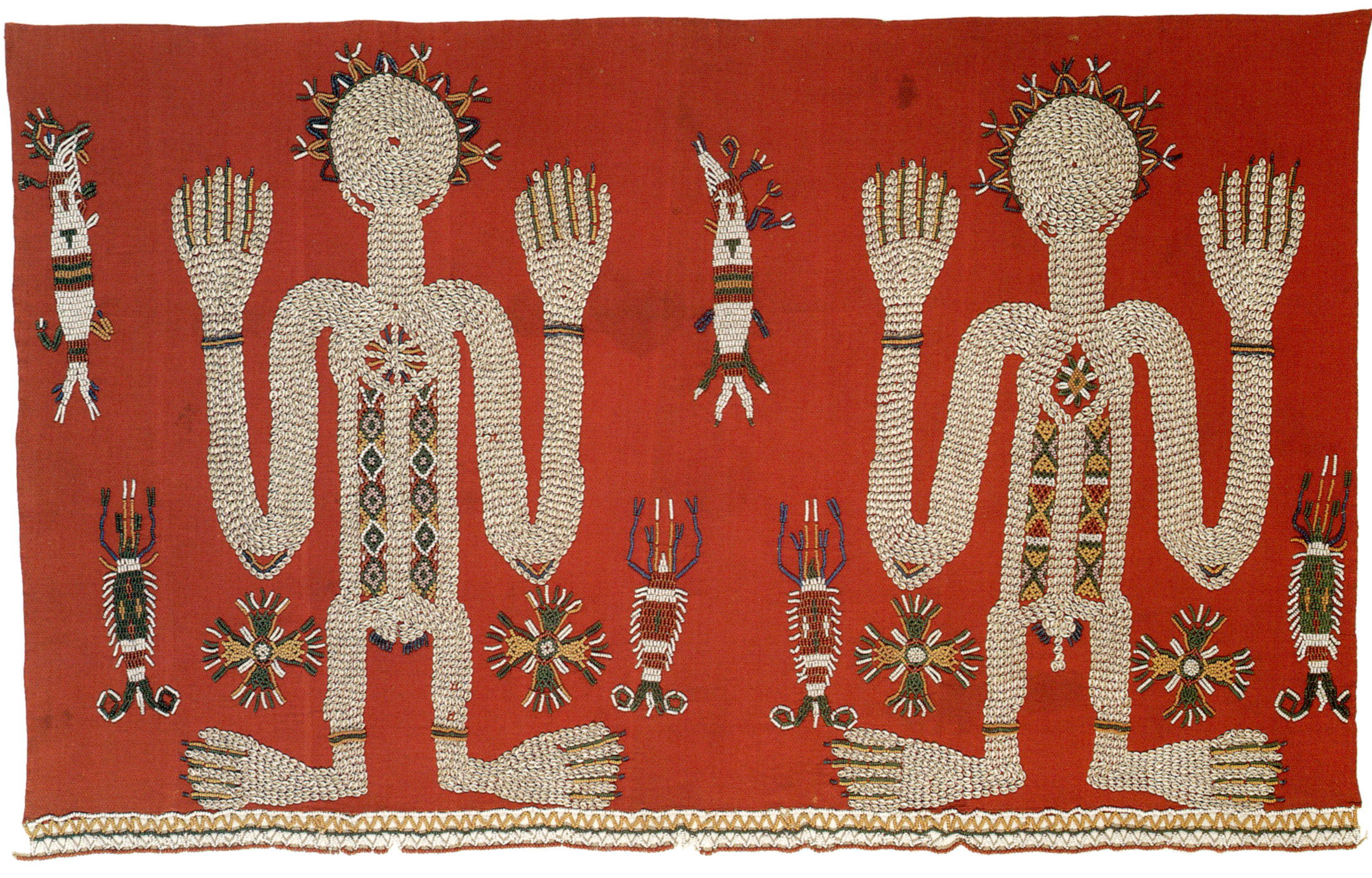

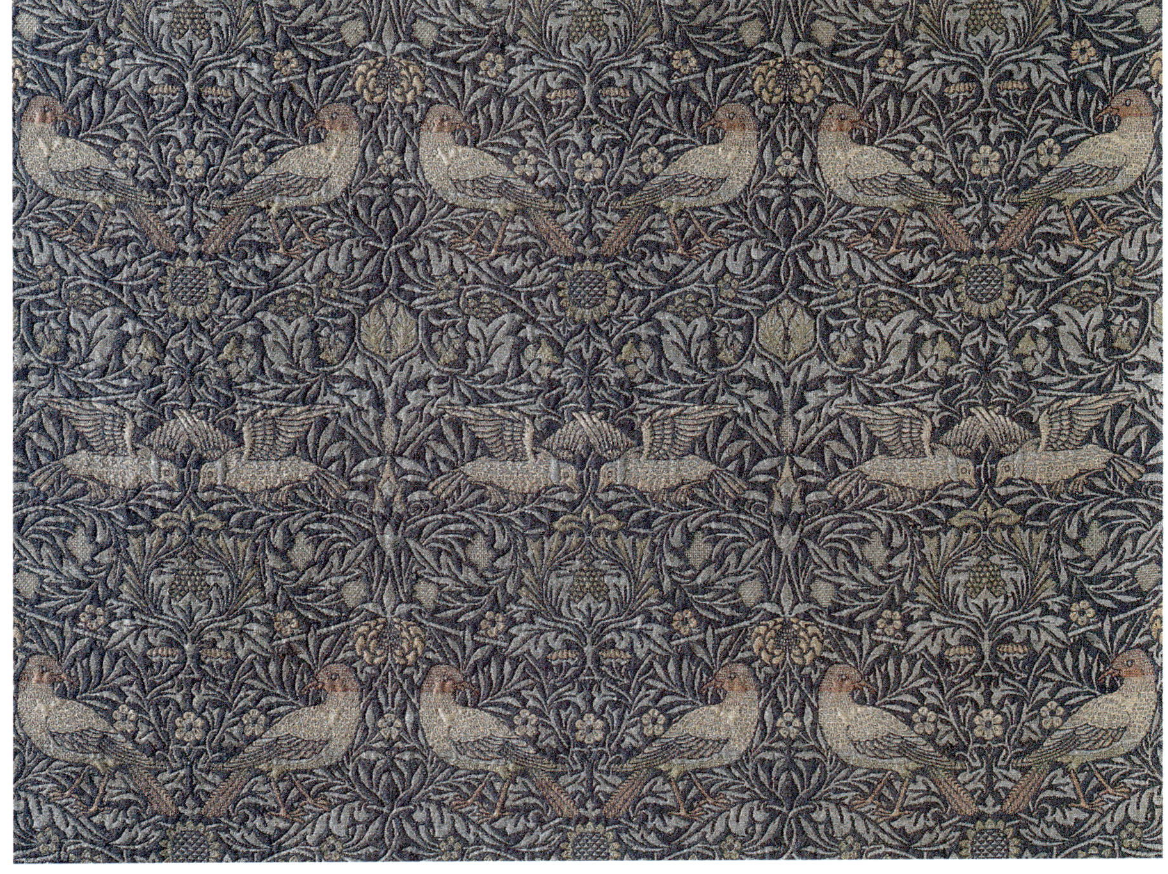

ABOVE:
Sumba, Indonesia
woman's wrapper, 19th century
cotton plain weave,
embroidered with shells and
beads, 29 x 46 1/2 in.
Eliza M. and Sarah L. Niblack
Collection, 33.682

RIGHT:
William Morris
English, 1834-1896
Bird, 1877-78
wool, 86 1/2 x 51 in.
Bequest of Mrs. Cornelius
O. Alig by exchange
1997.143

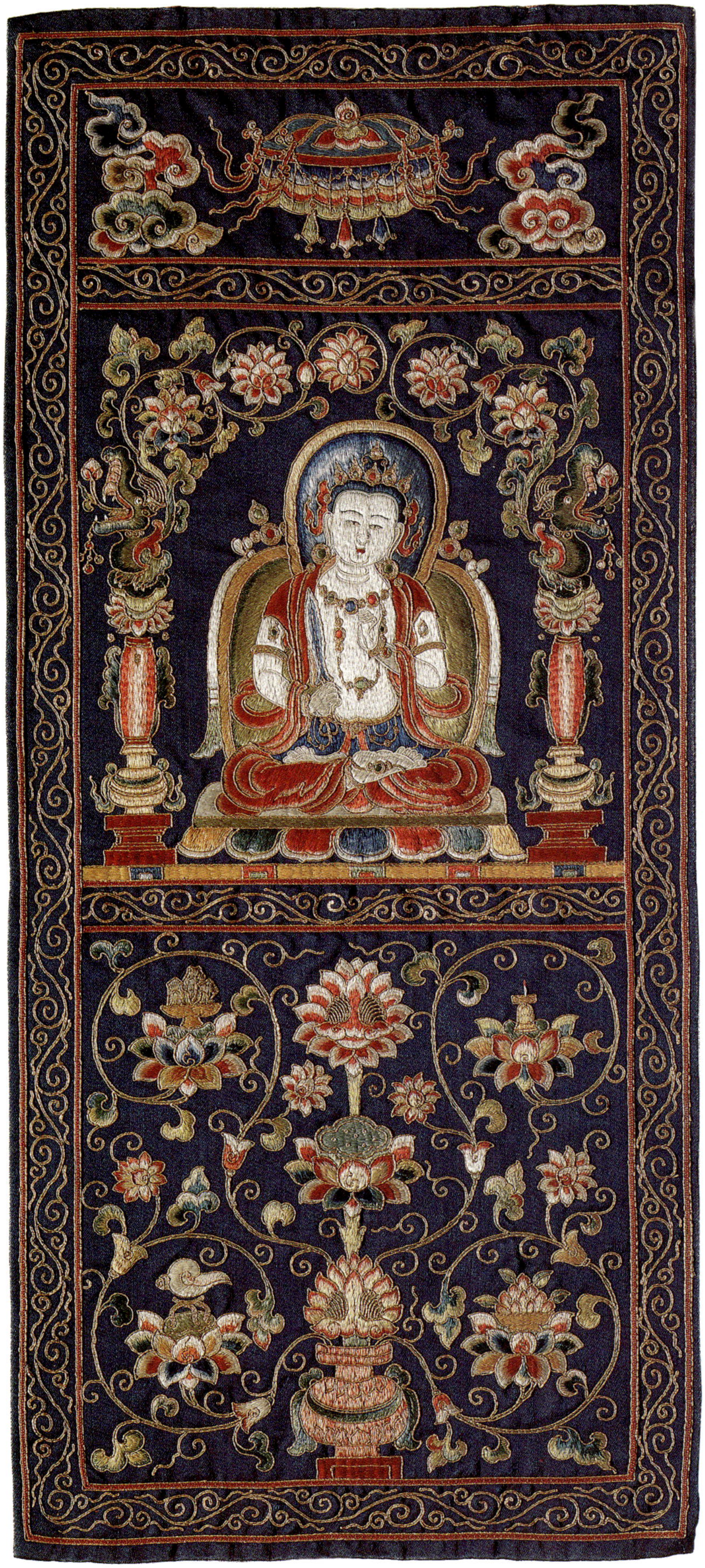

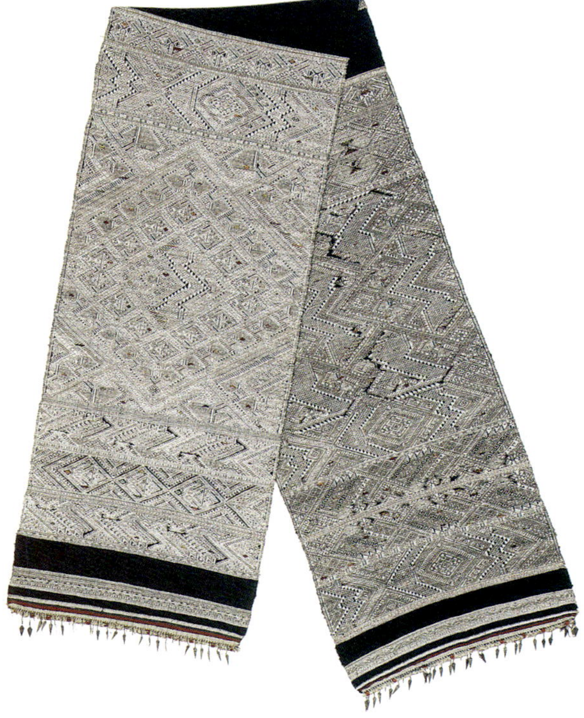

ABOVE:
Laos
shaman's shawl
late 19th century
silk, cotton, silver tassels
94 3/8 x 17 1/8 in.
Gift by exchange of Mrs. George Philip Meier, Mrs. George Monroe Dixon, bequest of Mrs. Cornelius O. Alig, 1997.148

LEFT:
China, Yuan dynasty
1279-1368
Bodhisattva of Wisdom (Manjusri)
13th–14th century
silk embroidered with silk and gold wrapped threads
17 3/8 x 7 5/8 in.
Martha Delzell Memorial Fund, 1992.66

RIGHT:
Berber people
Morocco
saddle rug
late 19th century
wool, cotton
89 1/2 x 46 1/4 in.
Gift of Frank Hall
1994.60

OPPOSITE:
Baluchi people
Northeastern Iran
prayer rug
third quarter of 19th century
wool, 63 x 30 in.
Colonel Jeff W. Boucher
Collection, 1996.62

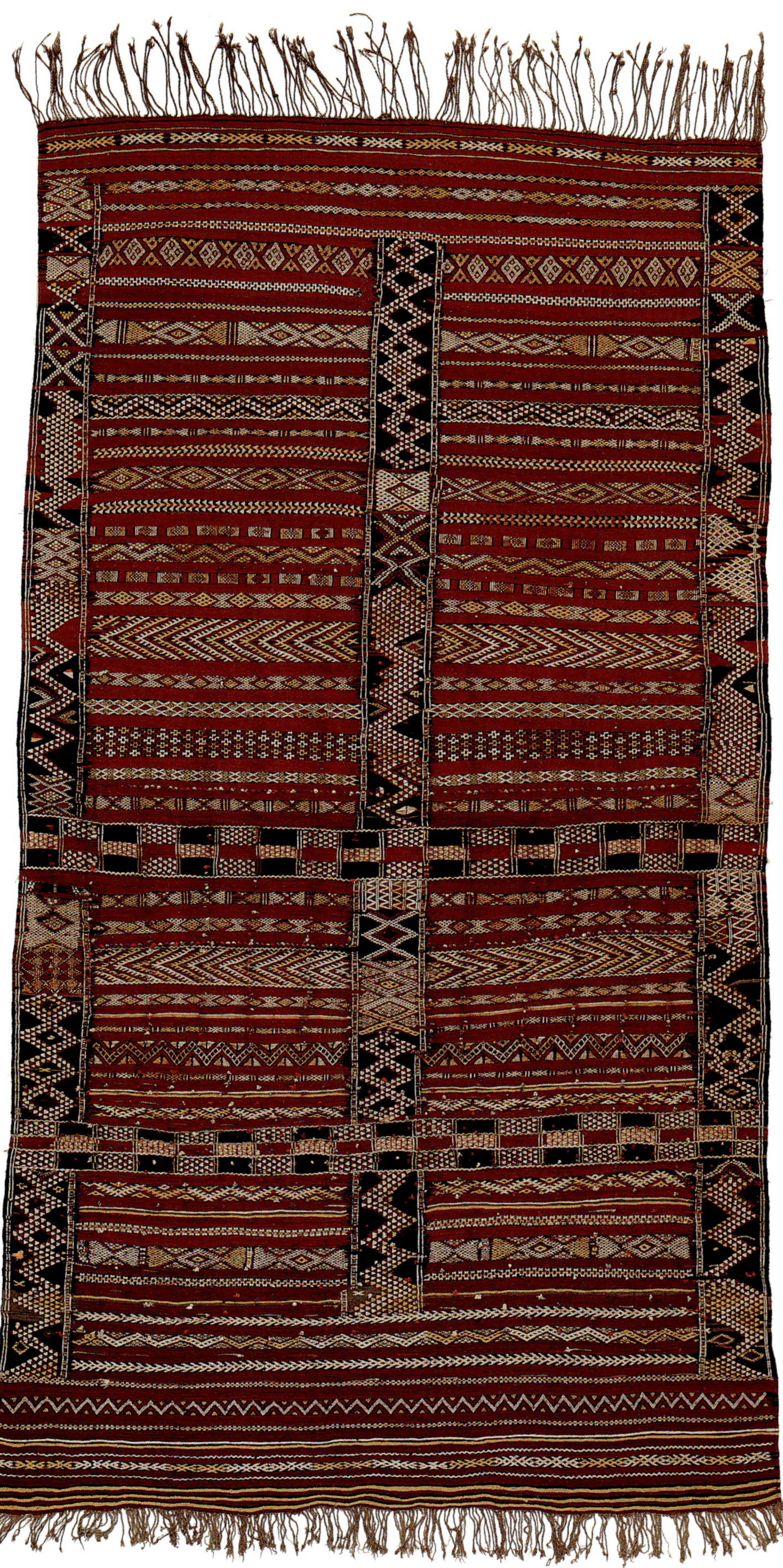

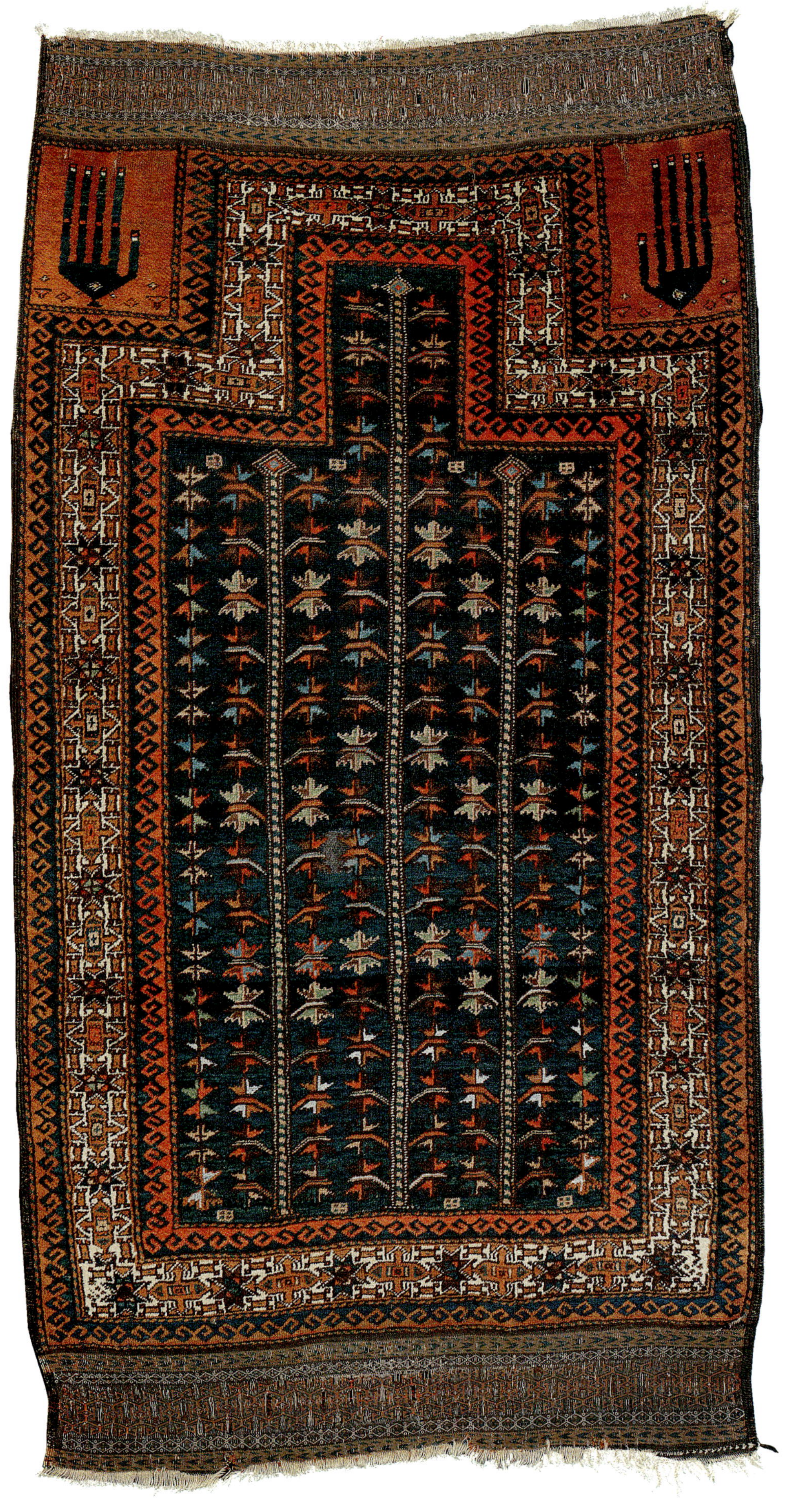

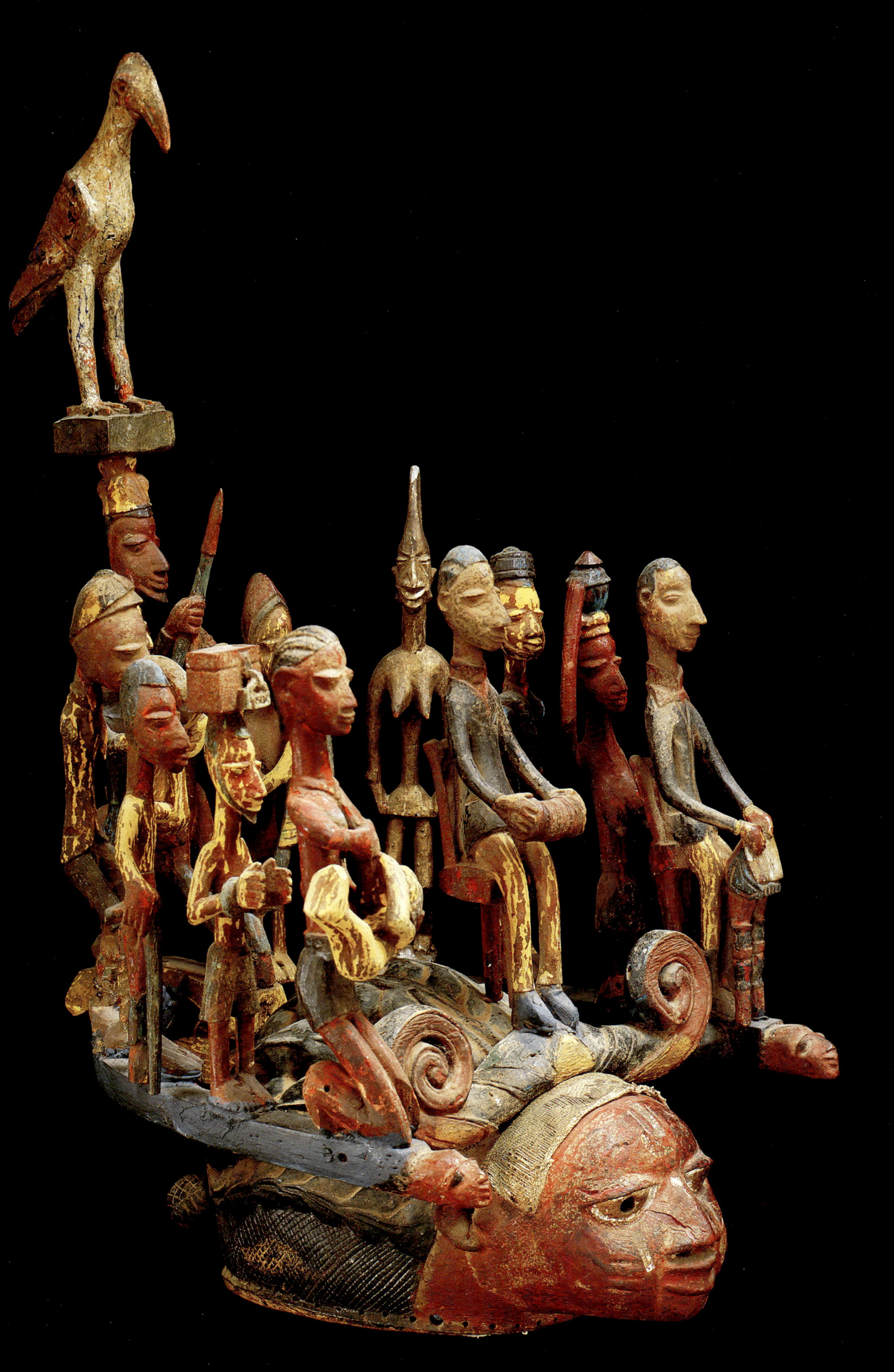

African, South Pacific, Precolumbian and American Indian Collections

The IMA has exhibited African art for more than a generation. During the 1970s, the museum began to acquire African textiles and other items that would complement the anticipated gift of approximately 1,200 items from Mr. and Mrs. Harrison Eiteljorg. This major gift, which came to the museum in 1989, made possible the establishment of the Eiteljorg Gallery of African Art and the Eiteljorg Gallery for Special Exhibitions, permanent installations on the second floor of the Hulman Pavilion. Since receiving the Eiteljorg gift, the museum has enhanced its African collection with purchases and donations.

This collection of more than 1,600 objects is among the most important collections of African art in the nation. It represents all major art-producing regions of Africa, including ancient Egypt. The strength of the collection is art from Western Africa, with significant holdings from the Yoruba people and the Benin Kingdom of Nigeria. Included are ritual masks and figures, crowns and other accouterments of leadership, articles of dress, and stools and other utilitarian objects. A special group of pieces is used for educational purposes. Most objects in the collection were made within the past one hundred years, although some date from the fourth millennium B.C. The museum has a small collection of ancient Egyptian art, most of which was acquired in the 1920s. The collection also includes a number of contemporary African art objects.

More than one hundred examples of South Pacific art—from Polynesia, Micronesia, Melanesia and Indonesia—are also in the museum's collection. Most of these objects, which include masks, figures, utilitarian items, architectural elements, and fabrics, were part of the 1989 gift of Mr. and Mrs. Harrison Eiteljorg.

OPPOSITE:
Yoruba people, Ijegbu subgroup, Ikorodu town
possibly carved by Onabanjo
Nigeria (Western Africa)
Magbo headpiece for *Oro* society
first half of 20th century
wood, pigment, cloth, iron, metal foil, mastic
h: 28 5/16 in.
Gift of Mr. and Mrs. Harrison Eiteljorg, 1989.754

BELOW:
probably Efik people
Nigeria (Western Africa)
head crest
early 20th century
wood, skin, pigment, metal, bone, fiber, basketry
w: 32 3/4 in.
Gift of Mr. and Mrs. Harrison Eiteljorg, 1989.900

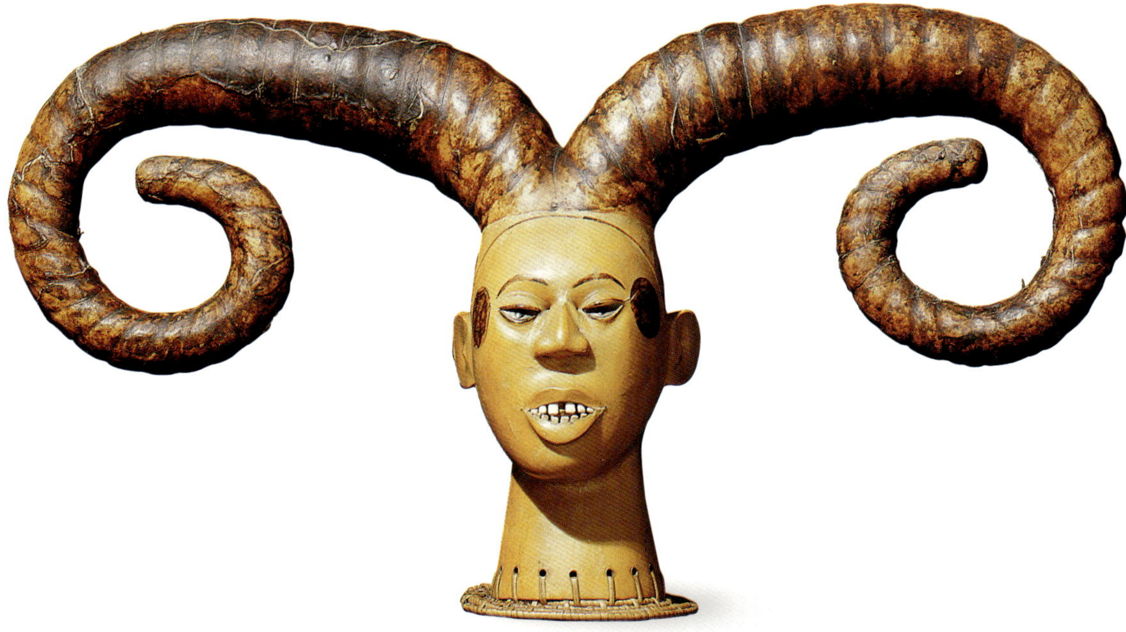

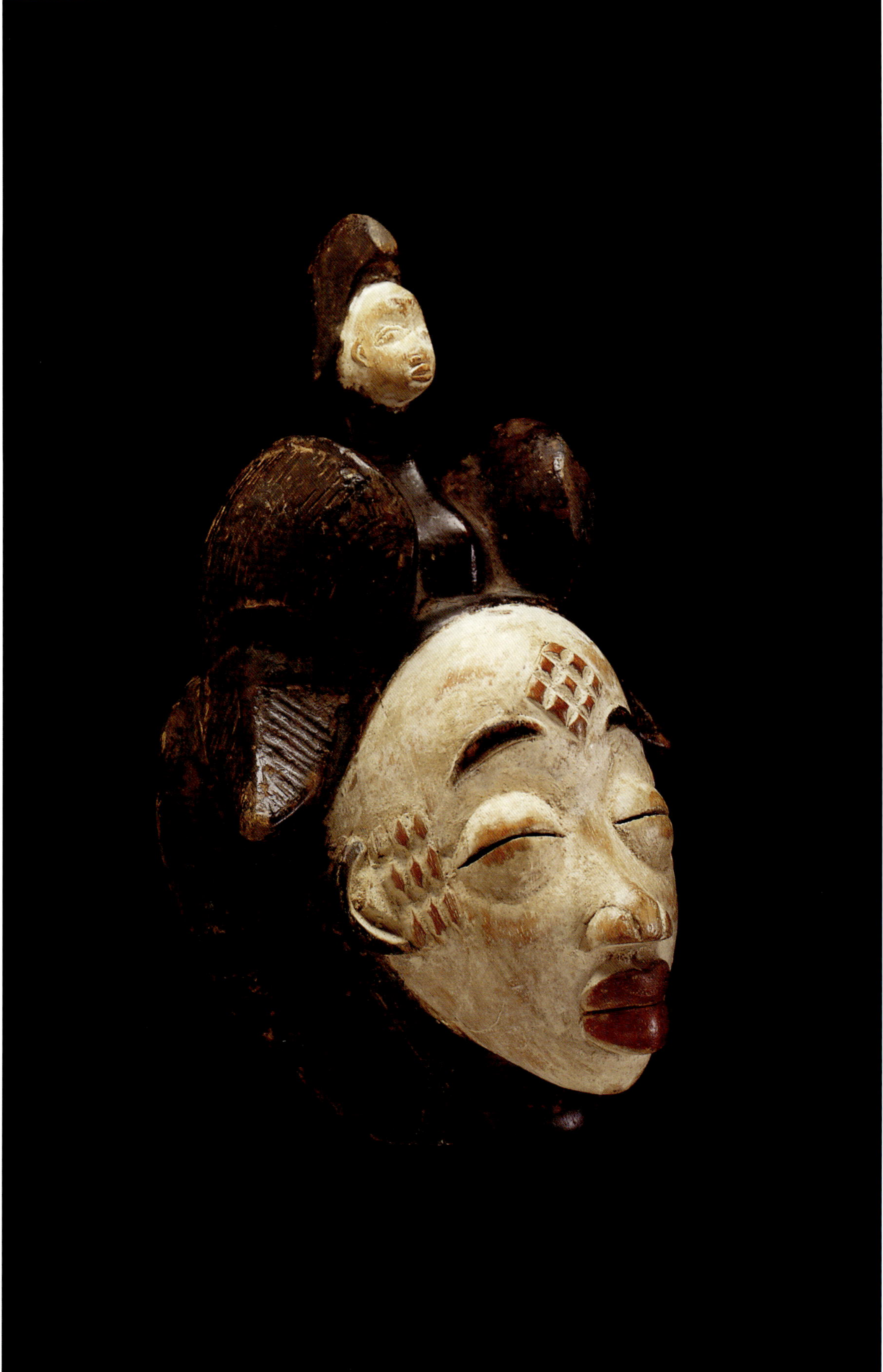

RIGHT:
probably Punu, Lumbo, or Shira people
Ngounié River region
Gabon (Central Africa)
face mask for *Mukudj* (*Mukuyi, Okuyi*) men's association
early 20th century
wood, pigment, iron
h: 10 1/4 in.
Gift of Mr. and Mrs. Harrison Eiteljorg, 1995.116

OPPOSITE:
Berber or Jewish people
Morocco (Northwestern Africa)
clasp for woman's garment
early 20th century
silver, enamel, glass
36 5/8 in.
Mr. and Mrs. William B. Ansted, Jr. Art Fund and Mary Black Fund, 1997.9

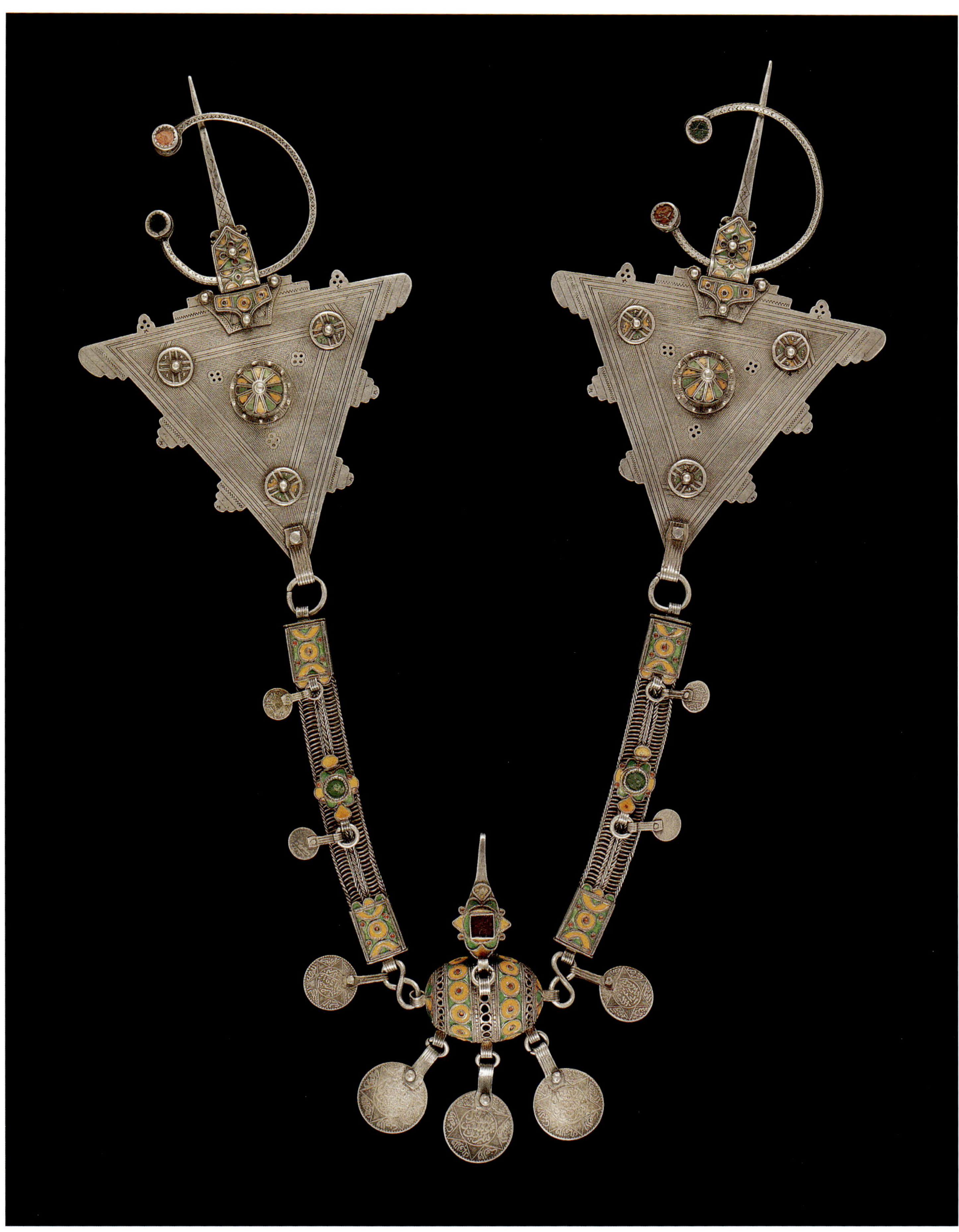

RIGHT:
Yoruba people, Owo subgroup
Nigeria (Western Africa)
ceremonial sword and sheath (*udamalore*) for the *olowo* (king) or high-ranking chief
19th or 20th century
iron, cloth, ivory, glass beads, thread, leather, and other materials, l: 18 in.
Gift of Mr. and Mrs. Harrison Eiteljorg, 1995.115a-b

BELOW RIGHT:
Mixtec culture, Mexico
pedestal bowl, 1200-1500 A.D.
ceramic, pigment
w: 12 1/2 in.
Gift of Bonnie and David Ross, 1996.118

OPPOSITE:
Edo people, Benin kingdom
Nigeria (Western Africa)
vessel lid in the form of a leopard head
probably 16th century
brass, h: 7 3/4 in.
Alliance Income Fund
1992.61

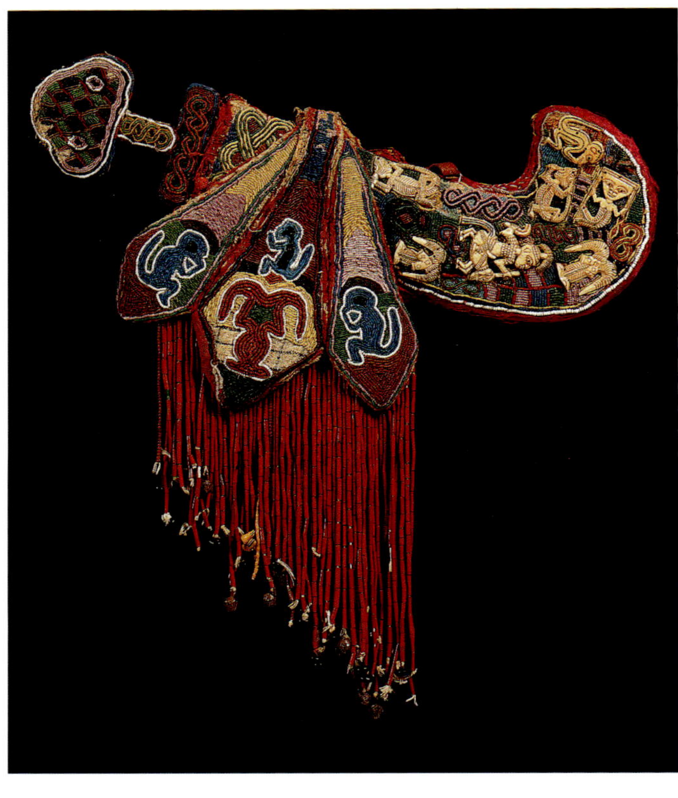

The collection contains a sampling of American Indian art that geographically reaches from Alaska to Peru and chronologically extends from 3,000 B.C. to the twentieth century. A variety of materials, techniques, forms and functions are represented.

The Precolumbian collection has examples of art from most of the major Mesoamerican cultures, including Olmec, West Mexico, Teotihuacan, Veracruz and Maya. The strength of the Precolumbian collection is Peruvian stirrup-spout pottery, with examples from the Chavin, Moche, and Nazca cultures. The museum also has ancient North American Indian art of high quality. Many historic North American Indian cultures are represented, including several from the Southwest. Objects from the Haida people of Alaska and British Columbia are of special interest.

In 1930, several Northwest Coast Indian objects collected by Vice Admiral Albert P. Niblack during his travels were donated to the IMA. Members of his family gave many other gifts in the years that followed, most notably textiles from the Andes. The museum began to receive donations of Precolumbian art in the late 1940s. During the late 1950s and 1960s many pieces of Precolumbian and historic American Indian art were given to the museum by Mr. and Mrs. J. W. Alsdorf, collectors from Chicago. The 1960s brought the greatest expansion of the collection, in part through purchases. Throughout this decade, the museum was the recipient of numerous gifts from Mr. and Mrs. Earl C. Townsend.

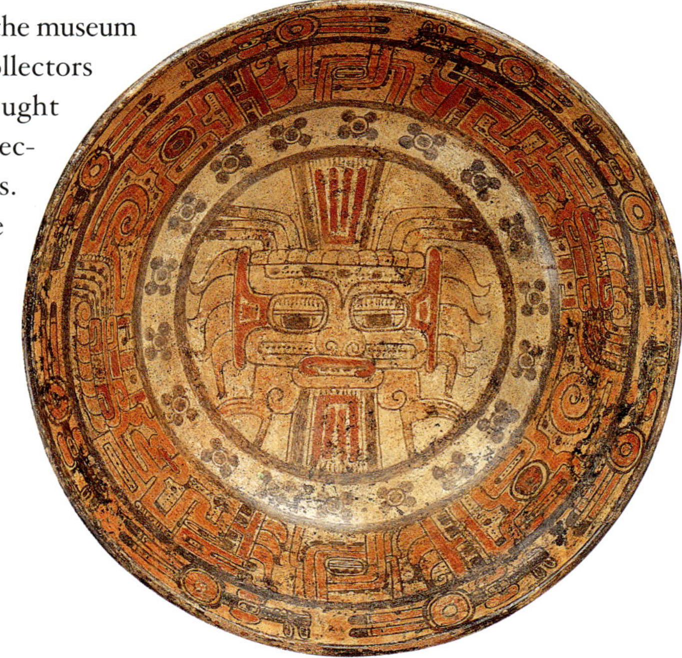

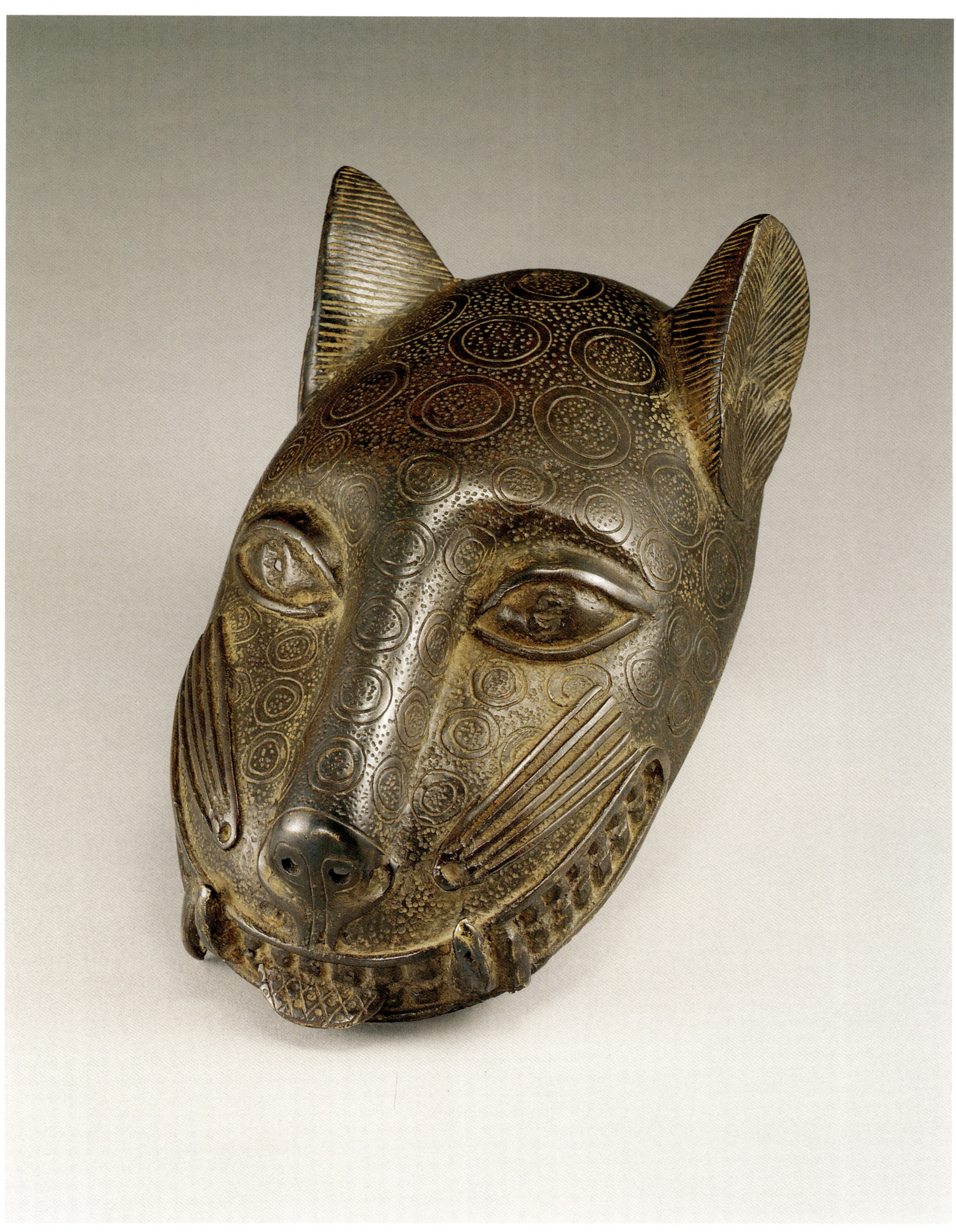

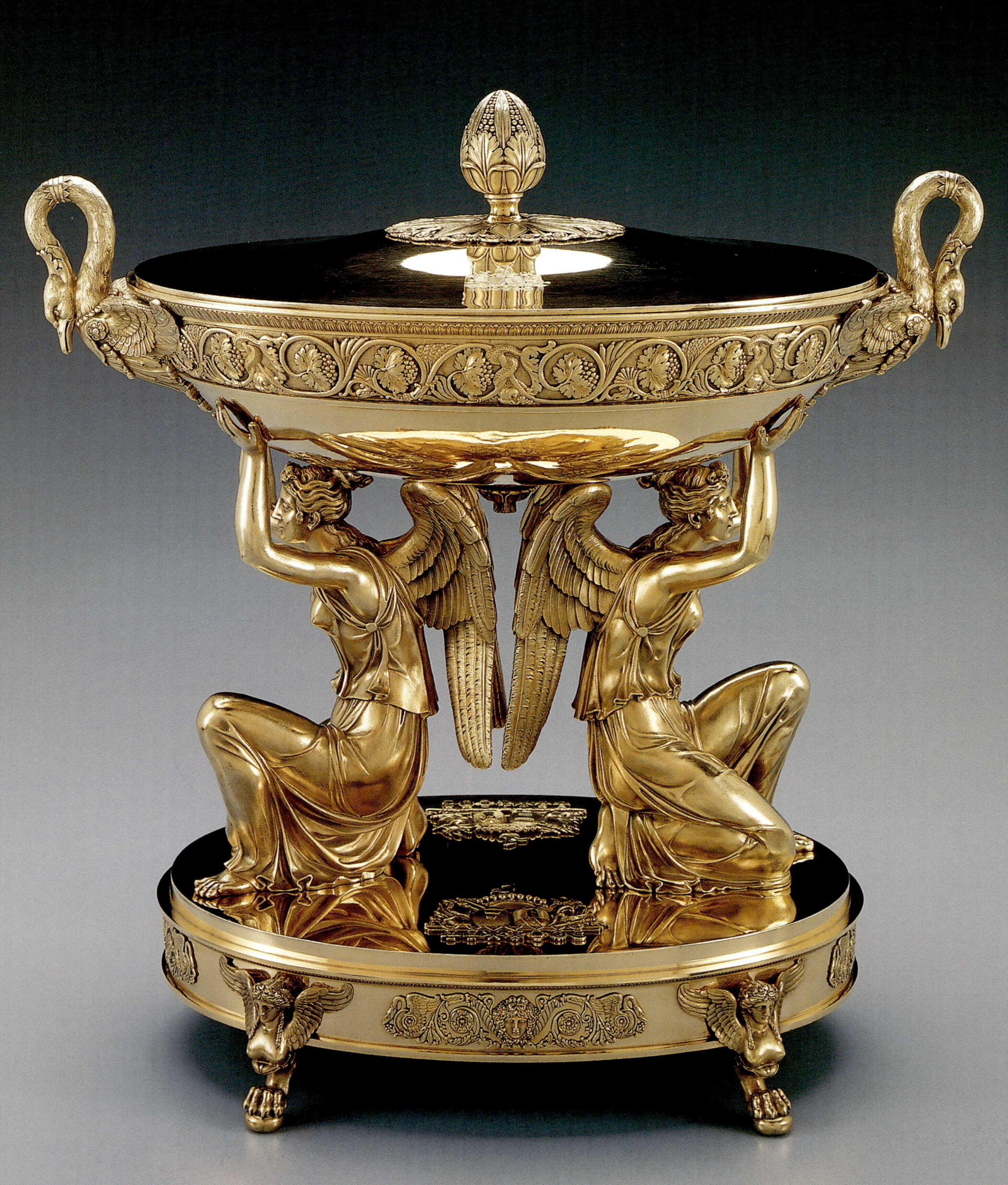

Decorative Arts

The decorative arts collection comprises American and European furniture, metalwork, ceramics and glass from the Renaissance to the present. Some of the most important artists are represented, and some areas of the collection are particularly strong.

Many of the objects in the ceramics collection are English eighteenth-century porcelain, and such manufacturers as Wedgwood, Worcester, Chelsea and Derby are represented. The museum is fortunate to have a rare Wedgwood Portland Vase, made by Josiah Wedgwood in about 1790. Numerous French (Sèvres), German (Meissen and Nymphenburg), and Austrian (Vienna) objects are also on display. The majority of the objects in the porcelain collection are eighteenth-century, but there are nineteenth-century examples as well. Renaissance Italian majolica, made in such centers as Urbino, is also represented in the collection. A group of French Art Nouveau ceramics includes a Sèvres porcelain vase of 1902, an earthenware charger made by Clément Massier in 1900, and a turn-of-the-century vase by Edmond Lachenal.

The strength of the furniture collection is the American objects, dating from about 1680 to the present, the majority from the colonial period through early Victorian times. The museum has a particularly impressive group of objects made from the 1820s through 1830s in the American Empire style, and from the 1850s through 1880s. Approximately twenty-five Art Deco objects from the 1930s are in the collection. An important and rare French Baroque longcase clock attributed to André-Charles Boulle, the cabinetmaker to Louis XIV, is among the examples of European furniture. A splendid pair of English Rococo side chairs, made in London about 1755 after a design by Thomas Chippendale, are also noteworthy.

The collection of glass is unusually strong in contemporary material. Because of the generosity of Marilyn and Eugene Glick, the Indianapolis Museum of Art has become one of the major centers for the study of contemporary studio glass. Such masters as Harvey Littleton, Dale Chihuly, Howard Ben Tré and Bertil Vallien are represented in the Caroline Marmon Fesler Gallery, which shows late nineteenth- through twentieth-century glass, ceramics, and metalwork. With the museum's many examples of glass by such important artists as René Lalique (French), Emile Gallé (French), Louis Comfort Tiffany

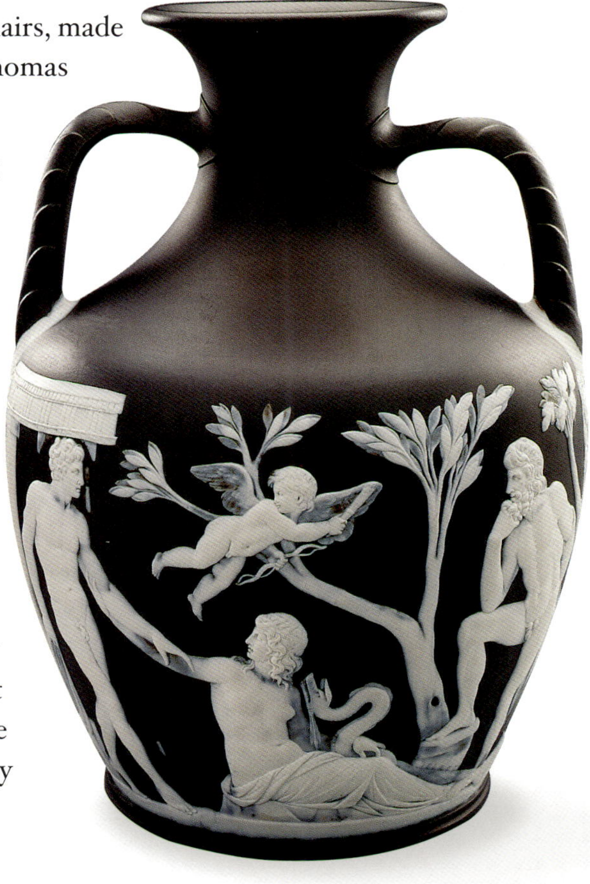

OPPOSITE:
Jean-Baptiste-Claude Odiot (maker)
French, 1763-1850
Pierre-Paul Prud'hon (designer of female figures)(attr.)
French, 1758-1823
Adrien-Louis-Marie Cavelier (designer)(attr.)
French, 1785-1867
soup tureen from the Branicki Service, 1819
gilded silver, h: 21 1/16 in.
Gift of Steve and Tomisue Hilbert and the Marian and Harold Victor Fund
1997.129a-c

BELOW:
Henry Webber (modeler)
English, 1754-1826
William Hackwood (modeler)
English, act. 1769-1832
William Wood (modeler)
English, act. after 1762
Josiah Wedgwood II (modeler)
English, d. 1843
Josiah Wedgwood (manufacturer)
Staffordshire, England
est. about 1759
vase, about 1790
stoneware, h: 10 in.
Ann McClelland Ropkey Decorative Arts Fund
1994.2

BELOW:
Paul de Lamerie
English (b. Holland), 1688-1751
covered cup, 1742
silver, h: 15 in.
Harold Victor Decorative Arts Fund, Ann McClelland Ropkey Decorative Arts Fund, Josephine Cowgill Jameson Fund, Nicholas H. Noyes Fund and Marian and Harold Victor Fund, 1994.159

OPPOSITE:
Nicolas Gribelin (movement)
French, 1637-1719
André-Charles Boulle (attr.)(case and dial mount)
French, 1642-1732
longcase pendulum clock
about 1673
ebony, oak, tortoiseshell, pewter, ebonized wood, gilt bronze, h: 82 1/2 in.
Gift of the Decorative Arts Society, the Alliance of the Indianapolis Museum of Art, and in memory of Dorothy Pettis Bookwalter
1989.72

(American), and Josef Hoffmann (Austrian), the development of glass can be traced from about 1870 to the present. *Angel of the Resurrection* (1904), a large stained-glass window by Tiffany Studios, was given to the museum by First Meridian Heights Presbyterian Church of Indianapolis. It was commissioned by the wife of President Benjamin Harrison.

One of the major highlights in the collection of metalwork—and the most significant object in the department of decorative arts—is the magnificent gilded silver soup tureen, cover and liner by Jean-Baptiste-Claude Odiot. This tureen was originally part of the 140-piece service made in Paris in 1819 for Count François-Xavier Branicki (1731-1819). The collection of metalwork also includes several pieces of sixteenth- and seventeenth-century European and American silver. The majority of works are eighteenth- through twentieth-century, and among them are important Georgian silver objects by Paul de Lamerie, Hester Bateman, and Paul Storr. A significant object in the English silver collection is the Nottingham Race Cup, made in 1775-1776 by Robert Smith and Daniel Sharp. The museum has the largest collection in existence of metalwork created by the Indianapolis Arts and Crafts designer Janet Payne Bowles. These objects, made for such celebrated individuals as J. P. Morgan and the Broadway actress Maude Adams, were made from about 1910 to 1930.

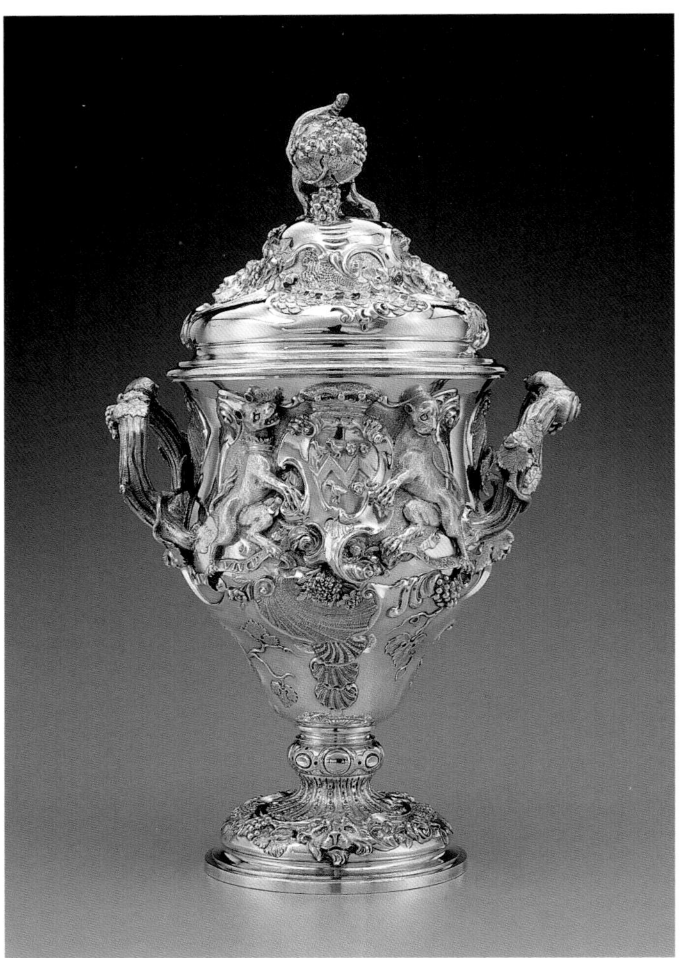

Objets de vertu (small precious objects) consist mainly of a small group of enameled and carved gemstones by the Russian goldsmith and jeweler Carl Peter Fabergé. The Ruth Allison Lilly Collection of approximately one hundred watches, some of which are major horological achievements, is significant. Most of the watches are nineteenth-century pocket watches, and a number are form watches, with cases shaped like harps, apples, and other objects.

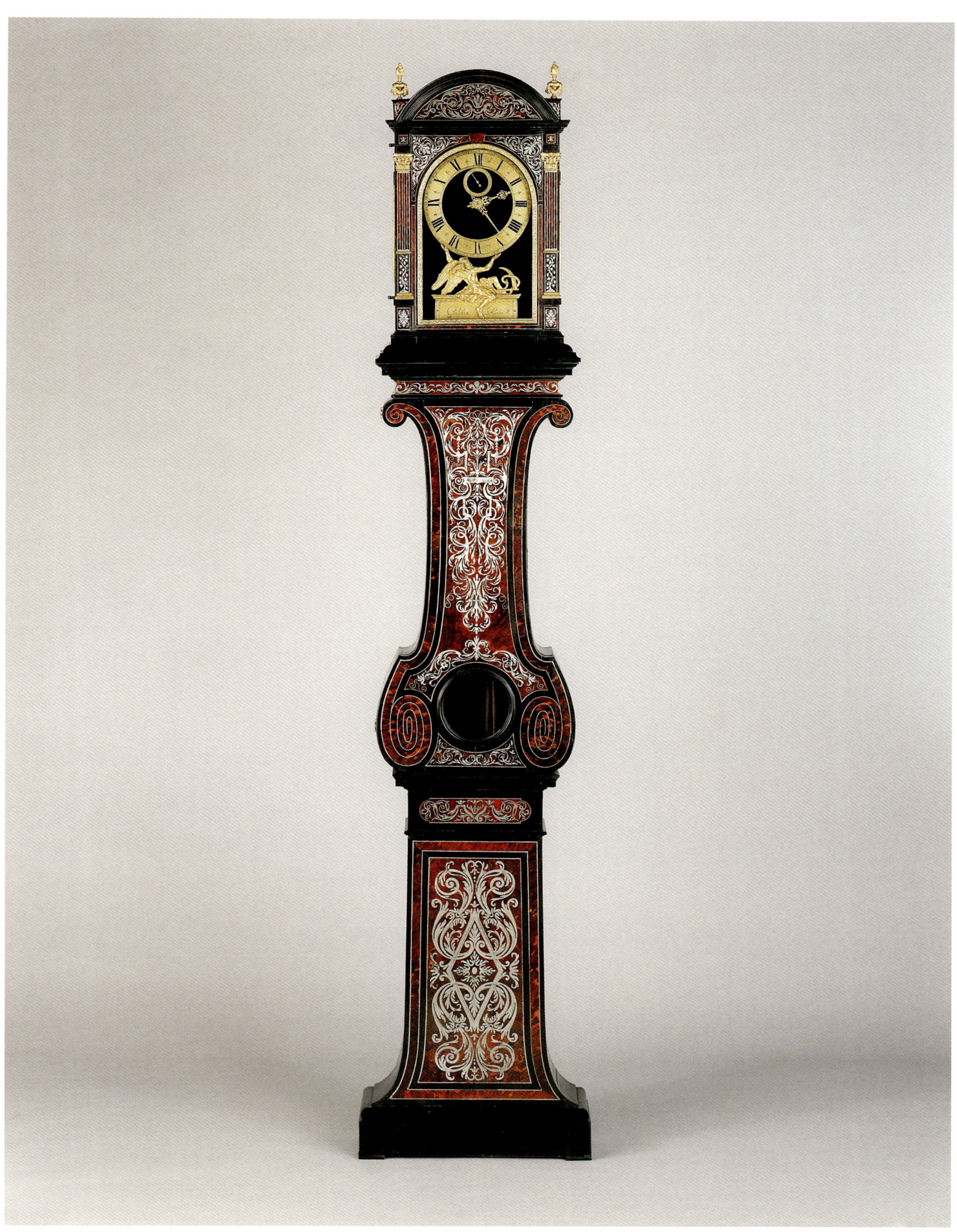

RIGHT:
American (Philadelphia)
18th century
high chest, about 1760-1780
walnut, brass mounts
98 x 43 1/4 x 22 1/4 in.
Gift of the National Society of the Colonial Dames of America in the State of Indiana, 75.99

OPPOSITE:
Howard Ben Tré
American, b. 1949
Second Vase, 1989
cast glass, gold leaf, and bronze powder
h: 71 1/2 in.
Gift of Marilyn and Eugene Glick, 1989.113

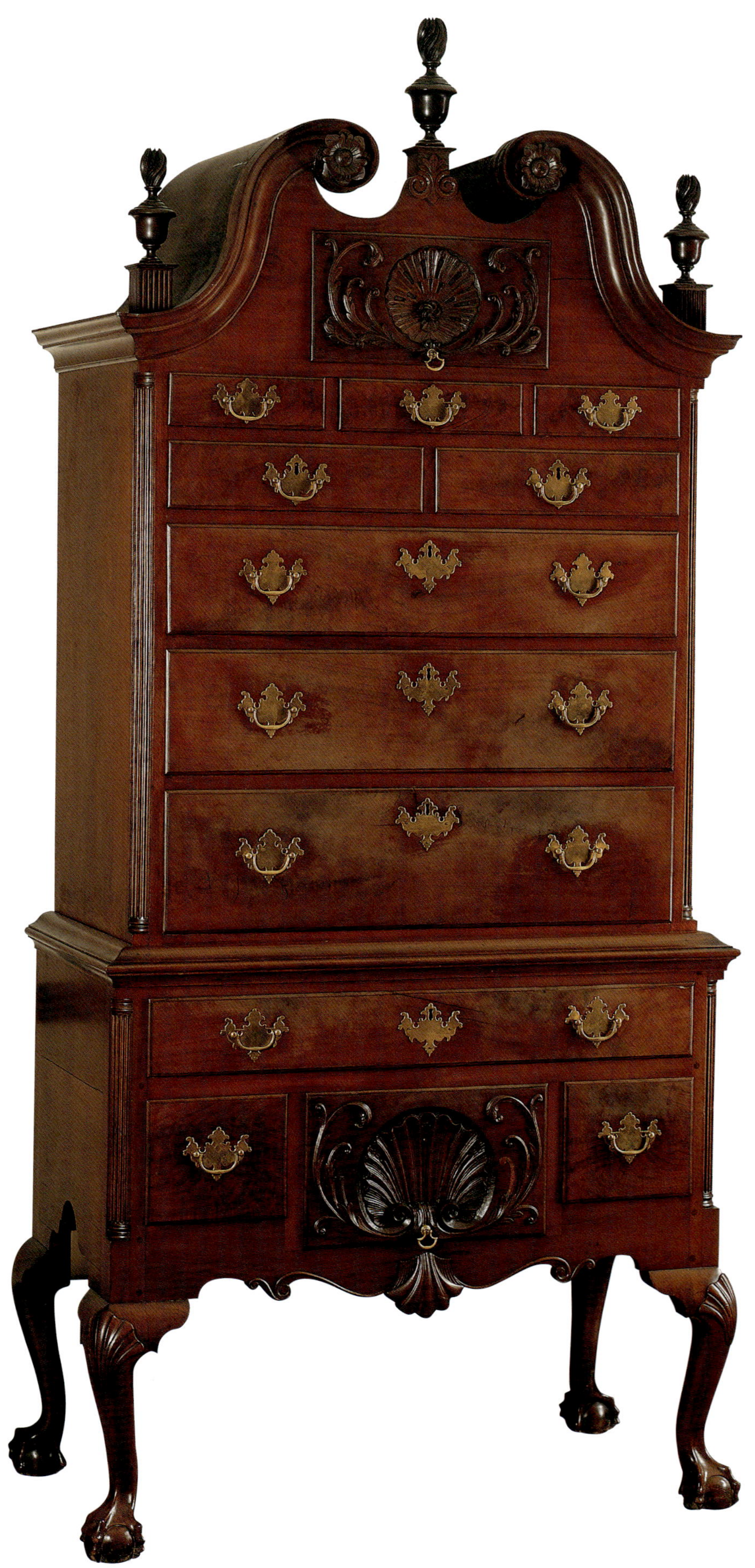

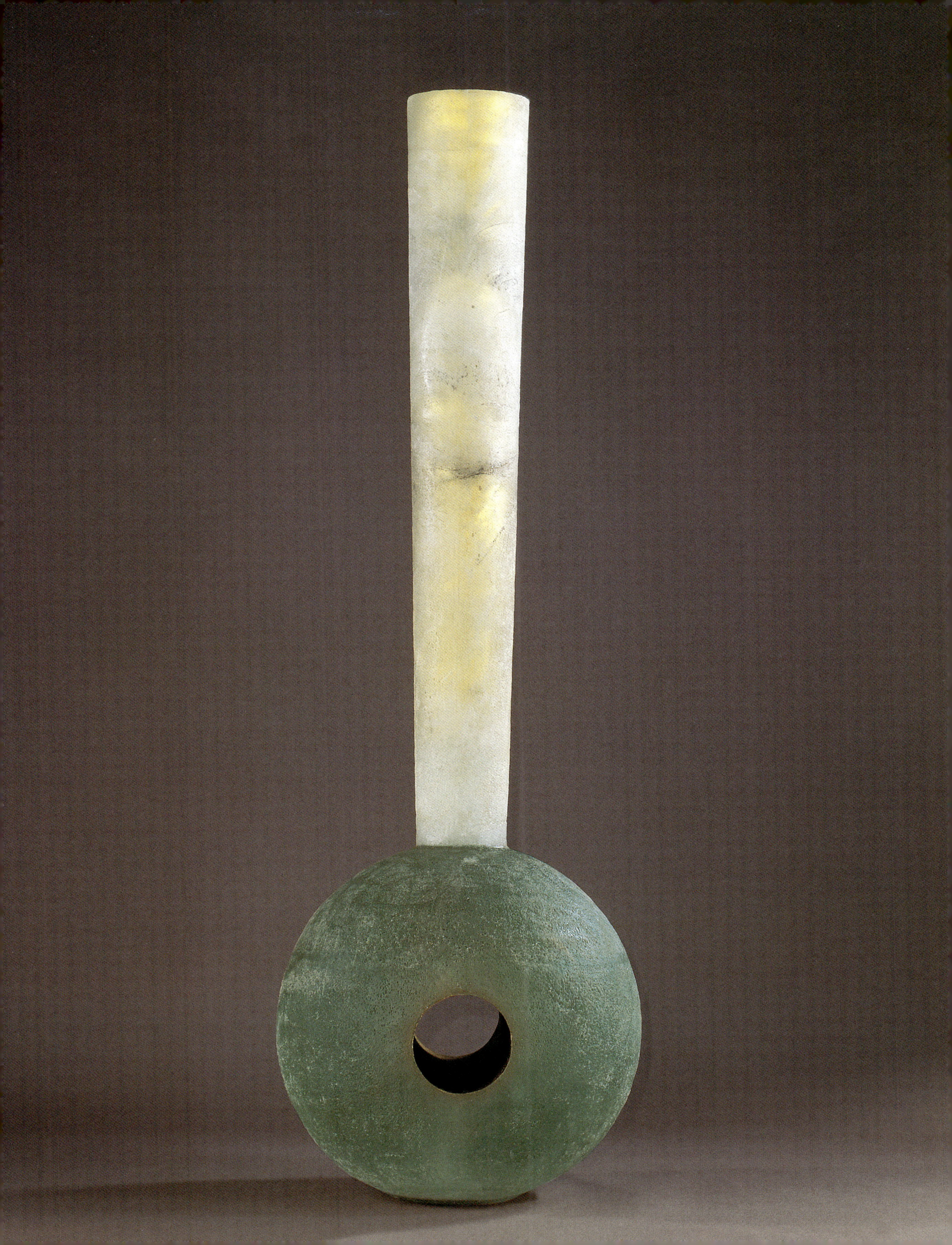

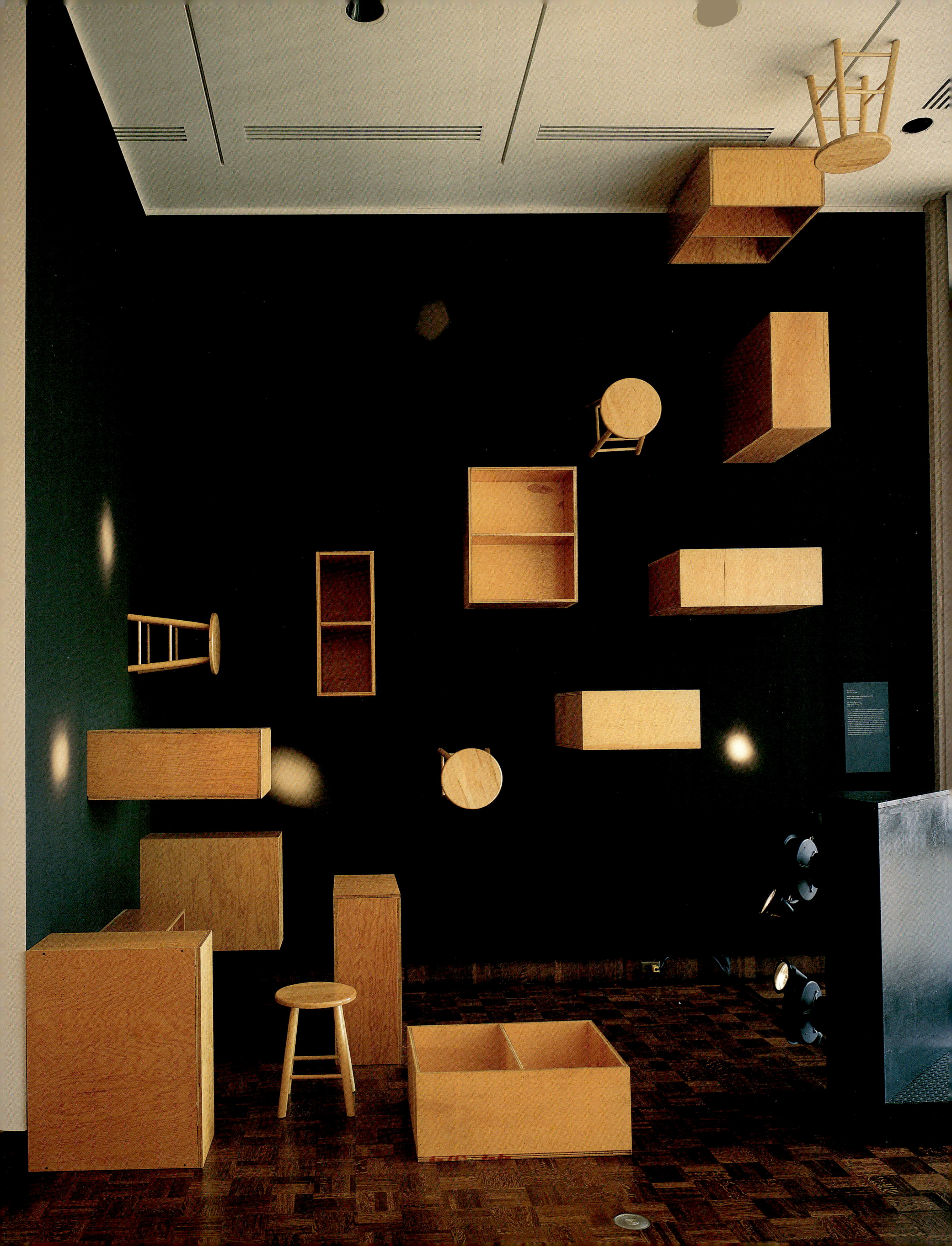

Contemporary Art, post-1945

This collection of art made since 1945 came into existence as a collection separate from American and European collections of painting and sculpture in 1985. Although the IMA had acquired works by living artists in the late nineteenth and early twentieth centuries, the practice languished until 1962, when the Contemporary Art Society was formed to assist the museum in actively acquiring works made after 1945. Approximately one-fourth of the collection was acquired through purchases of the Contemporary Art Society. These include *Poème d'amour,* by Hans Hofmann, purchased in 1963, and *Acton*, by James Turrell, acquired for the occasion of the reinstallation of the collection in renovated space in Krannert Pavilion in 1990.

About 535 works of post-1945 art have been acquired, either as gifts or purchases. In addition, the IMA has acquired a substantial number of works from the contemporary period that are part of the prints and drawings, decorative arts, and textile collections.

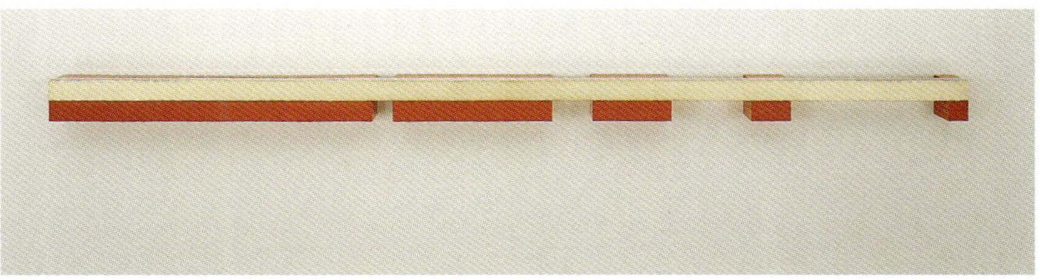

ABOVE:
Donald Judd
untitled, 1967
brass and light cadmium red enamel on cold-rolled steel
6 1/8 x 138 x 6 in.
Morris Goodman Sculpture Fund and Alliance Fine Arts Fund, 1992.362

OPPOSITE:
Vito Acconci
American, b. 1940
Round Trip (A Space to Fall Back On), 1975
stools, plywood boxes, audio tape equipment, spotlights, black paint
15 x 12 x 8 ft., installed
Gift of the Alliance of the Indianapolis Museum of Art
1989.35

The largest group of works given to the IMA is the Joseph Cantor Collection, consisting primarily of pre-1960 European works and including artists such as Balthus and Antoni Tapies. However, notable American works in this collection are two 1948 paintings by Josef Albers and an Alexander Calder mobile from 1958.

Another strength of the IMA collection is a group of paintings and sculptures by artists from Indiana. These works include sculptures by David Smith, George Rickey, John Chamberlain, Robert Indiana, and Bruce Nauman and a painting by William Wiley, as well as a substantial number of works by artists currently living in Indiana.

In the late 1980s and early 1990s the museum acquired a number of installations by artists including Robert Irwin, Vito Acconci, Donald Lipski, and the aforementioned James Turrell. Perhaps the most spectacular of these installations is the Sol LeWitt wall drawing installed in 1990 in the staircase connecting the Long Gallery to the museum's main lobby, Herron Hall.

In addition to the indoor collection, the IMA's contemporary works include a number of outdoor sculptures, which are displayed on the museum's grounds. These works include Robert Indiana's multicolored numerals 0-9 and the famous *LOVE* sculpture, as well as sculptures by Barbara Hepworth, Mark DiSuvero, and Dennis Oppenheimer.

Recently, the department has added a number of major works that strengthen the collection in its earlier decades; they include Donald Judd's 1967 progression of forms in cadmium red and brass, Hans Hofmann's *Radiant Space* (1958) and Ellsworth Kelly's eleven painted panels of 1981. Other recent additions capture the artistic spirit of Europe and America of the 1990s; among them are a 1996 book by Anselm Kiefer, Martin Puryear's untitled 1993 sculpture, and a 1992 multi-part Cibachrome by Lorna Simpson.

RIGHT:
Mimmo Paladino
Italian, b. 1948
La Tempesta, 1983
oil on canvas
84 x 108 in.
Henry F. and Katherine DeBoest Memorial Fund
1986.1

LOWER RIGHT:
Jean Dubuffet
French, 1901-1985
*Courre Merlan (*Whiting Chase), 1964
oil on canvas
38 1/4 x 51 in.
Gift of Gerald and Dorit Paul
1992.394

OPPOSITE:
Hans Hofmann
American (b. Germany)
1880-1960
Radiant Space, 1955
oil on canvas, 60 x 48 in.
Kathryn A. Simmons Contemporary Art Fund, Alliance Income Fund, Mr. and Mrs. Richard Crane Fund, James E. Roberts Fund, Dan and Lori Efroymson Fund, Martha Delzell Memorial Fund, William Dyer Bequest Fund, Mary Pearl Art Fund, Alliance Fine Arts Fund, Roger G. Wolcott Fund, Now and Future Purchase Fund. Joseph Cantor Collection and The Robert and Traude Hensel Collection by exchange, 1996.247

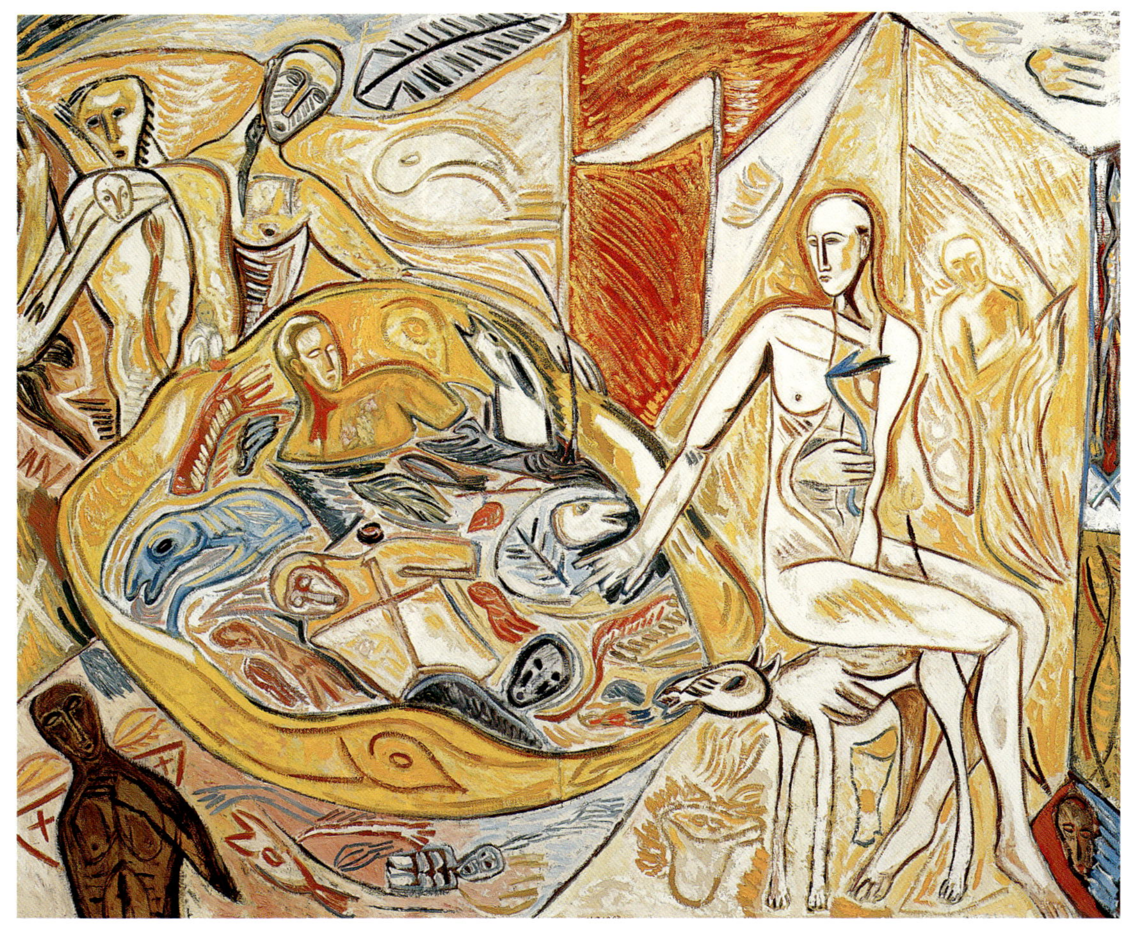

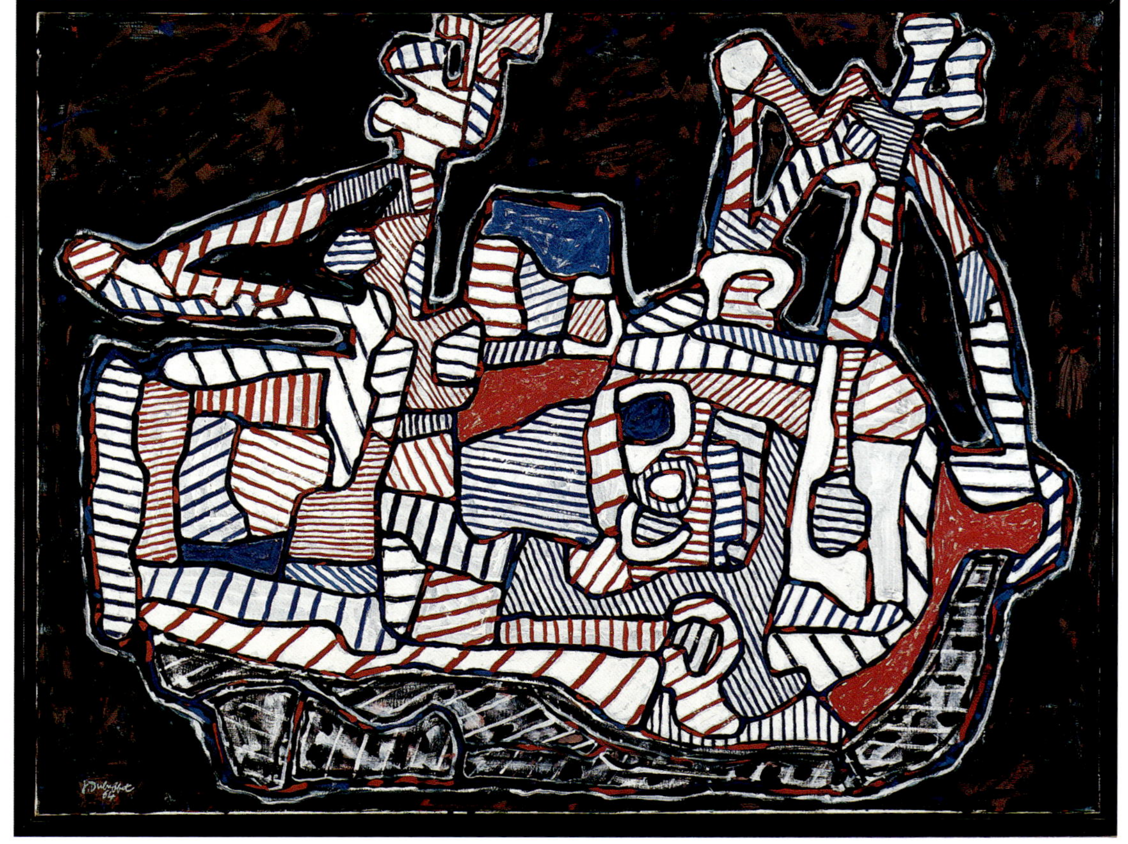

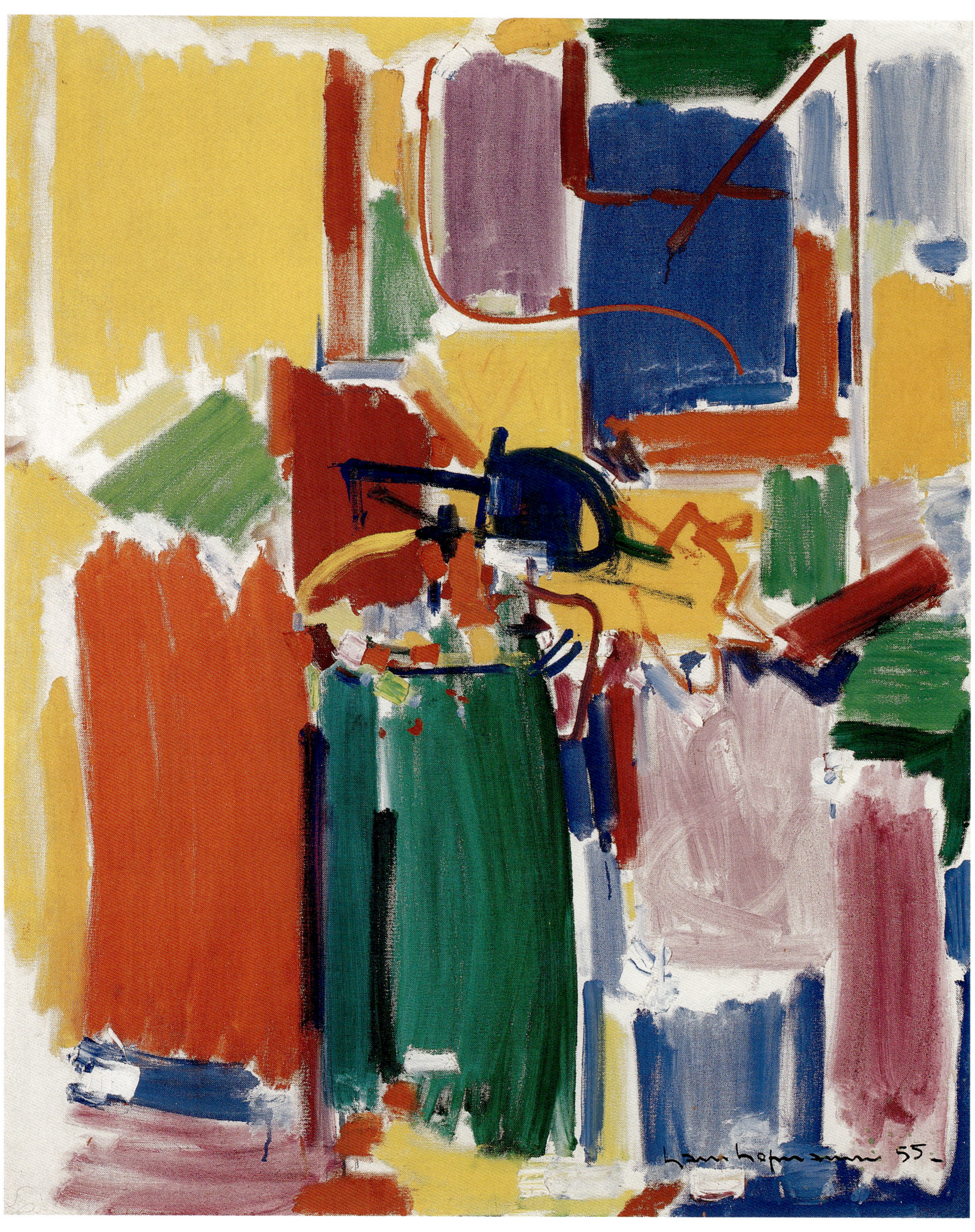

RIGHT:
Bruce Nauman
American, Fort Wayne,
Indiana, b. 1941
untitled (Hand Circle), 1996
phosphorus patinated
bronze with wire
Edition 3/9, 4 x 24 x 28 in.
Henry F. and Katherine
DeBoest Memorial Fund and
Mr. and Mrs. Richard Crane
Fund, 1996.248

BELOW:
David Smith
American, b. Decatur,
Indiana, 1906-1965
Egyptian Barnyard, 1954
wrought and soldered silver
14 1/2 x 24 in.
Gift of Mr. and Mrs.
J. W. Alsdorf, 60.279

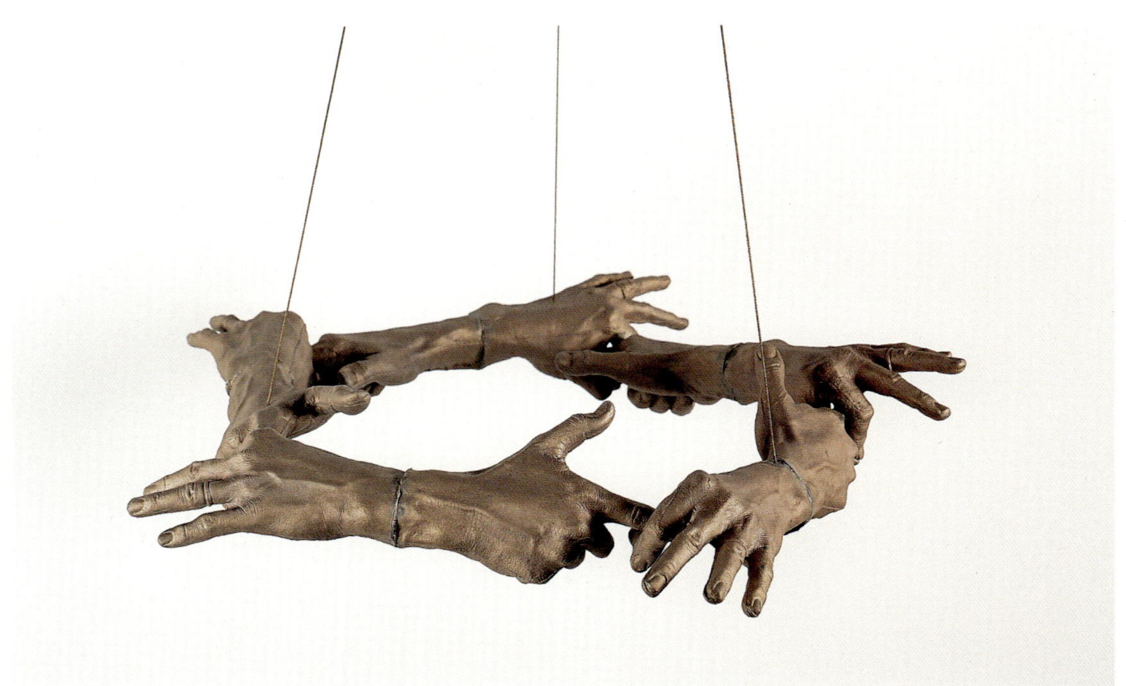

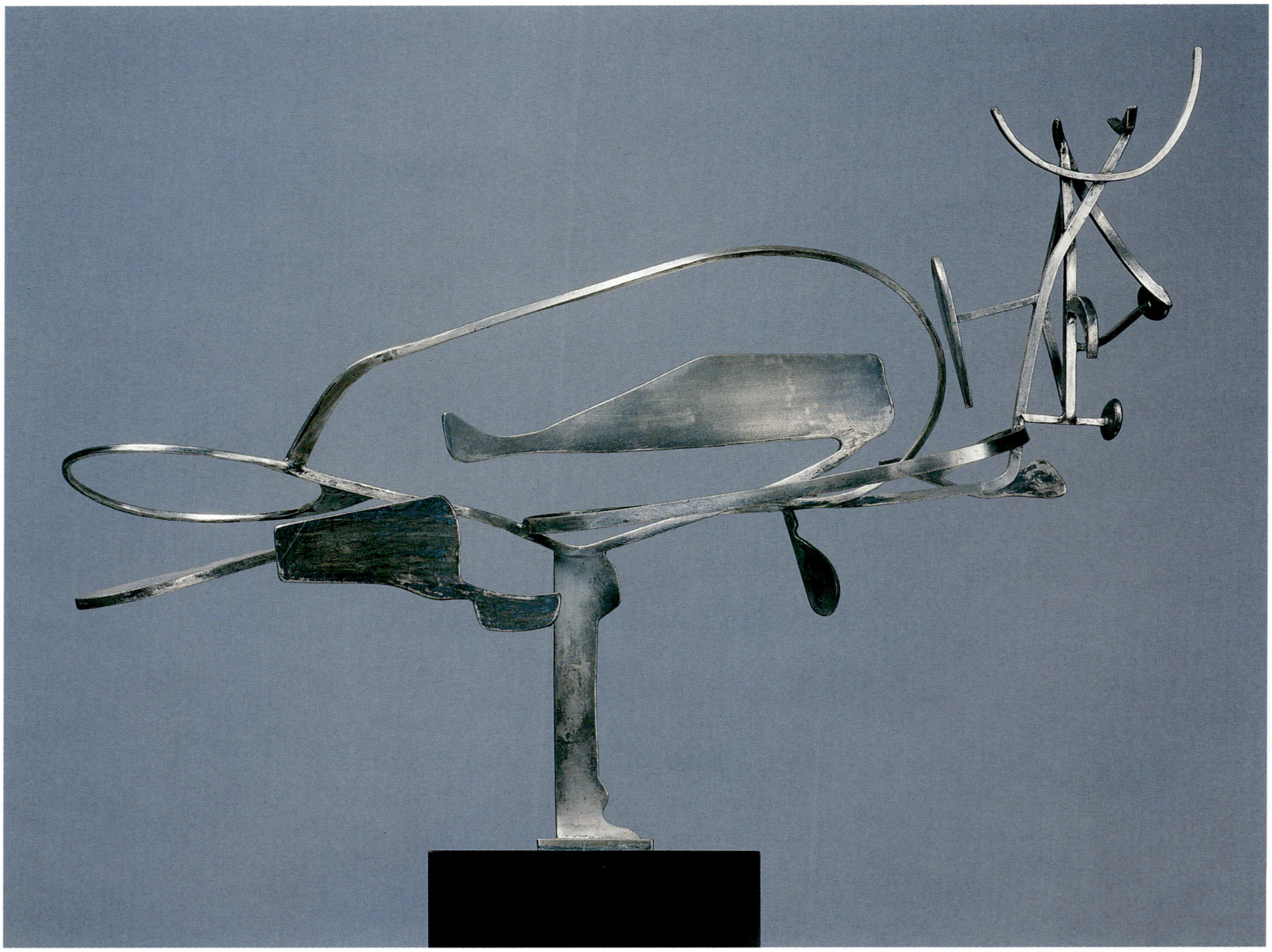

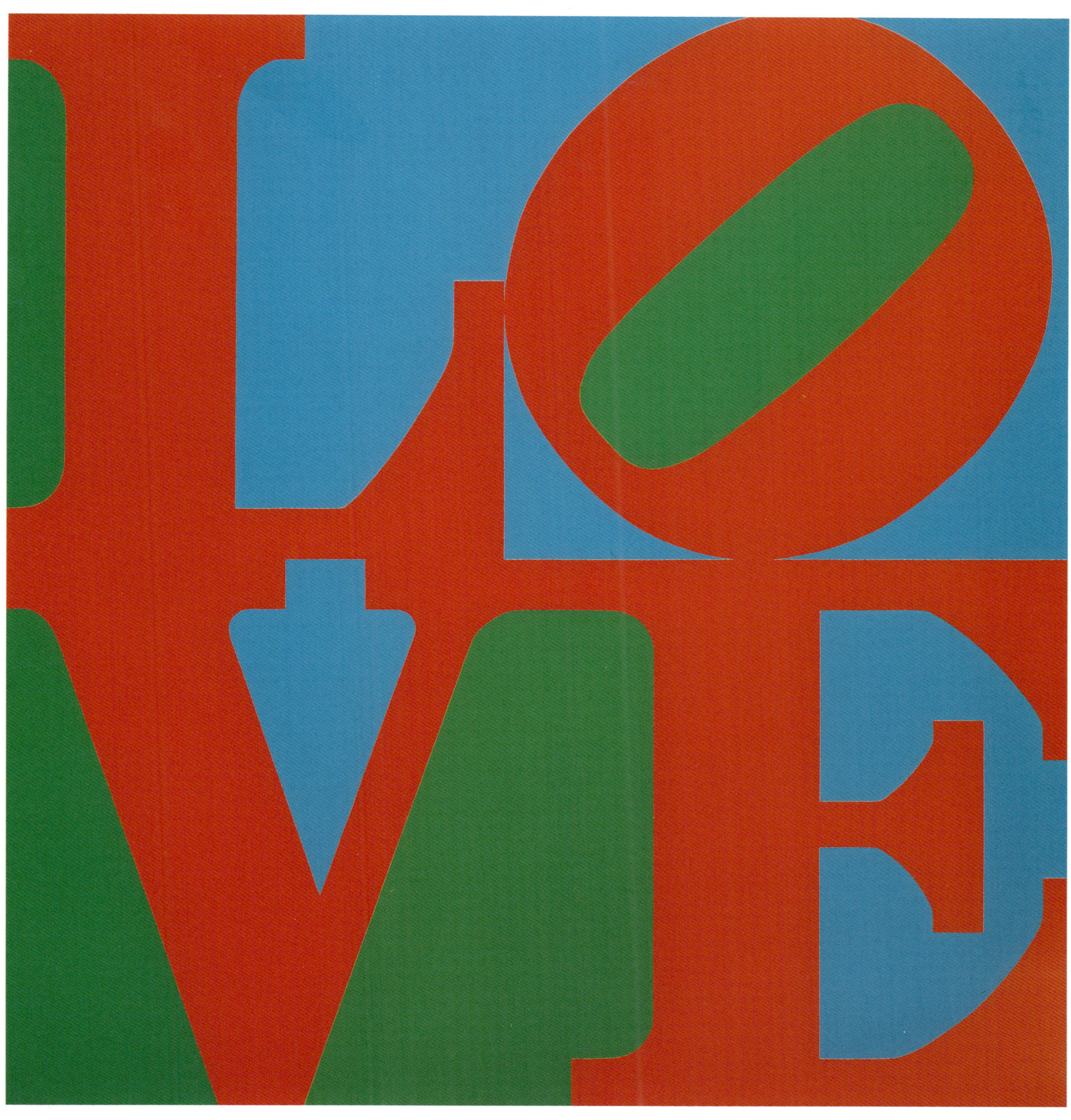

Robert Indiana
American, New Castle, Indiana, b. 1928
LOVE, 1966
acrylic on canvas
71 7/8 x 71 7/8 in.
James E. Roberts Fund
67.08

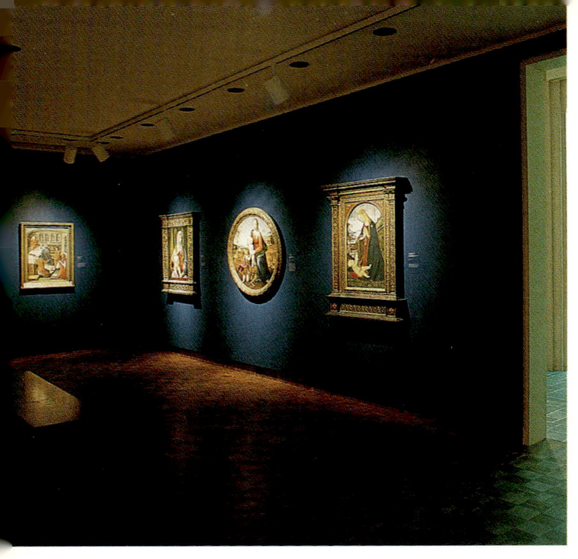
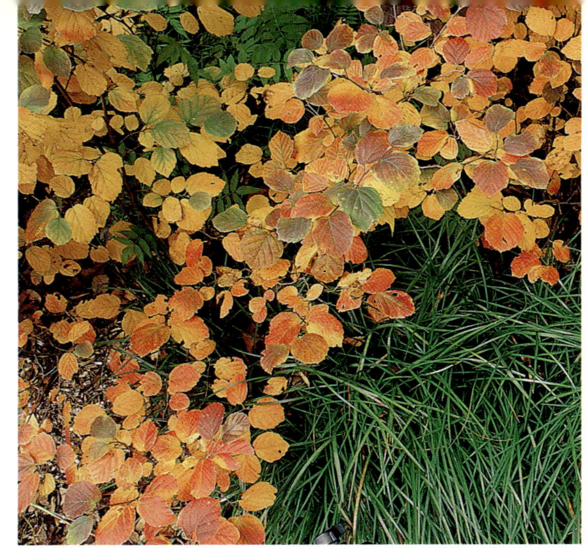
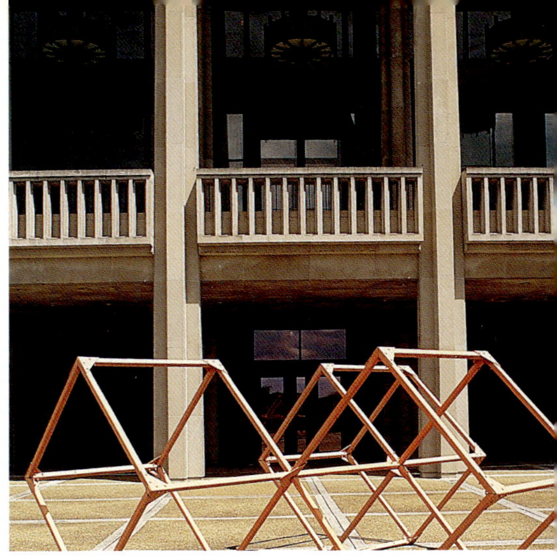
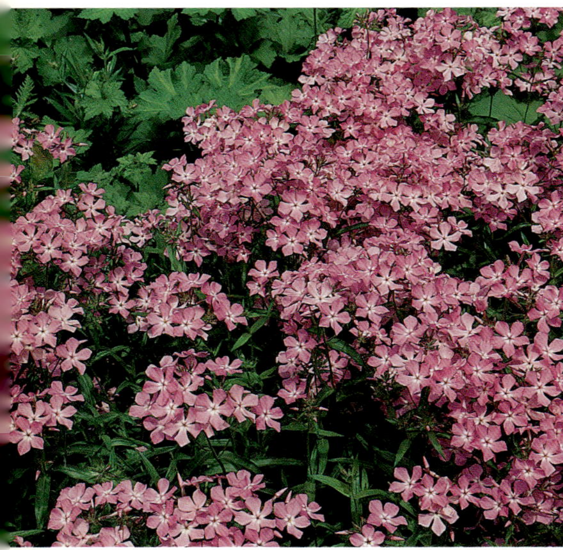
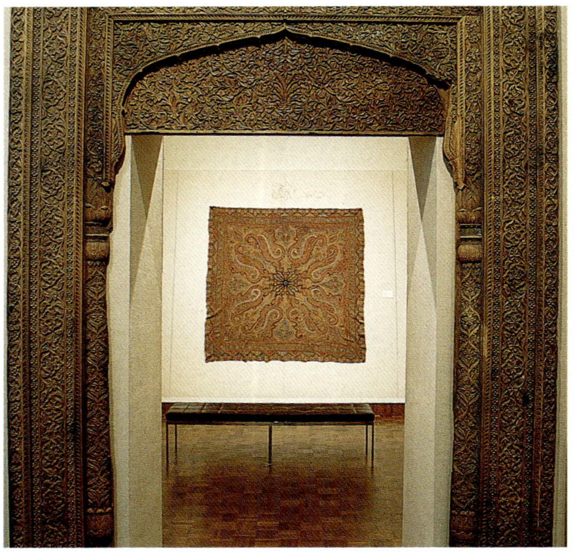
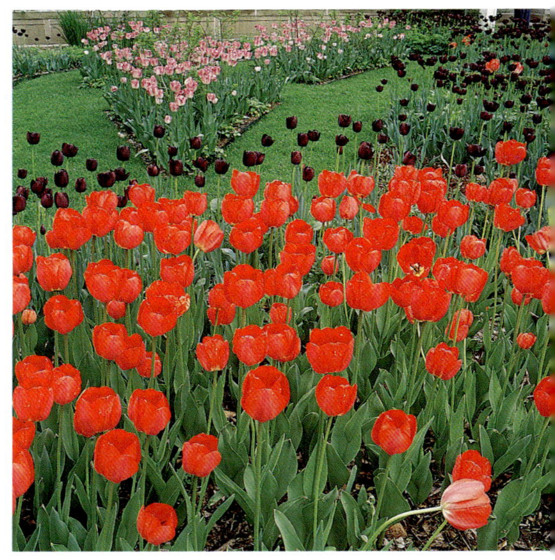
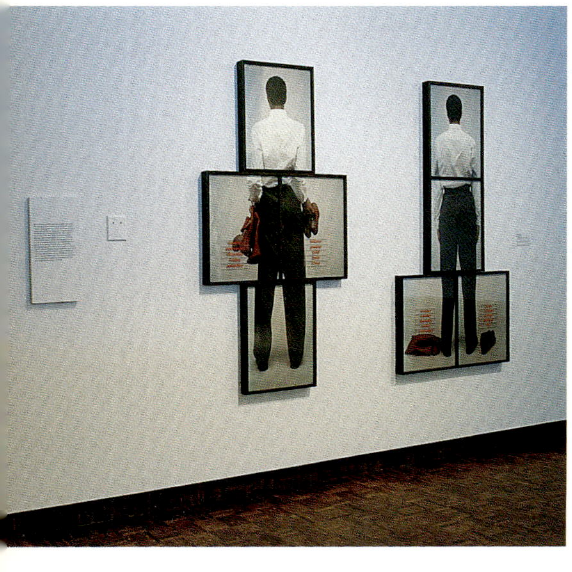
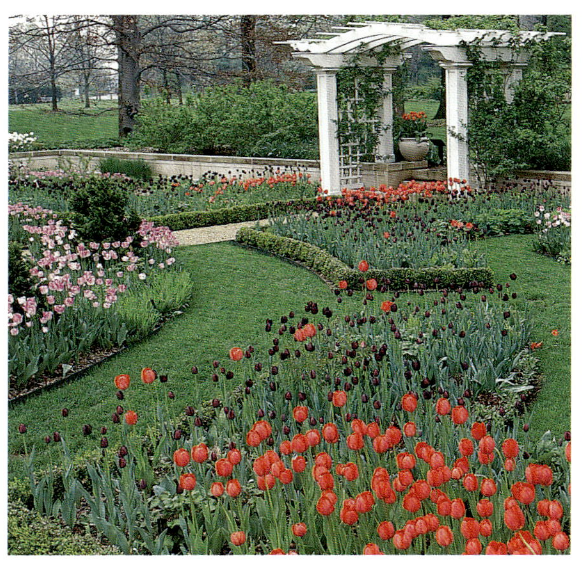
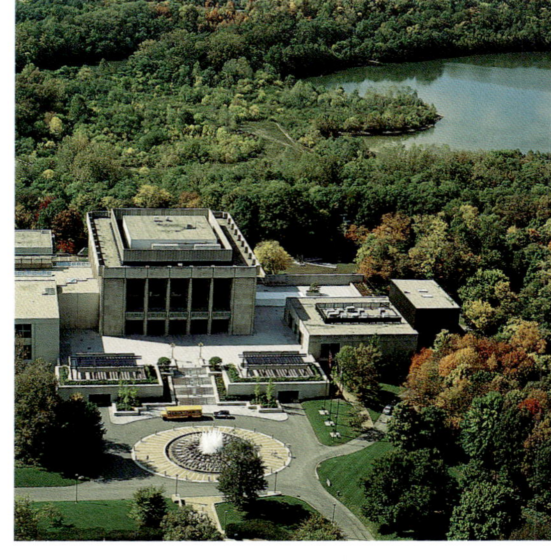
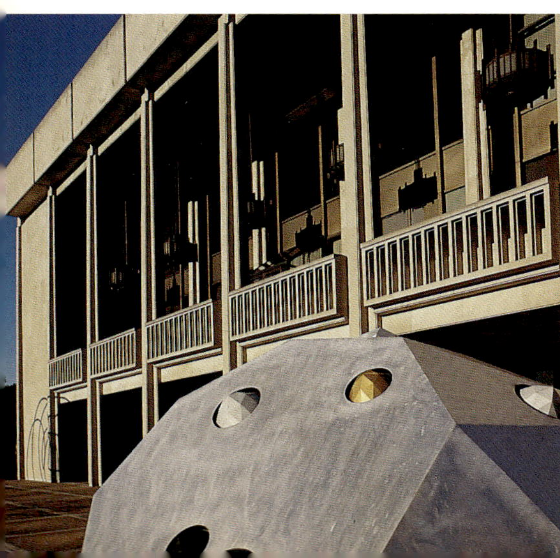
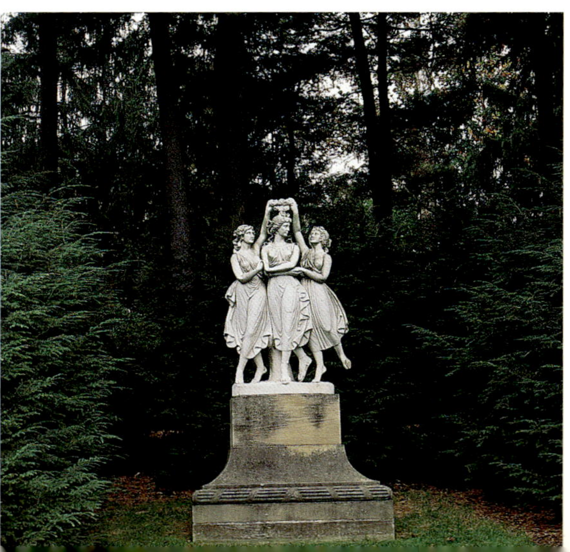
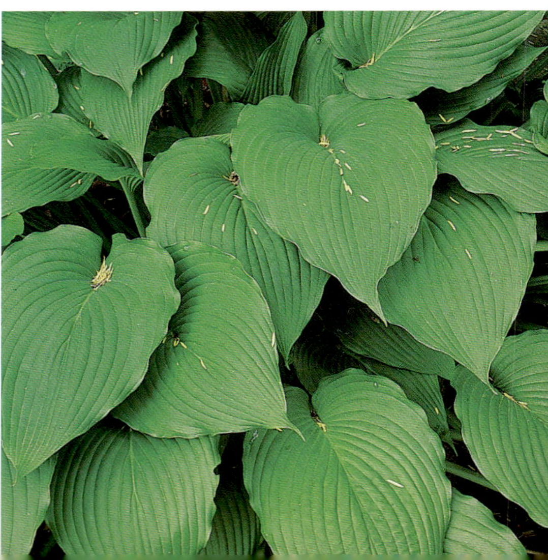

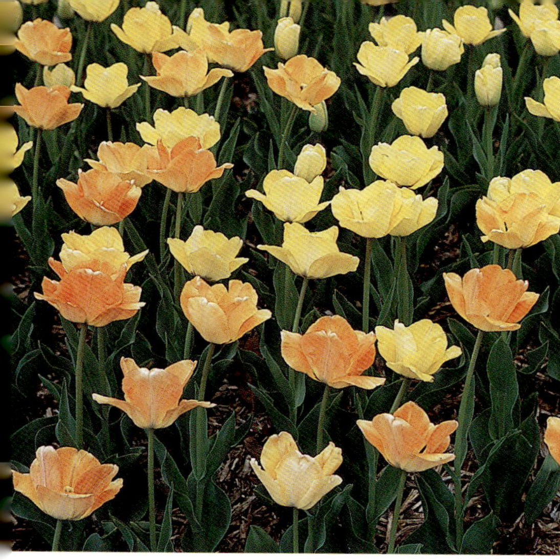
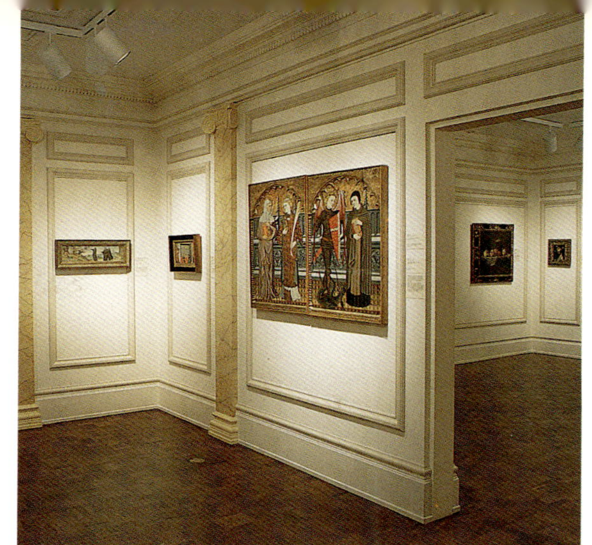
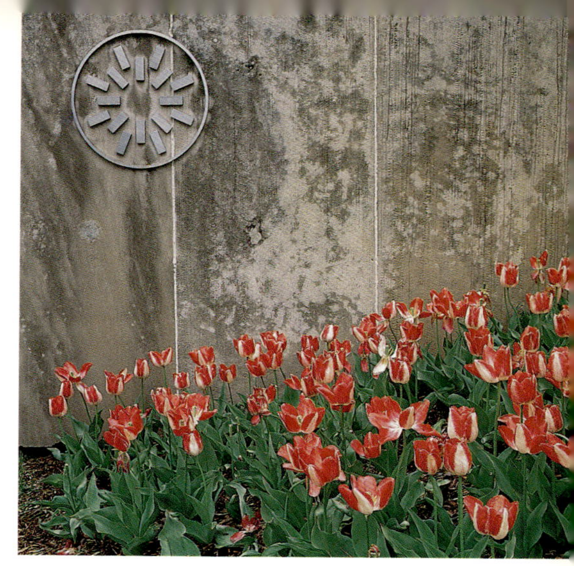
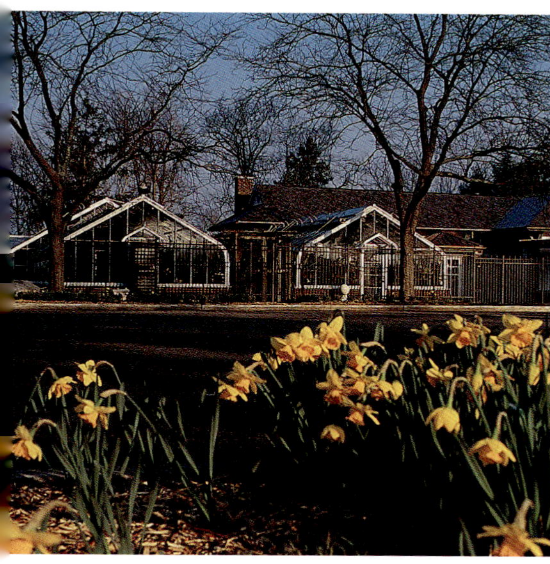
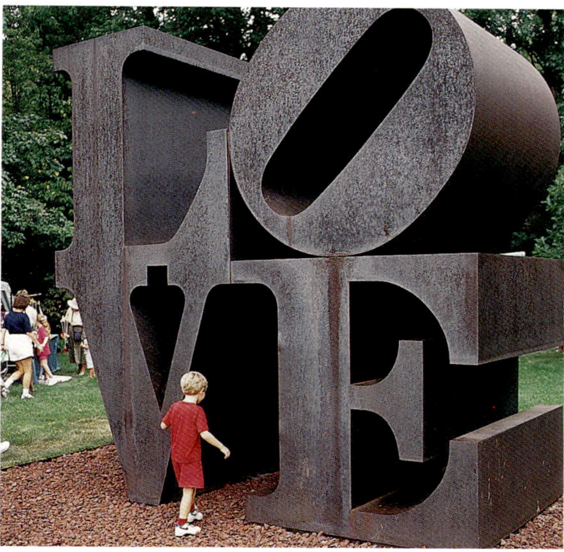
LOVE
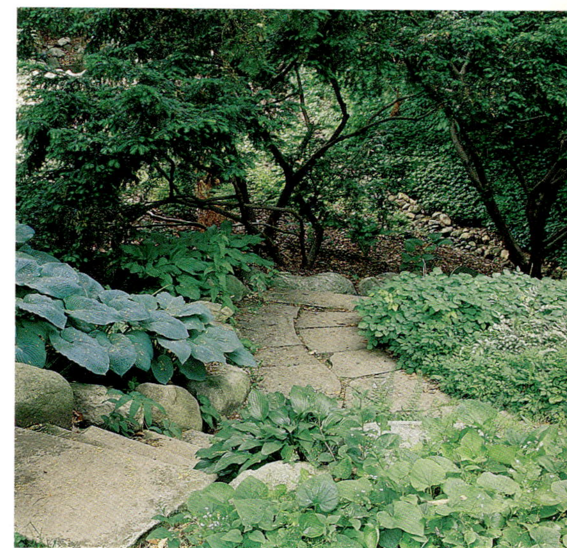
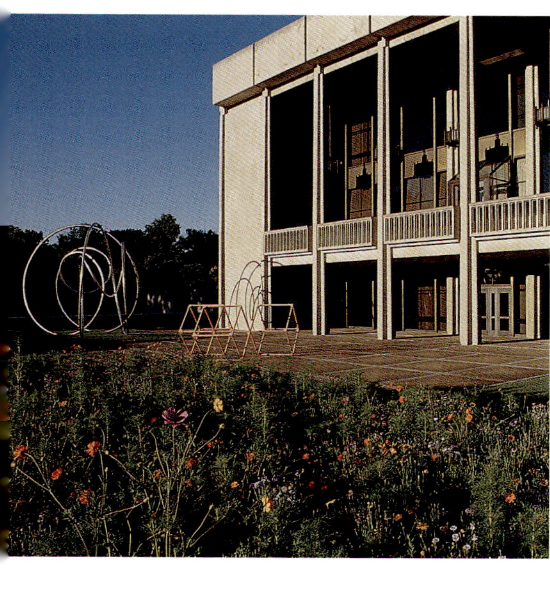
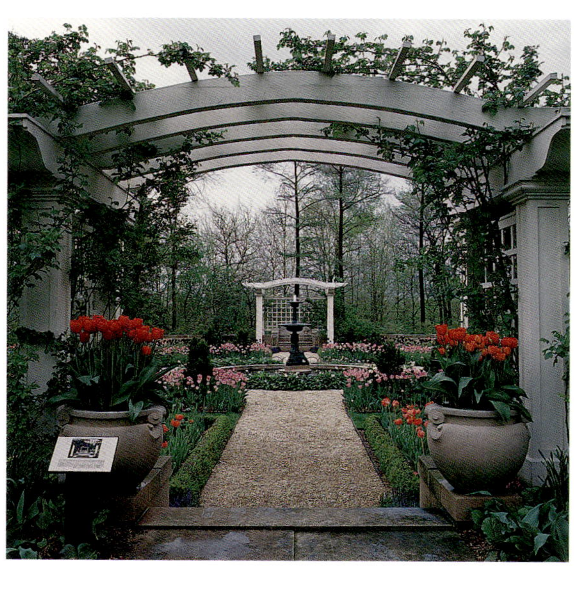
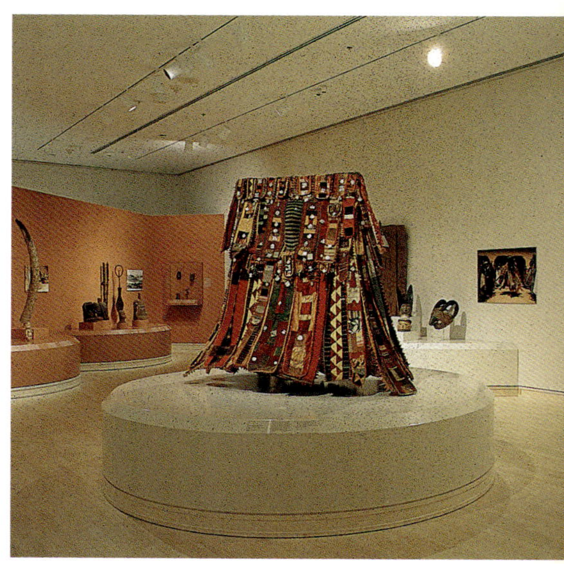
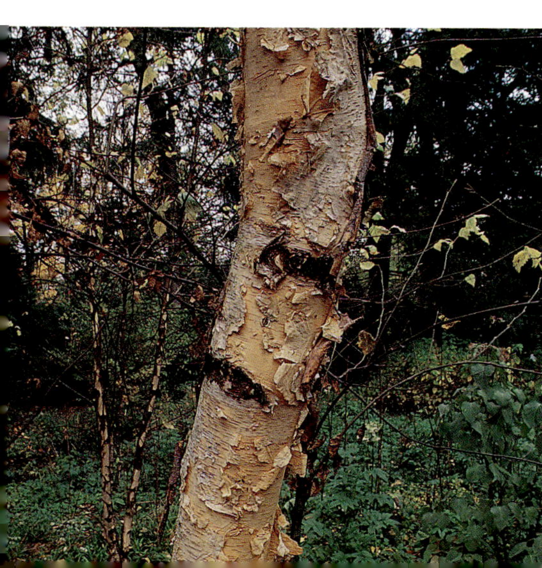
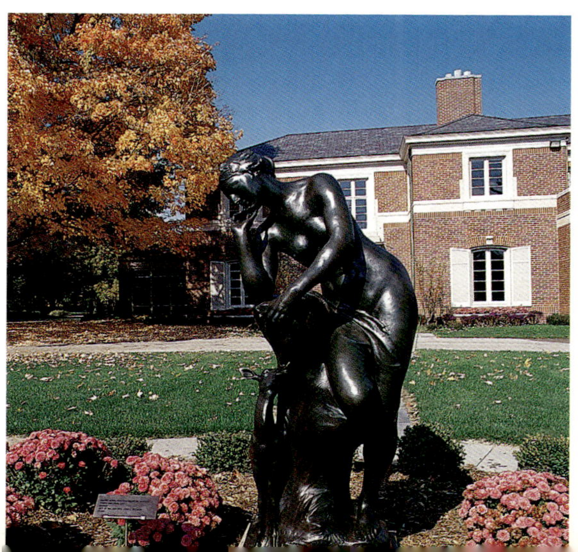
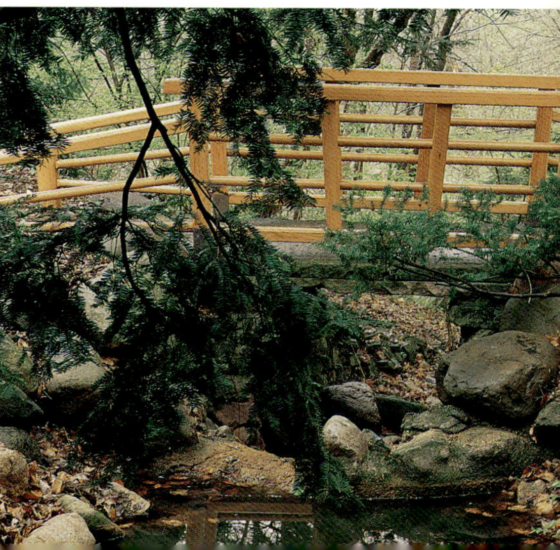

The Oldfields Story

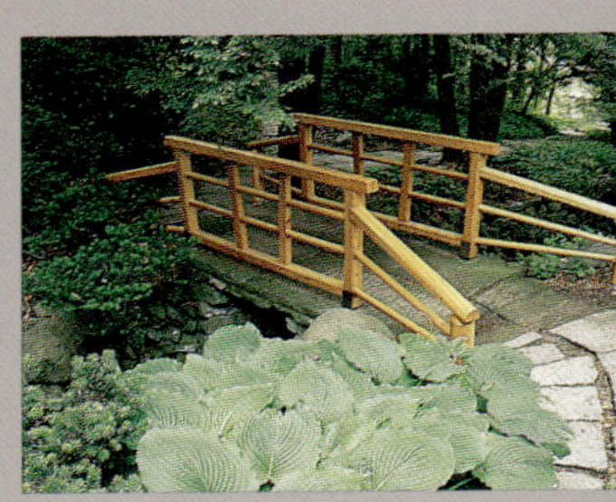

Among the IMA's treasures are its gardens, sweeping lawns, and tree-shaded paths, its panoramic views of woods and river, and its buildings, both historic and contemporary. The fifty-two acres that now contain the IMA's buildings and landscaped grounds were originally laid out as the town of Woodstock early in the twentieth century. Hugh McK. Landon, an executive with the Indianapolis Water Company, and his family were among the first residents of the town, and their home, Oldfields, is now the museum's Lilly Pavilion of Decorative Arts. The house was designed by Mrs. Landon's brother, Lewis Ketcham Davis, and built in 1912. In 1920, Percival Gallagher, of the famous Olmsted Brothers firm, was commissioned to develop the landscape design for the 26-acre estate.

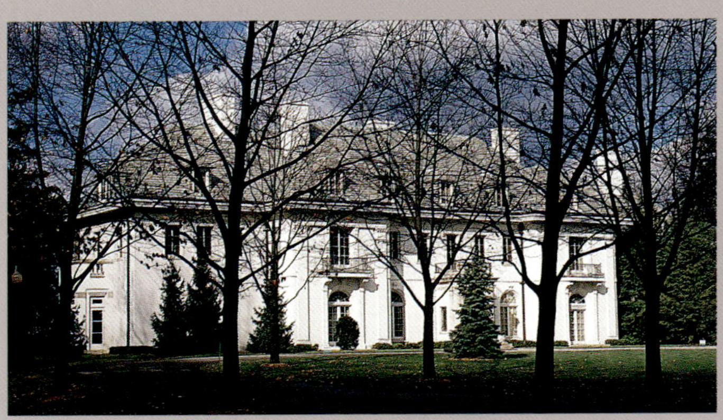

In 1932, Oldfields was purchased by Josiah K. Lilly, Jr., who with his brother, Eli, guided the family pharmaceutical company for many years. Over the years Mr. Lilly bought other Woodstock property, and when it was donated to the Indianapolis Art Association in 1966 by Mr. Lilly's children, the Lilly estate covered more than 40 acres. In 1972, the wooded flood plain west of the museum was donated by the Indianapolis general contracting company Huber, Hunt and Nichols, adding approximately 100 acres to the museum's property.

Today, Oldfields—the 22-room mansion and its Grand Allée and gardens—is a rare Midwestern example of the gracious estates of the Country Place era. Restoration of the house and gardens and renovation of the surrounding grounds are continuing projects for the museum.

The Formal Garden at Oldfields, distinguished by its rose-entwined trellises and arbors, was restored in 1993. The restoration was made possible by a gift from the friends and colleagues of Richard D. Wood to honor him upon his retirement from Eli Lilly and Company. He has served as a trustee and as president and chairman of the Indianapolis Museum of Art.

OPPOSITE:
The Ravine Garden at Oldfields in the 1920s

Another major landscape project for the IMA is the Ravine Garden, which descends nearly 50 feet from the terrace of Oldfields to the canal below, covering more than an acre. When it is restored, it will provide ever-changing displays with its flowering shrubs and trees, evergreens, perenniels, bulbs, ferns and wildflowers. Three pools and a recirculating stream, the limestone paths, and the Arts and Crafts bridge are also part of the restoration.

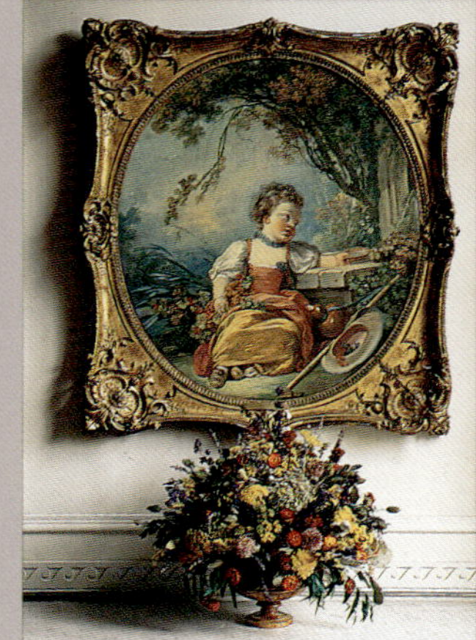

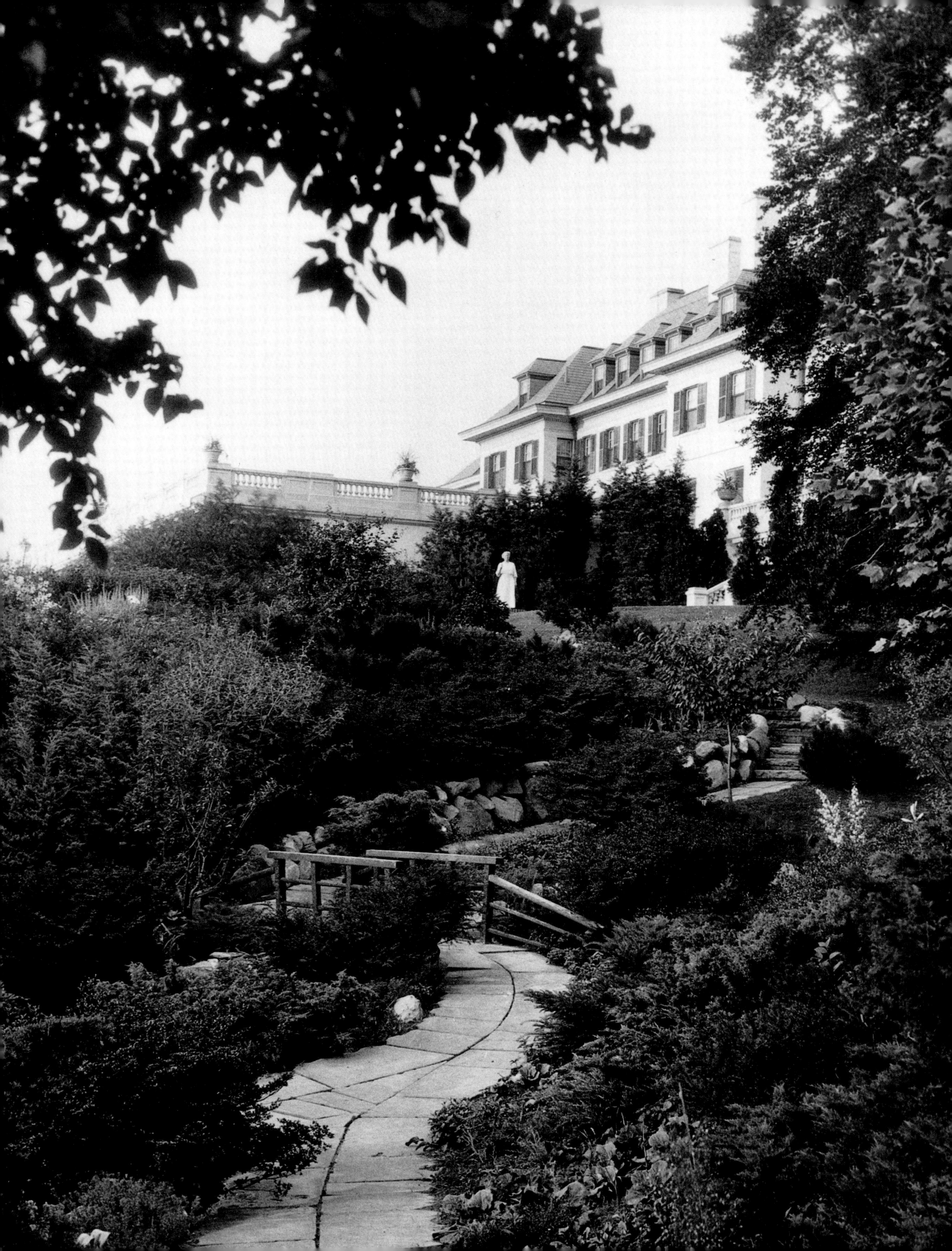

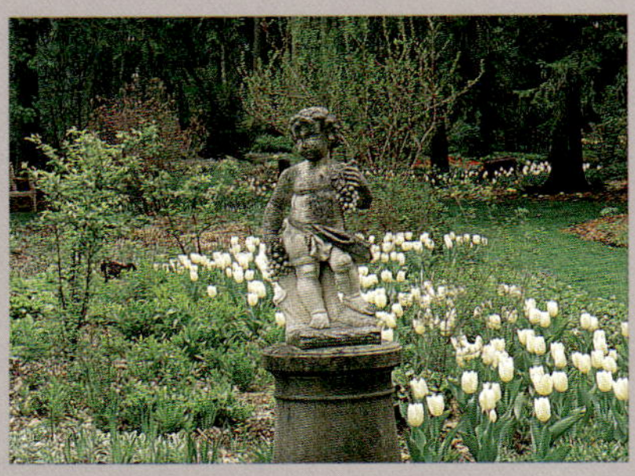

The mansion itself displays works from the IMA's extensive collections of furniture, porcelains, and silver. Galleries contain exhibitions of rare porcelains, silver, and period antiques and textiles.

The Madeline F. Elder Greenhouse, just north of the Lilly Pavilion, originally provided fresh vegetables and garden plants for the Landon and Lilly families. For many years, it has offered plants for sale to museum visitors, and has been used for plant production by the horticultural staff. The greenhouse reopened in April 1995 with a new wing after almost a year of construction and renovation and was renamed to honor Mrs. Elder, its long-time patron. The enlarged facility provided a new sales area as well as enlarged office, work, and storage space. Plants, gardening tools and books, and related merchandise are available for sale year-round, and the greenhouse also displays its permanent plant collections, including orchids and succulents. The greenhouse renovation was made possible by the family and friends of Mrs. Elder.

Located under the rear terrace of the Lilly Pavilion, the Horticulture Study Center houses an extensive horticultural library. The library is maintained by the IMA Horticultural Society, which also sponsors lectures and other horticultural activities.

The Modern Pavilions

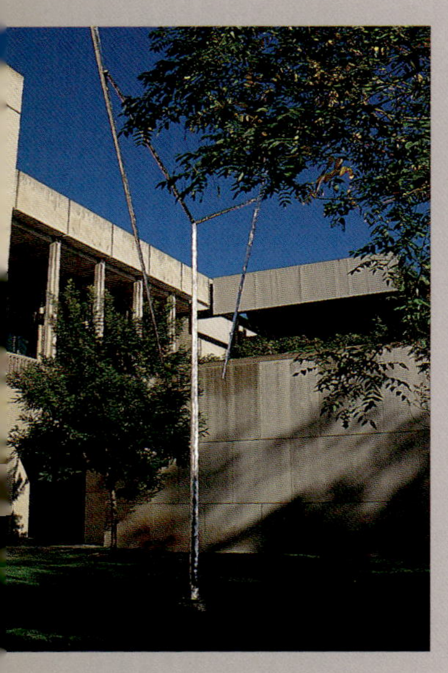

The main museum complex, which sits on a bluff overlooking the White River, is made up of four adjoining pavilions and encompasses three floors of galleries, DeBoest Lecture Hall and the Lila Wallace-Readers' Digest Fund Education Center, a theater, shops, offices, art storage and conservation areas, and a parking garage.

Krannert Pavilion

Named in honor of Ellnora Decker Krannert and Herman C. Krannert, its primary benefactors, Krannert Pavilion includes the museum's galleries of American, Asian, Precolumbian, early twentieth-century and contemporary art, textiles and costumes, and twentieth-century design. The Alliance Museum Shop and the Alliance Rental Gallery, which rents and sells original works of art, the Stout Reference Library, and the Jane S. Dutton Educational Resource Center are also located in this pavilion.

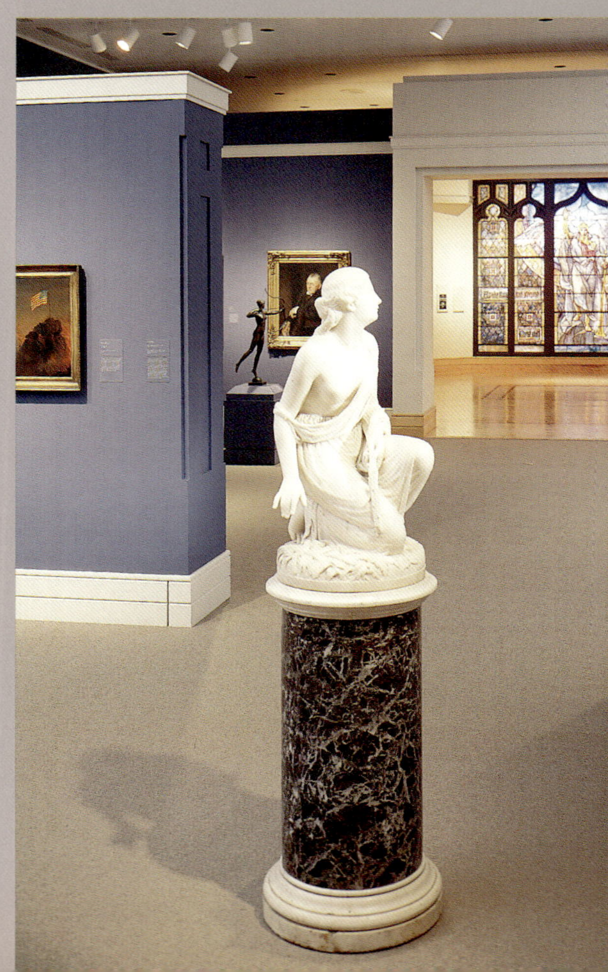

Clowes Pavilion

With its courtyard surrounded by cloisters and its series of intimate rooms—library, music room, and chapel—the Clowes Pavilion is more in keeping with the Old Masters paintings of the Clowes Fund

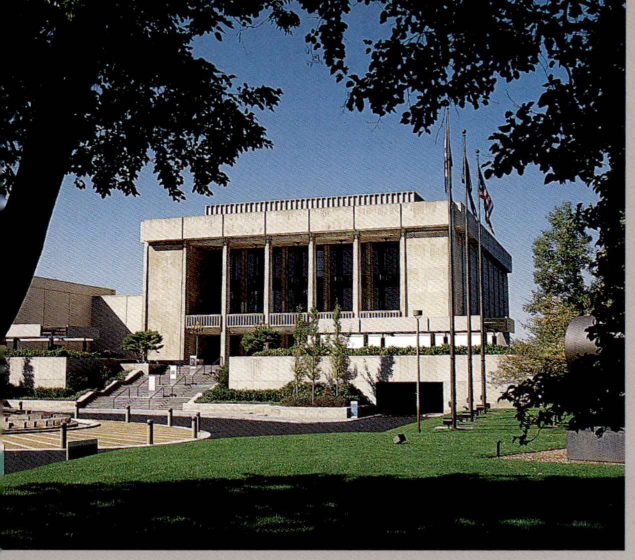

Collection that are exhibited there. It is dedicated to the memory of Edith Whitehill Clowes, who with her husband, Dr. George H. A. Clowes, formed this important collection. Connected to the Krannert Pavilion by a gallery that houses the museum's collection of classical works, the Clowes Pavilion also has a gallery for the display of prints and the suite of rooms in which the museum's superb collection of works by J. M. W. Turner are exhibited.

Hulman Pavilion

The Mary Fendrich Hulman Pavilion, completed in 1990, houses the museum's European painting and sculpture collections and the Eiteljorg Collection of African and South Pacific Art, the Lila Wallace-Readers' Digest Fund Education Center, the 12,000-square-foot Allen Whitehill Clowes Special Exhibition Gallery, a theater for visitor orientation, a prints and drawings study, and the Harold R. Victor Office Plaza (the museum's administrative offices and conference rooms). Curators' offices and the museum's Art Conservation Department are located on the service level of Hulman Pavilion.

Showalter Pavilion

The Grace M. Showalter Pavilion is the home of the Indianapolis Civic Theatre—one of the oldest civic theaters in the country—and includes an 800-seat auditorium and stage, dressing rooms, lobby, and reception area.

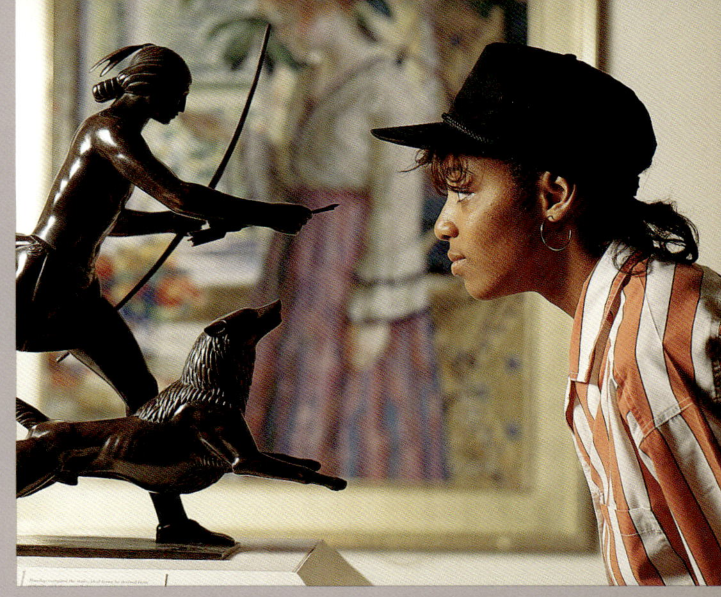

Also on the museum grounds are two buildings that have been integral to the functioning of the museum since it opened in 1970 in its new quarters. Formerly the home of J. K. Lilly III and, later, Ruth Lilly, children of of J. K. Lilly, Jr., the recently renovated Better Than New Shop is operated by the Alliance of the Indianapolis Museum of Art. The Better Than New Shop has raised more than $1.5 million over the last twenty-five years for the benefit of the museum from the sale of used clothing, furniture, and other household items at the shop. The Garden on the Green Restaurant, once the Lilly family's recreation house, has served lunch and brunch to museum visitors for more than twenty-five years.

OPPOSITE:
Randolph Rogers
American, 1825-1892
Ruth Gleaning, 1860
marble on plum marble pedestal
Gift in honor of Mr. and Mrs. William L. Fortune by their children and Gift of the Alliance of the Indianapolis Museum of Art, 1988.219

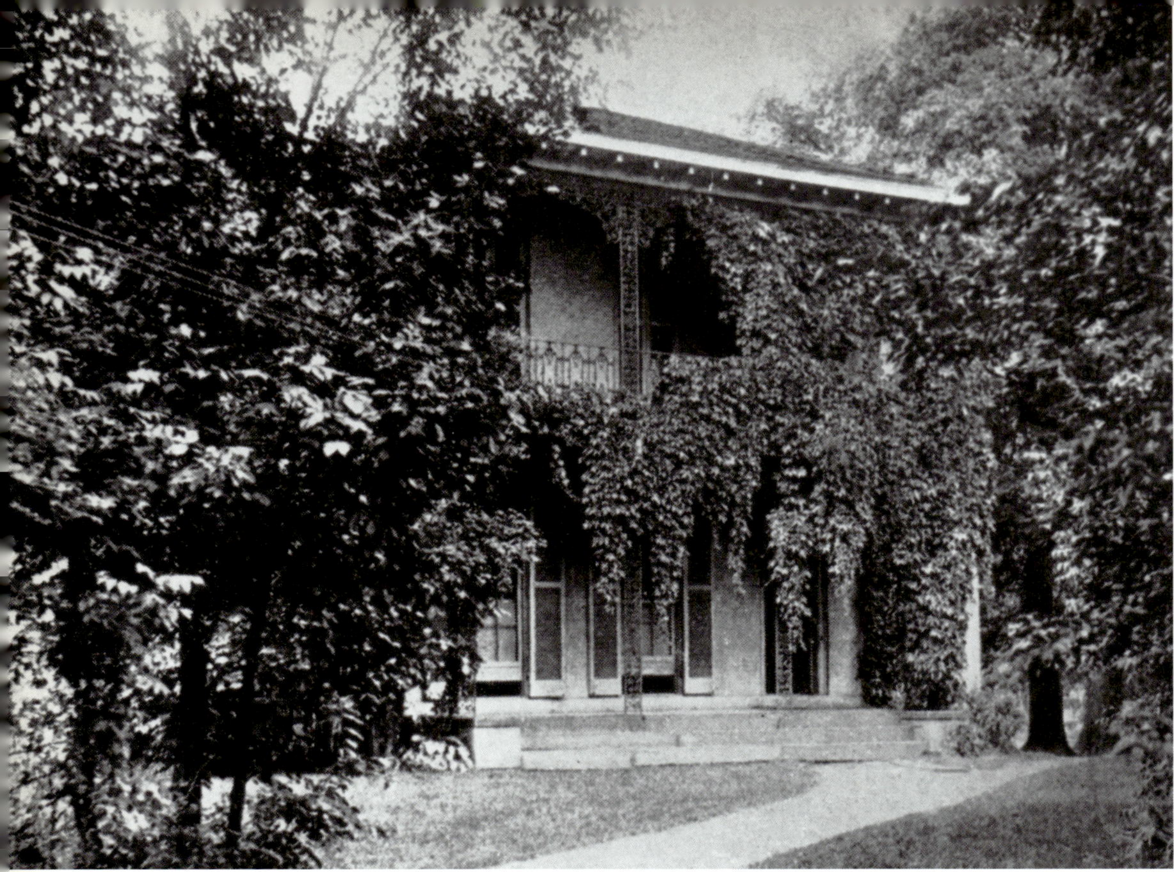

The Talbott House at Tinker Place, first home of the John Herron Art Institute, 1901-1905

A Brief History of the Indianapolis Museum of Art

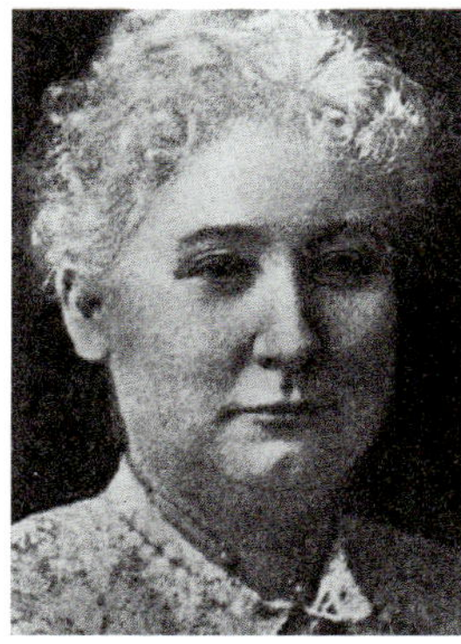

May Wright Sewall

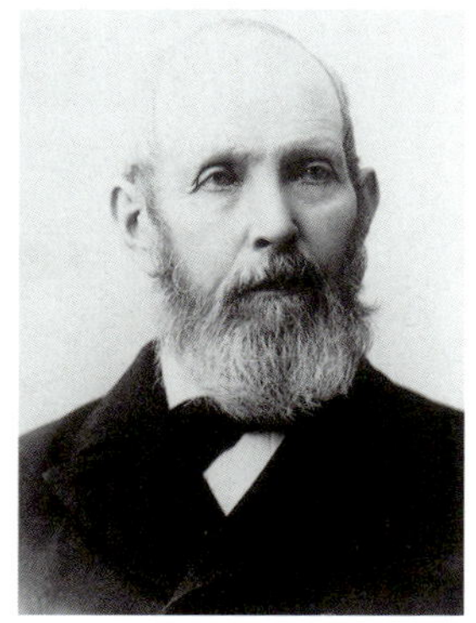

John Herron
Herron School of Art Library, IUPUI

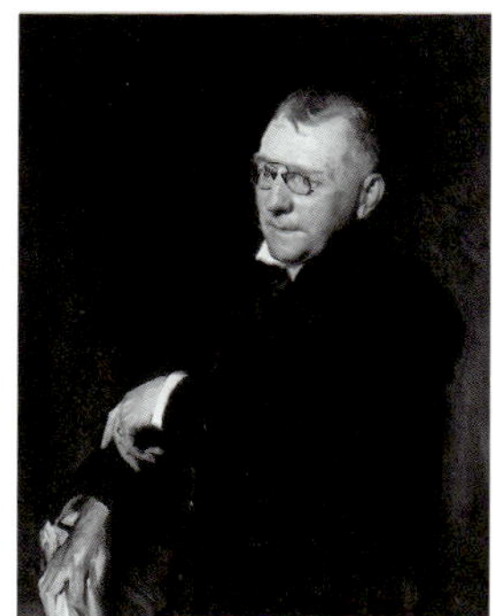

Portrait of James Whitcomb Riley, 1903, John Singer Sargent

1883 May Wright Sewall, principal of the Girls' Classical School in Indianapolis, and seventeen other residents of the city sign articles of incorporation on October 11 to found the Art Association of Indianapolis. The Association has its first exhibition in November, including paintings by William Merritt Chase and Alfred Thompson Bricher.

1885 The second art exhibition—*The Hoosier Colony in München*—shows seventy-one pictures by Indiana artists Theodore C. Steele and William Forsyth.

1895 The Association learns that it will receive $225,000 from the estate of Indianapolis real estate investor John Herron to build a permanent art gallery and school.

1899 James Whitcomb Riley gives a reading of his poetry as a benefit for the Art Association. The proceeds will be used to pay John Singer Sargent for his portrait of Riley.

John Herron Art Institute

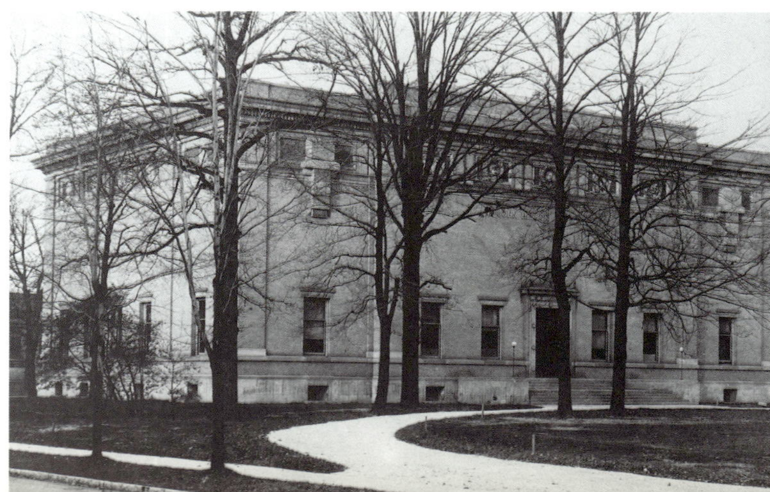

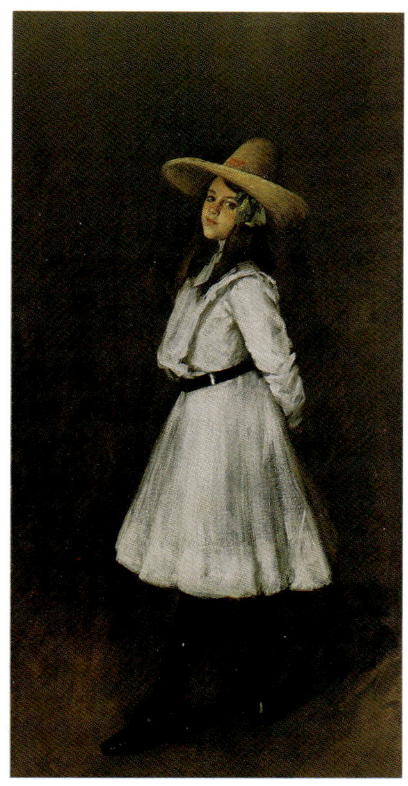

Dorothy, 1902,
William Merritt Chase

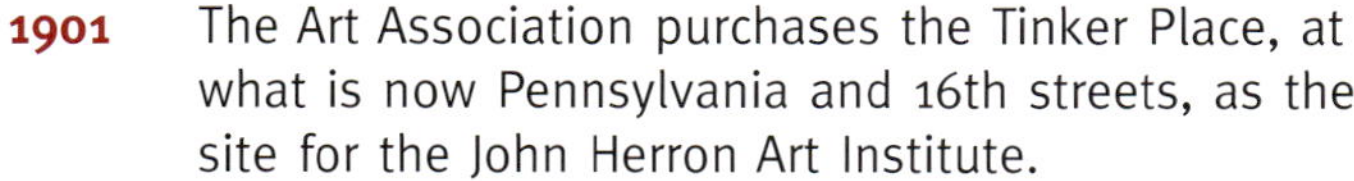

1901 The Art Association purchases the Tinker Place, at what is now Pennsylvania and 16th streets, as the site for the John Herron Art Institute.

1902 On January 13, the art school opens at the new site in T. C. Steele's studio, with five teachers and ten students. In February, the Art Association moves into the Talbott House at Tinker Place, and John Herron Art Institute formally opens on March 4.

1903 The Association acquires *Dorothy*, by Indiana native William Merritt Chase, through the John Herron Fund.

1905 William Henry Fox is hired as managing director of the Association.

1906 The new buildings for the John Herron Art Institute and Herron School of Art open to the public on November 22.

1907 Evans Woollen, an Indianapolis banker and candidate for U. S. president in 1923, becomes the sixth president of the Art Association. He will continue in the position for 34 years. The Association purchases *Cliff Rock, Appledore*, by Childe Hassam, through the John Herron Fund.

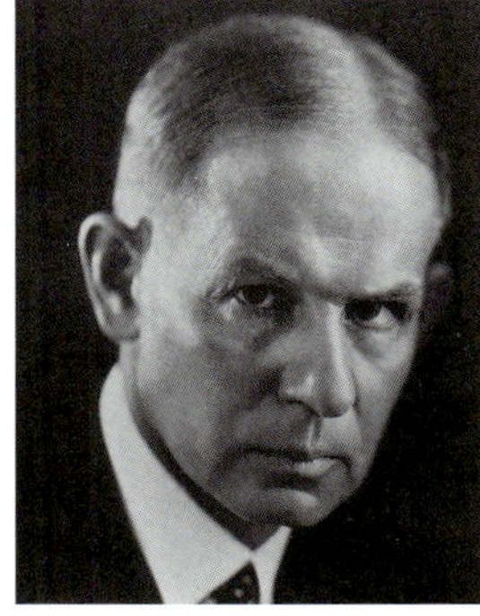

Evans Woollen, 1923

1910 The Augustus Saint-Gaudens Memorial Exhibition, which opened on December 25, 1909, draws 56,574 visitors by the time it closes in March. Professor Alfred M. Brooks is appointed curator of the new department of prints in July.

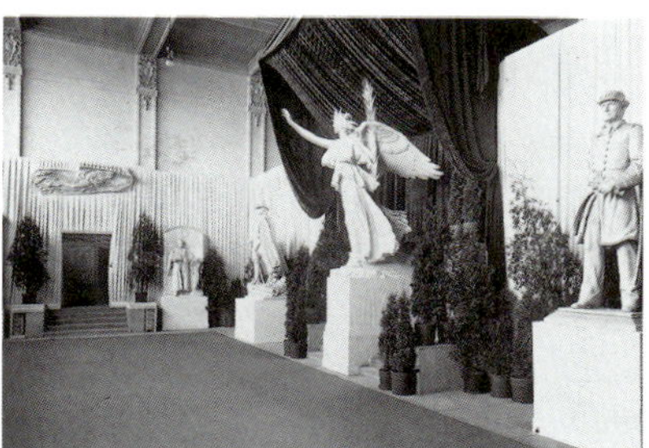

Augustus Saint-Gaudens exhibition Herron School of Art Library, IUPUI

BELOW:
An early exhibition at the new Art Institute Herron Collection, Ruth Lilly Special Collections and Archives, IUPUI

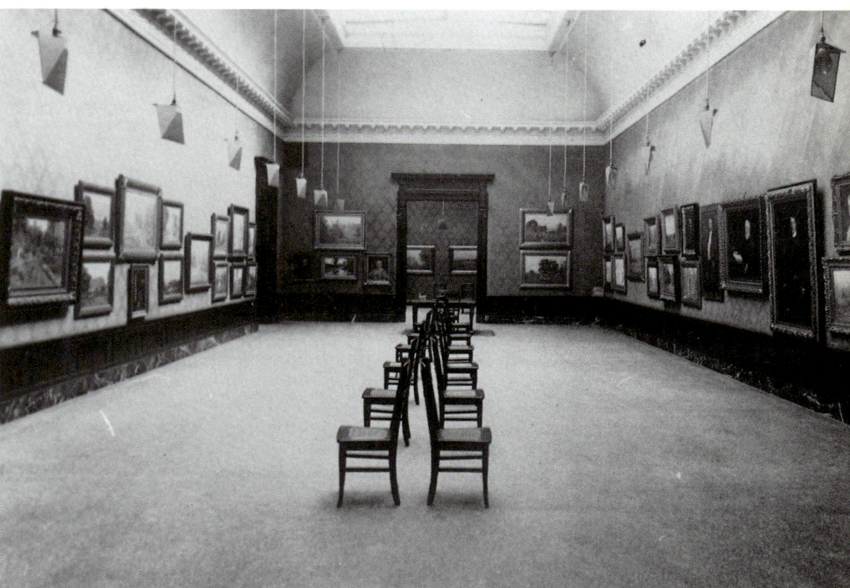

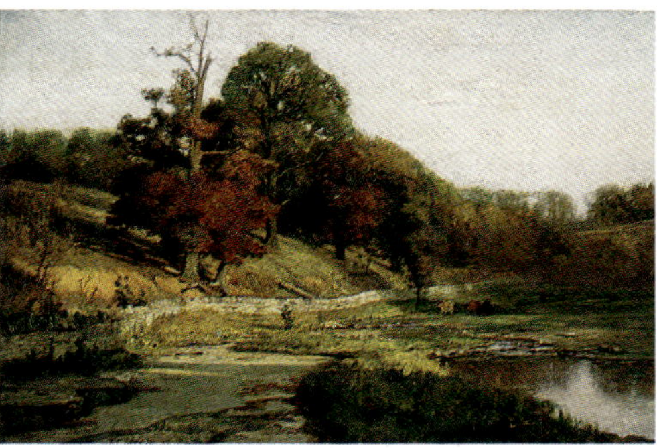

The Oaks of Vernon, 1887,
T. C. Steele

1911 Milton Matter is acting director of the Association, serving in this capacity until 1912. Mrs. Addison Bybee gives Albert Bierstadt's painting *Alaska* to the museum. Purchases include 69 color woodcuts by Hiroshige.

1912 Frederic Allen Whiting is the new director of the museum. An exhibition of paintings and drawings by Winslow Homer is presented in the fall.

1913 Harold Haven Brown is appointed director of the museum. Museum purchases include prints by Albrecht Dürer, drawings by Thomas Hearne, Samuel Prout, John Ruskin and J. M. W. Turner, and watercolors by John Frederick Lewis and John Ruskin.

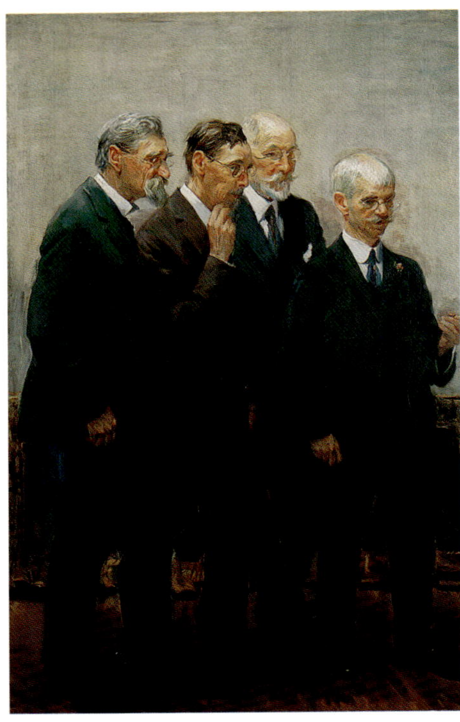

The Art Jury, 1921, Wayman Adams

1922 The Art Association receives $95,000 from the estate of Indianapolis businessman James E. Roberts for the purchase of art.

1923 J. Arthur MacLean, curator of oriental art, serves as director and will remain in the position until 1926.

1924 An endowment fund for operating expenses is established; it will total $341,015.36 by 1928.

1926 Wayman Adams's group portrait of T. C. Steele, William Forsyth, J. Ottis Adams and Otto Stark is purchased by subscription for $5,000 as a permanent memorial to these deans of Indiana art.

1927 Sixteen civic leaders found the Gamboliers. For the next few years they will gamble on "promising artists," adding works by Modigliani, Prendergast, Matisse, Toulouse-Lautrec, and others to the collection—167 works in all, for a little more than $2,000.

1929 Wilbur David Peat becomes director of the museum, a position he will hold until 1965. A new building for the art school, donated anonymously by Caroline Marmon Fesler, opens.

1932 An exhibition of American paintings from the museum's collection includes canvases by Rembrandt Peale, John Henry Twachtman, Asher B. Durand, William Merritt Chase, John Singer Sargent, Frank Benson, Mary Cassatt, Frank Currier, Frederick Frieseke, Albert Bierstadt, Childe Hassam, Victor Higgins, and Edward Hopper.

1933 Donald Magnus Mattison is appointed the new director of the art school at Herron Art Institute.

1937 Author Booth Tarkington, Muncie industrialist Frank Ball, and Lilly Company executive George H. A. Clowes are among the lenders to an exhibition of portraits, landscapes and genre paintings by Dutch Masters, including Rembrandt, Hals, Ruisdael, Steen, and Vermeer. Attendance for this exhibition totals 32,455. Tarkington calls it "a distinguished and brilliant event in art, the first of such magnitude in our history."

1941 Caroline Marmon Fesler is the new president of the Association, a position she will hold until 1947. Accessions include Camille Pissarro's *Banks of the Oise, near Pontoise*, purchased through the James E. Roberts Fund. In June, the museum reopens after extensive remodeling and the addition of new galleries.

1942 The Association receives a bequest of $100,000 from the estate of Walter L. Milliken.

1943 Caroline Marmon Fesler gives a number of important paintings to the museum, including works by Corneille de Lyon, Aelbert Cuyp, and Meindert Hobbema.

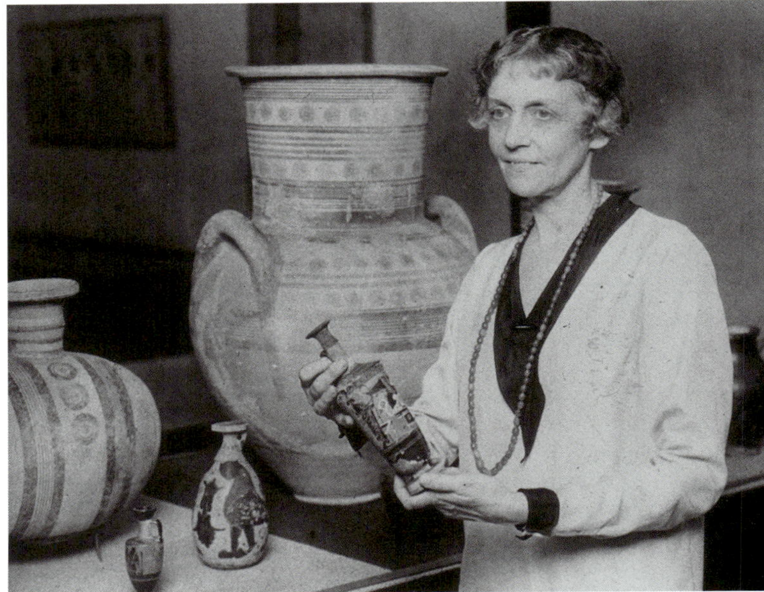

Museum curator Anna Hasselman was acting director between 1926 and 1929. Herron School of Art Library, IUPUI

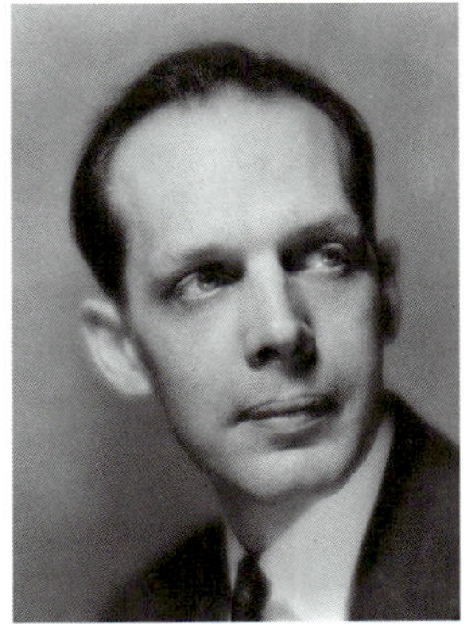

Wilbur David Peat, 1932

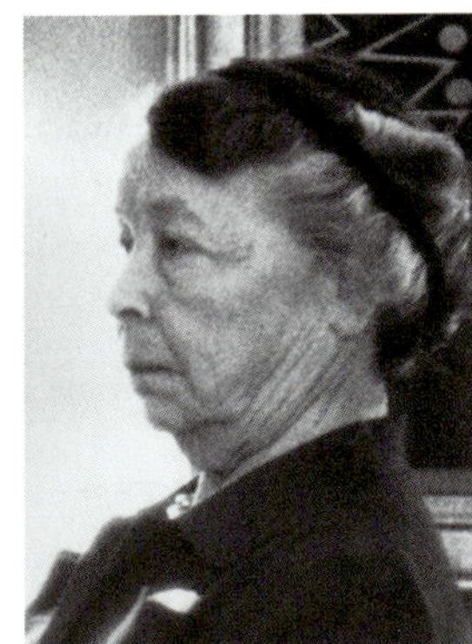

Caroline Marmom Fesler, 1950s

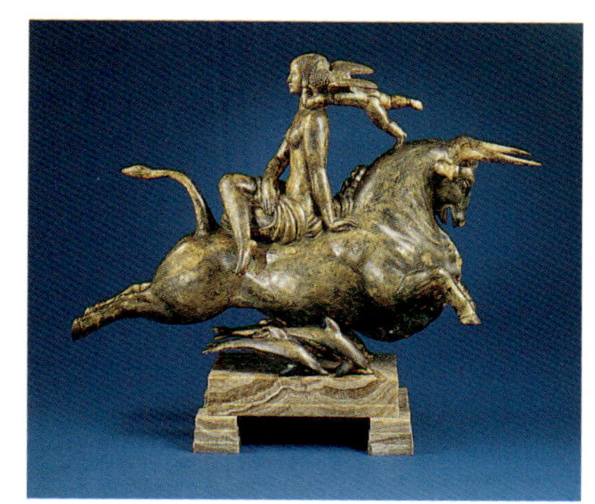

The Flight of Europa, 1925, Paul Manship

1947 Josef Anton Scherrer becomes president of the Association. Eli Lilly, president of the pharmaceutical company, begins his collection of Chinese art, and makes his first loans and gifts to the IMA.

1950 Gifts to the Art Association include Paul Manship's *Flight of Europa*, given by Lucy M. Taggart in memory of Thomas Taggart.

1955 The museum organizes the major loan exhibition *Turner in America*, which includes J. M. W. Turner's painting *Fifth Plague of Egypt*.

1956 The John Herron Art Institute celebrates its 50th anniversary.

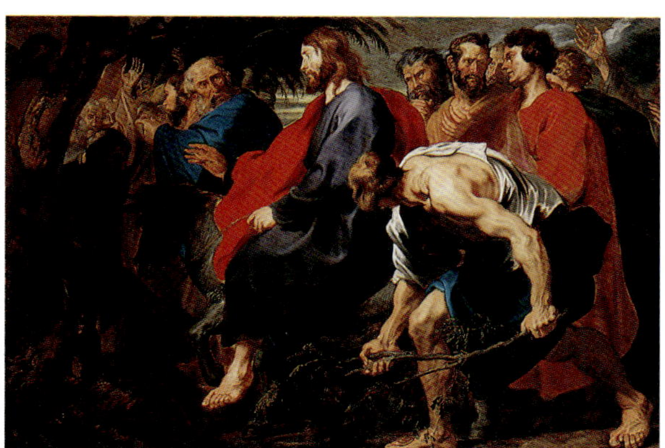

Entry of Christ into Jerusalem, about 1619, Anthony van Dyck

1958 *Entry of Christ into Jerusalem,* by Anthony van Dyck, is added to the collection, a gift of Mr. and Mrs. Herman C. Krannert. The Herron Museum Alliance (now the Alliance of the Indianapolis Museum of Art) is organized by Mrs. Booth T. Jameson, Mrs. William Ansted, and Mrs. Beverly Carmichael. Among its stated purposes are "stimulating public interest in the collections, exhibitions, and programs, and carrying out projects that will increase the museum's revenues for operation and the acquisition of art."

1960 Herman C. Krannert, founder of Inland Container Corporation, is named chairman of the board and Eli Lilly is vice chairman. Attorney Robert Ashby becomes president, and attorney Kurt F. Pantzer persuades other civic leaders to join the board. Mr. Lilly presents the rest of his collection of Chinese art to the museum.

1962 The Contemporary Art Society is founded.

1963 The board of trustees commissions architects to study and make recommendations for renovating and expanding the museum. The Contemporary Art Society sponsors the first *Painting and Sculpture Today* exhibition. CAS will sponsor seventeen more contemporary art exhibitions in the next twenty-five years.

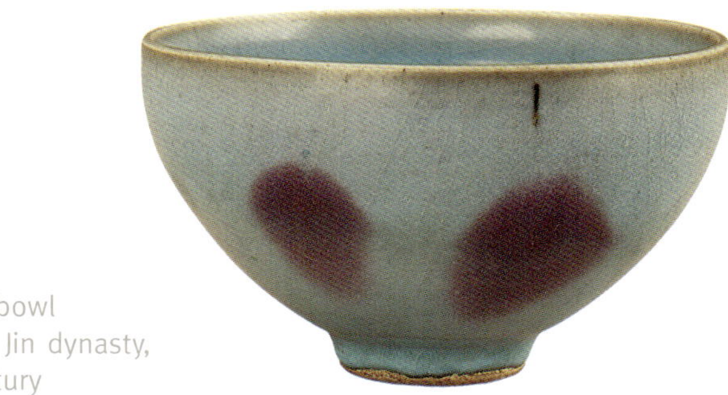

Chinese bowl from the Jin dynasty, 13th century

1965 Carl J. Weinhardt, Jr., is appointed director of the museum.

1966 Ruth Lilly and Josiah K. Lilly III donate their parents' estate, Oldfields, to the Art Association.

1967 Herron School of Art becomes part of Indiana University on July 1.

1968 The Alliance helps raise $25,500 during the operating fund drive, trains 143 docents for the new "Pavilion of Decorative Arts at Oldfields," and establishes the Craft Shop.

1969 The Art Association changes its name to Indianapolis Museum of Art.

1970 The new museum, at 1200 West 38th Street, opens to the public. The Decorative Arts Society and Business Group are founded.

1971 More than 300 Chinese jade objects and other Asian works of art are given to the museum by Professor R. Norris Shreve and Irene Shreve.

1972 Henry F. DeBoest is named chairman of the IMA. The Clowes Pavilion opens, a memorial to Edith Whitehill Clowes. A bequest of approximately $1 million from Mrs. Grace Showalter is received. It will be used to build the Showalter Pavilion, home of the Indianapolis Civic Theatre. The Sutphin Fountain is dedicated. The Horticultural Society is founded.

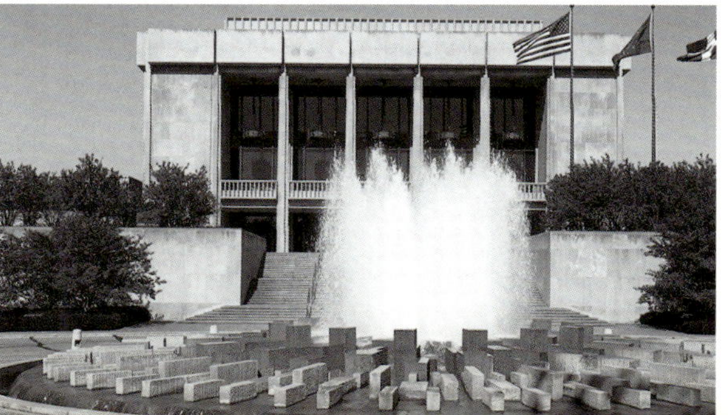

Exterior view, Krannert Pavilion, with Sutphin Fountain in foreground, 1970s

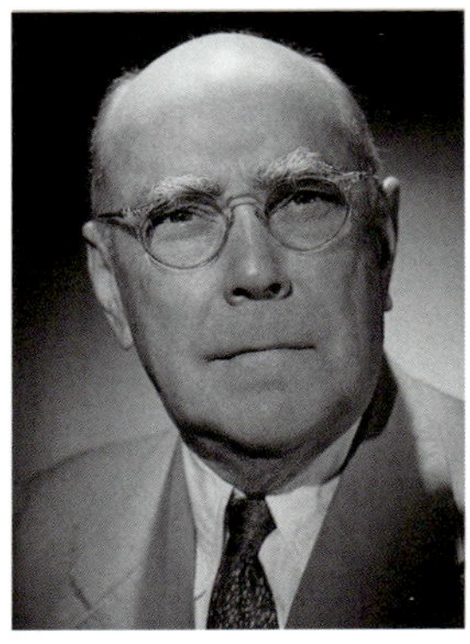

Eli Lilly, 1970

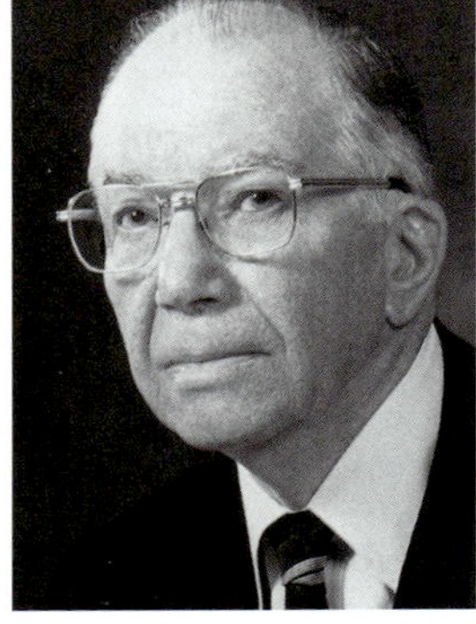

Kurt F. Pantzer

1973 IMA volunteers open the Better Than New Shop as a fund-raising project. The Better Than New Shop, managed by Alliance members, will raise more than $1.5 million over the next 25 years for the benefit of the museum. An additional $166,770 will be raised through moving and estate sales.

1974 Harrison Eiteljorg is named chairman of the IMA, a position he will hold for more than nine years. The Indianapolis Museum of Art-Columbus Gallery opens at the Columbus Visitors' Center in September.

1975 Robert A. Yassin, former chief curator of the IMA, is named director. The Oriental Art Society (now the Asian Art Society) is founded. The Krannert Charitable Trust announces a $5-million matching grant for operating endowment for the museum. The Enchanted Owl Craft Shop merges with the bookstore and Museum Shop to become the Alliance Museum Shop.

1977 After the death of Eli Lilly in January, the museum learns of his bequest of more than $14 million, the largest in the museum's history.

1979 The museum receives W. J. Holliday's collection of Neo-Impressionist paintings, now the largest public collection of Neo-Impressionist paintings in the U.S. The largest collection of works by J. M. W. Turner outside Great Britain, amassed over many years by Indianapolis attorney Kurt F. Pantzer, becomes a permanent part of the museum's collection.

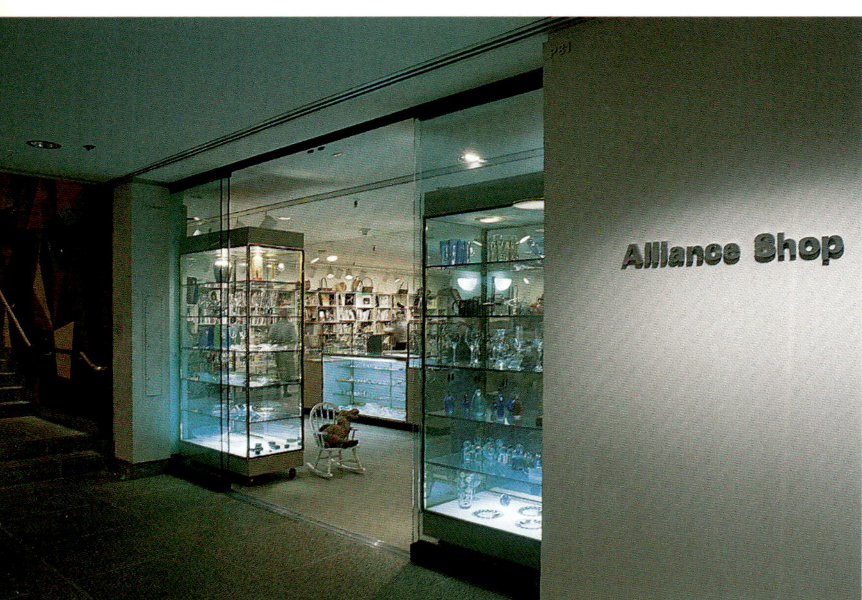

Alliance Museum Shop

1981 The Andrew J. Mellon Foundation awards a major grant to the museum for the support of exhibiitions and publications.

1983 Robert S. Ashby becomes chairman of the museum; he will serve for five years. The IMA celebrates its centennial with a series of exhibitions of art from the permanent collection. The Alliance celebrates its 25th anniversary and the completion of its $350,000 endowment pledge for the maintenance of the Alliance Sculpture Court.

1984 A bequest of $1 million from the estate of Glenn Warren is the first in a series of major gifts in the building fund campaign.

1985 The museum organizes *Art of the Fantastic, Latin America 1920-1987* in conjunction with the Tenth Pan American Games in Indianapolis.

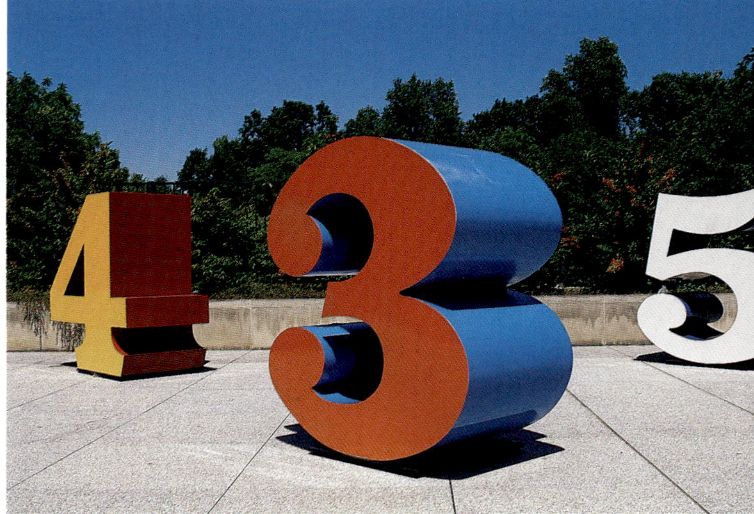

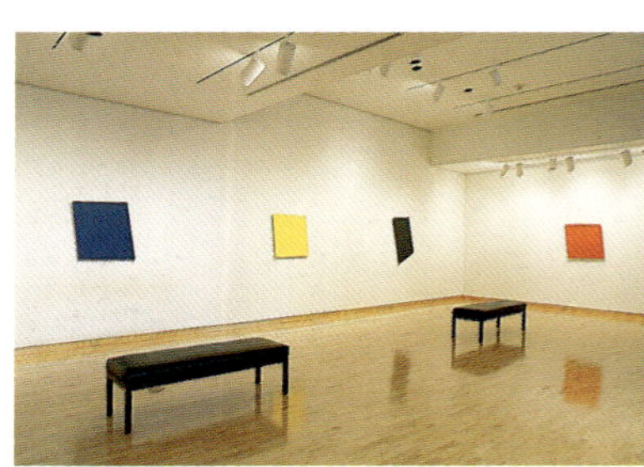

ABOVE: The Alliance Sculpture Court, with Robert Indiana's ten polychrome numerals

LEFT: *Ellsworth Kelly: Colors and Forms,* at the IMA-Columbus Gallery. The eleven painted panels were purchased through the Xenia and J. Irwin Miller Fund.

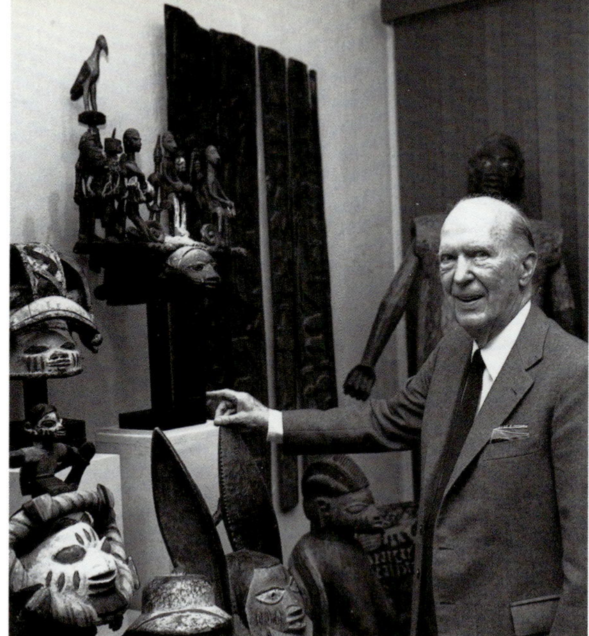

Harrison Eiteljorg, 1990

1986 The Young Friends of Art is founded, with the goal of diversifying and expanding the membership of the museum.

1987 E. Kirk McKinney is appointed president and chief executive officer of the Indianapolis Museum of Art. He will direct the museum through a period of major renovation and construction.

1988 Dudley Sutphin is chairman of the IMA. In February, the Alliance pledges $500,000 to the building fund for the new Alliance Special Events Area. Mary Fendrich Hulman turns the first shovel of soil at the groundbreaking ceremonies for a new pavilion on October 12. In December, the Alliance has its first fund-raising Holiday Ball.

1989 An anonymous bequest adds $29 million to the endowment fund.

1990 Bret Waller is appointed the museum's director, and Anna S. White is chairman of the museum. The new Mary Fendrich Hulman Pavilion is dedicated and the renovated Krannert and Clowes pavilions are reopened. Mr. and Mrs. Harrison Eiteljorg donate their collection of African and South Pacific art, more than 1,500 objects, to the IMA. Paintings by the Hoosier Group travel to Cologne, Germany, in the exhibition *The Passage: Return of Indiana Painters from Germany, 1880-1905.*

1991 The new American Galleries and other new and renovated galleries open to the public. The bronze door by Richard Pousette-Dart is installed, a gift of Susan and Robert Ashby. The first International Wine Auction, organized by the Alliance, raises $40,000.

1992 The IMA receives a grant of $1.533 million from the Lila Wallace-Reader's Digest Fund to enhance accessibility to the IMA's collections.

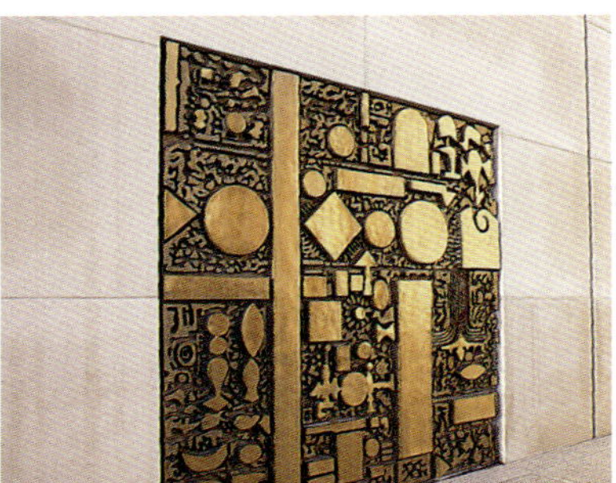

Cathedral, 1990, Richard Pousette-Dart

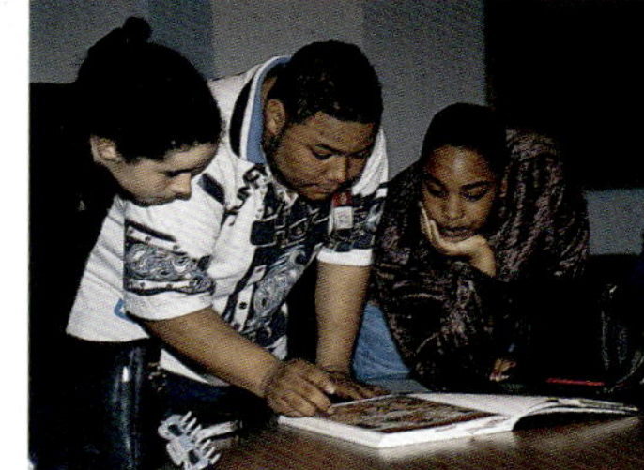

Community Connection Program participants learn about an upcoming exhibition of art from India.

1993 Mark Holeman is named chairman of the IMA. The new 4,600-square-foot Indianapolis Museum of Art-Columbus Gallery, funded by a gift from Xenia S. Miller, opens at The Commons in Columbus.

1995 The Lila Wallace-Reader's Digest Fund Education Center, the completely renovated classroom area, is dedicated. The expanded and renovated greenhouse reopens and is renamed for its longtime patron, Madeline Fortune Elder.

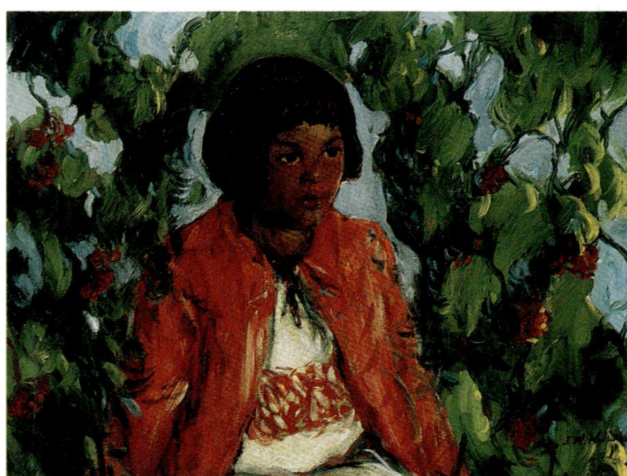

Little Brown Girl, 1927, John Wesley Hardrick

1996 Richard D. Wood is named chairman of the IMA. The Alliance supports three major exhibitions—*A Shared Heritage: Art by Four African Americans, Egypt in Africa*, and *Painting in Spain in the Age of Enlightenment: Goya and His Contemporaries*—with donations totaling $152,500. In the fall, twenty-five ASID designers and three landscape design companies transform the Better Than New Shop for the Alliance fund-raiser *Newfields—An ASID Designer Showcase.*

1997 The museum receives a bequest of more than $40 million from the estate of Enid P. Goodrich. The Jane S. Dutton Educational Resource Center, a gift of Mrs. Ben Dutton, opens. The Alliance Fine Arts Endowment Fund passes the $2 million mark.

1998 The IMA celebrates its 115th anniversary. The Alliance celebrates its 40th year.

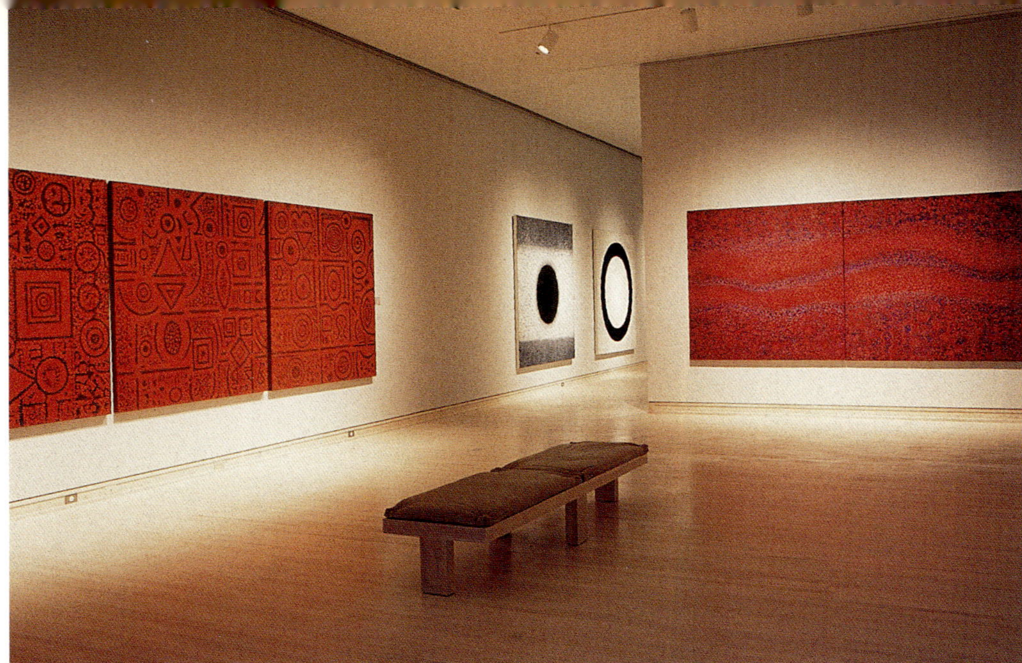

Richard Pousette-Dart: *A Retrospective*, 1990

Major Exhibitions Organized by the Indianapolis Museum of Art since 1970

1970 *Seven Outside*, an exhibition of contemporary outdoor sculpture

1973 *Alfred Thompson Bricher, 1837-1908,* the first comprehensive exhibition documenting this American marine painter

1976 *Mirages of Memory: 200 Years of Indiana Art,* a bicentennial survey of Indiana painting, sculpture, and graphics from the late eighteenth century to the present

1978 *William McGregor Paxton*, a retrospective of one of the leading painters of the Boston School

1980 *Freedom of Clay and Brush through Seven Centuries in Northern China: Tz'u-chou Type Wares, 960–1600 A.D.*, the first exhibition devoted to ceramics that have been continuously produced in China since the tenth century

1983 *The Aura of Neo-Impressionism: The W. J. Holliday Collection*, pointillist paintings by French, Belgian, German, and Dutch followers of Georges Seurat, bequeathed to the IMA in 1977

Beauty and Tranquility: The Eli Lilly Collection of Chinese Art, 167 bronzes, jades, ceramics, and paintings from one of the finest comprehensive collections of Chinese art, now part of the museum's permanent collection

1985 *African Art from the Harrison Eiteljorg Collection,* more than 150 pieces revealing the aesthetic range, technical sophistication, and complex social contexts of traditional African art, from the permanent collection

1987 *Ice and Green Clouds: Traditions of Chinese Celadon,* eighty-seven pieces of the green-glazed ware representing the longest tradition in the history of Chinese ceramics

The Art of the Fantastic: Latin America, 1920-1987, a groundbreaking exhibition of more than 100 pieces by three generations of Central and South American artists who express themselves through use of fantastic imagery

1988 *Views from Jade Terrace: Chinese Women Artists, 1300-1912,* the first exhibition ever devoted to this subject

1989 *African Improvisation: Textiles from the Collection,* twenty-eight fabrics from West, Central and North Africa whose design can be described in musical terms

1990 *Seurat at Gravelines: The Last Landscapes,* an exhibition reuniting Seurat's last landscape paintings for the first time in a century

Richard Pousette-Dart: A Retrospective, the first comprehensive view of the achievements of Pousette-Dart, one of the originators of the American Abstract Expressionist movement

1991 *POWER: Its Myths and Mores in American Art,* 1961-1991, an exhibition identifying images of power that permeate contemporary American society

The Passage: Return of Indiana Painters from Germany, 1880-1905, an exhibition of paintings, drawings, and watercolors produced by Indiana's four most highly regarded turn-of-the-century painters: Theodore Clement Steele, J. Ottis Adams, William Forsyth and Samuel Richards

1993 *The Poetry of Form: Richard Tuttle Drawings from the Vogel Collection* (at the National Gallery of Art), works by this Post-Minimalist artist that incorporate the simplicity of Minimalism but retain the expressive gestures of the artist's hand

American Traditions: Art from the Collections of Culver Alumni, an exhibition of American paintings presented on the occasion of the centennial of this northern Indiana school

1994 *The Arts & Crafts Metalwork of Janet Payne Bowles,* a survey of the work from the museum's collection by the Indianapolis metalsmith, who achieved international recognition for her designs

Garo Antreasian: Written on Stone, prints, drawings and paintings, spanning more than fifty years, by the Indianapolis-born artist

Walt Disney's Snow White and the Seven Dwarfs: An Art in Its Making, animation drawings, hand-painted cels and watercolor backgrounds from the collection of Stephen H. Ison

1996 *A Shared Heritage: Art by Four African Americans,* paintings and prints by nationally recognized artists with roots in Indianapolis and John Herron Art Institute

Patterned Elegance: West Asian Rugs from the Markarian Collection, fifty rugs from one of the most comprehensive collections of Oriental rugs in the United States

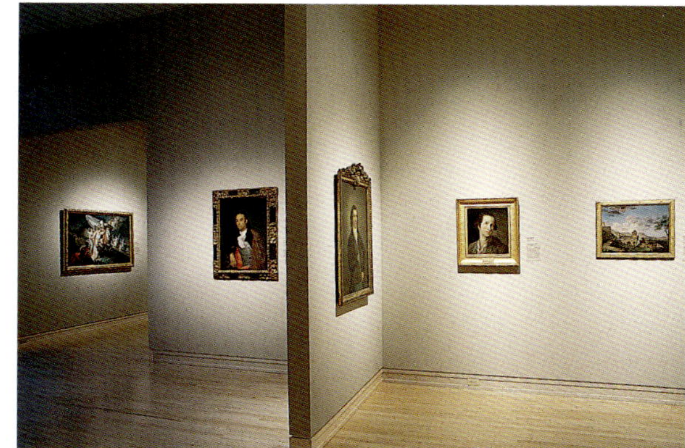

Painting in Spain in the Age of Enlightenment: Goya and His Contemporaries, 1996

Egypt in Africa, an exhibition addressing the widespread misconception that Egypt is separate from Africa, with ninety objects from many African cultures

Painting in Spain in the Age of Enlightenment: Goya and His Contemporaries, sixty-six paintings by Goya, Giaquinto, Mengs, Tiepolo, and others, conveying the richness and variety of artistic expression in Spain in the eighteenth and early nineteenth centuries

1997 *Baluchi Woven Treasures: The Boucher Collection,* weavings by the Baluchi people of Iran and Afghanistan, from one of the finest collections of its kind, given to the IMA in 1996

Turner Watercolors from Manchester and Indianapolis, 116 drawings and watercolors from three of the world's finest collections of works by the great English landscape artist

Masters of Contemporary Glass: Selections from the Glick Collection, an overview of the contemporary studio glass movement, comprising sixty-five objects committed to the IMA by Marilyn and Eugene Glick

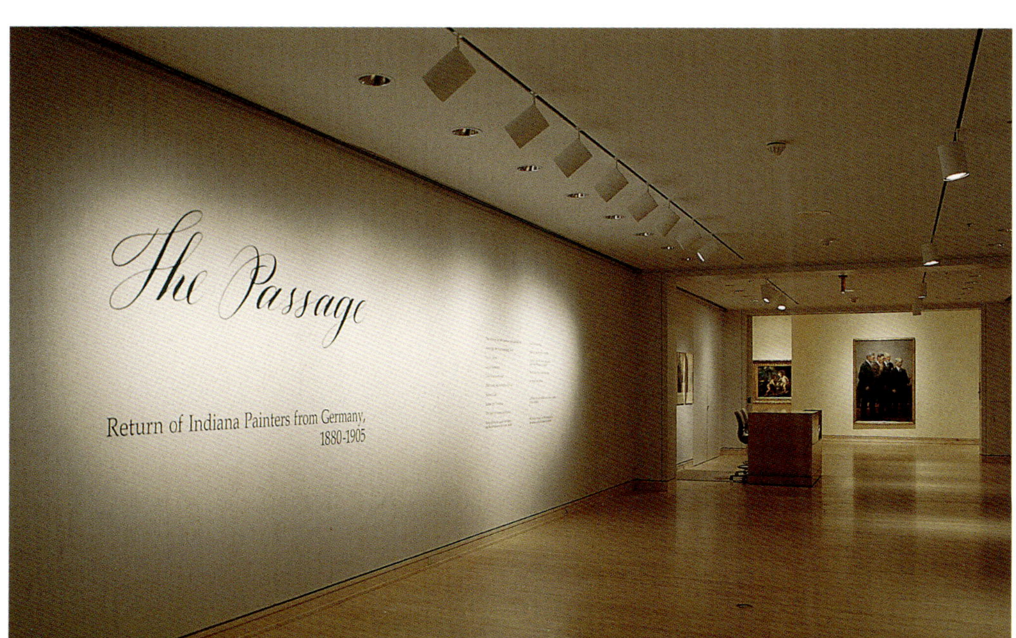

The Passage: Return of Indiana Painters from Germany, 1880-1905, 1991

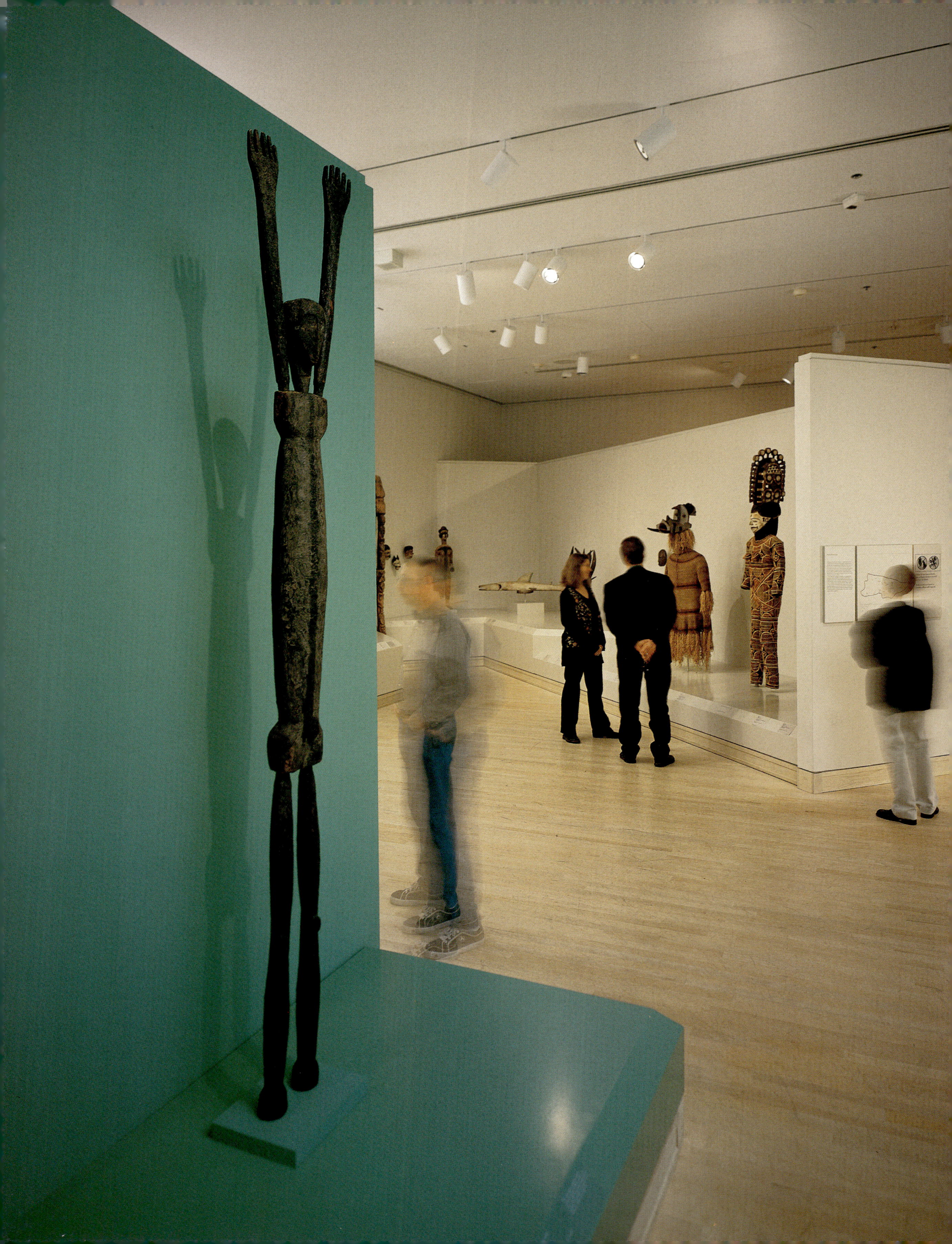